RENE DESCARTES
MEDITATIONS
ON FIRST PHILOSOPHY
in focus

This volume contains the excellent and popular Elizabeth S. Haldane and G. R. T. Ross translation of René Descartes' *Meditations on First Philosophy*, and a portion of the Replies to Objections II in which Descartes discusses how the method employed in the *Meditations*, which he calls "analysis," differs from the method of "synthesis" employed by the geometer.

In the Editor's Introduction, Stanley Tweyman provides a fresh and detailed discussion of the relationship between Descartes' *Rules for the Direction of the Mind* and the method of 'analysis', insofar as each has application to the *Meditations*. The six critical papers which Professor Tweyman has drawn together in this book present a broad and exegetical commentary on the *Meditations* and give an indication of the diversity of scholarly opinion which exists on the topic of method in Descartes' philosophy. An extensive bibliography is also included.

Stanley Tweyman is Professor of Philosophy at York University, Toronto.

ROUTLEDGE PHILOSOPHERS IN FOCUS SERIES

Series editor: Stanley Tweyman
York University, Toronto

ARISTOTLE'S *DE ANIMA* IN FOCUS
Edited by Michael Durrant

GEORGE BERKELEY: *ALCIPHRON* IN FOCUS
Edited by David Berman

CIVIL DISOBEDIENCE IN FOCUS
Edited by Hugo Adam Bedau

GODEL'S *THEOREM* IN FOCUS
Edited by S. G. Shanker

DAVID HUME: *DIALOGUES CONCERNING NATURAL RELIGION* IN FOCUS
Edited by Stanley Tweyman

WILLIAM JAMES: *PRAGMATISM* IN FOCUS
Edited by Doris Olin

JOHN LOCKE: *LETTER CONCERNING TOLERATION* IN FOCUS
Edited by John Horton and Susan Mendus

J. S. MILL: *ON LIBERTY* IN FOCUS
Edited by John Gray and G. W. Smith

RENE DESCARTES

MEDITATIONS ON FIRST PHILOSOPHY

in focus

Edited and with an introduction by
Stanley Tweyman

London and New York

First published 1993
by Routledge
11 New Fetter Lane, London EC4P 4EE

Simultaneously published in the USA and Canada
by Routledge
29 West 35th Street, New York, NY 10001

Selection and editorial matter © 1993 Stanley Tweyman; each article ©
respective contributor

Typeset in 10 on 12 point Bembo by
Florencetype Ltd, Kewstoke, Avon
Printed in Great Britain by TJ Press Ltd, Padstow, Cornwall

British Library Cataloguing in Publication Data
A catalogue record for this book is available from the British Library

Library of Congress Cataloging in Publication Data
Descartes, René, 1596–1650.
[Meditationes de prima philosophia. English]
Meditations on first philosophy / René Descartes : edited and with an
introduction by Stanley Tweyman.
(Routledge philosophers in foucus series)
"Contains the excellent and popular Elizabeth S. Haldane and
G.R.T. Ross translation."
Includes bibliographical references and index.
1. First philosophy–Early works to 1800. 2. God–Proof,
Ontological–Early works to 1800. 3. Methodology. 4. Knowledge,
Theory of. 5. Descartes, René, 1596–1650–Views on methodology.
6. Methodology. I. Tweyman, Stanley. II. Haldane, Elizabeth Sanderson,
1862–1937. III. Ross, G. R. T. (George Robert
Thomson) IV. title. V. Series.
B1853.E5H44 1993
194–dc20   92-47345   CIP

ISBN 0-415-07706-0 (hbk)
ISBN 0-415-07707-9 (pbk)

CONTENTS

CONTENTS

PREFACE

The *Meditations* was written by Descartes while he was living in Holland. The first edition, which appeared in Latin, was published in Paris, as *Meditationes de Prima Philosophia*, in 1641. Descartes had circulated the manuscript among his friends, in particular Friar Marin Mersenne, requesting comments and criticisms, and six "Objections and Replies" appeared in this first edition along with the six Meditations and introductory material. A seventh set of Objections and Replies, and a "Letter to P. Dinet" were added to the second Latin edition (1642), published in Amsterdam. Gassendi, the author of the Fifth Set of Objections, published his own Objections and Descartes' Replies, with the original *Meditations* as an appendix, in 1644 as *Disquisitio Metaphysica*. The first French edition, which included the *Meditations* translated by Duc de Luynes and the first six Objections and Replies translated by Clerselier, and a "Letter to Clerselier" (written in answer to Gassendi and originally intended by Descartes as a substitute for the Fifth Set of Objections) appeared in 1647. Descartes read and revised this edition, except the Fifth Set of Objections which was later added by Clerselier. Further Latin editions appeared in the next three years; the fourth Latin edition (1650) included the Clerselier letter, a "Letter to Voetius," "Notae in Programma" and the "Letter to P. Dinet," but omitted the Fifth Set of Objections. A second French edition was published by Clerselier in 1661, in which he corrected the earlier Duc de Luynes translation (Descartes may have also seen this new version); it included the preface to the reader, all seven sets of Objections and Replies, and the letters to Clerselier and Dinet. A third French edition (by René Fède) appeared in 1673. The comprehensive Adam and Tannery edition (Paris: Léopold Cerf, 1897) was based upon the second

Latin edition, as was the 1911 Haldane and Ross edition (these translators also utilized the second French edition). The present volume contains a reprint of the Haldane and Ross translation. Square brackets in the text of the *Meditations* indicate that Haldane and Ross provide an alternative reading from the French text. Minor typographical errors in the Haldane and Ross edition have been corrected.

Included in this present volume are Descartes' Dedication to the faculty of the Sorbonne (where he indicates that questions regarding God and the soul should be demonstrated by philosophical rather than theological argument), his "Preface to the Reader" (where Descartes writes that he would like to see if he can persuade others, by the same reasons which persuaded him, of certain and evident knowledge of the truth), and his Synopsis of the Meditations. A portion of the Replies to Objections II is also reprinted; in this passage, Descartes speaks of analysis – the method he employs in the Meditations – and contrasts this method of proof with synthesis, the method of the geometer. I wish to thank Cambridge University Press for permission to reprint the text of the Haldane and Ross translation of the *Meditations on First Philosophy* and this portion of the Replies (*The Philosophical Works of Descartes*, 2 vols, first published 1911; reprinted with corrections 1931).

This volume also contains six papers that are concerned with Descartes' method. Where reference is made in these papers to Descartes' *Meditations* and to reprinted passages from the Replies, the relevant page number from the present volume is added in square brackets. An extensive Selected Bibliography is included at the end of the volume.

The present project has benefited greatly from the advice and assistance of Beryl Logan. Her love of Descartes' writings and her sound philosophic sense are evident throughout this volume.

My efforts in this book, as usual, are dedicated to my parents, Fay and Dave Tweyman, my wife Barbara, my daughter Justine Susan, and my brother Martin.

ACKNOWLEDGMENTS

Desmond M. Clarke's essay, "Descartes' use of 'demonstration' and 'deduction' " first appeared in *Modern Schoolman* 54 (May 1977) and is reprinted by permission of the author and *Modern Schoolman*. Jaakko Hintikka's "A discourse on Descartes' method" is reprinted from *Descartes: Critical and Interpretive Essays*, ed. Michael Hooker (Baltimore, Md: Johns Hopkins University Press, 1978) by permission of the author and the publisher. "A point of order: analysis, synthesis, and Descartes' *Principles*," by Daniel Garber and Lesley Cohen, was first published in *Archiv für Geschichte der Philosophie* 64 (1982) and is reprinted by permission of the authors and *Archiv für Geschichte der Philosophie*. Stanley Tweyman's "Professor Cottingham and Descartes' methods of analysis and synthesis" was presented at the conference celebrating the 350th Anniversary of the publication of Descartes' *Meditations*, in Reading, UK, 3–5 September 1991, organized by Professor John Cottingham. It is a modified version of an earlier paper, "Descartes' Second Meditation and Seventh Principle," published in Stanley Tweyman, *Descartes and Hume: Selected Topics* (Delmar, NY: Caravan Press, 1989). "Analysis in the *Meditations*: the quest for clear and distinct ideas," by E. M. Curley, is reprinted from *Essays on Descartes' Meditations*, ed. Amélie Oksenberg Rorty (Berkeley: University of California Press, 1986) by permission of the author and the publisher. Georges J. D. Moyal's "The ontological proof within the order of reasons" is translated from the French, with minor additions and modifications, by the author and is printed by his permission and that of the *Revue de metaphysique et de morale*, where the original version of the article appeared in 1988.

INTRODUCTION

Stanley Tweyman

In the opening paragraph of the First Meditation, Descartes states that his aim in the *Meditations on First Philosophy* is to establish a firm and permanent structure in the sciences. In the *Preface to the Principles of Philosophy*, he speaks of the *Meditations* as his metaphysics "which contains the principles of knowledge, amongst which is the explanation of the principal attributes of God, of the immateriality of our souls, and of all the clear and simple notions which are in us". The *Meditations*, therefore, will contain what Descartes regards as the first principles of knowledge – those matters which must be known before any other matters can be known.

There has been considerable debate in the literature on Descartes' method in the *Meditations* in arriving at the first principles of human knowledge. In this Introduction, I propose to show that Descartes' method in the *Meditations* is not the new method or logic of discovery he began developing in the *Regulae*, a work he never completed and which was not published during Descartes' lifetime. Descartes' view in the *Regulae* is that philosophy can be successful, provided that a proper method of inquiry can be found. To this end, he urges that philosophy does not so much require a new method (one never before thought of, or employed) as it requires adapting a method used in other subjects in which indubitable knowledge has been obtained. In the *Regulae*, Descartes insists that, of the sciences already discovered, only arithmetic and geometry have been successful in providing sure and indubitable knowledge. Accordingly, Descartes' goal in the *Regulae* is to understand how arithmetic and geometry obtain knowledge, and to adapt understanding of method in these sciences to the pursuit of philosophic knowledge.

Although the *Meditations* fits into Descartes' overall view of philosophy – in the *Preface to the Principles of Philosophy* he tells us that the *Meditations* is to be studied after we have acquired the skills associated with the rules of the logic of discovery, and before we go on to study physics, which concerns the true principles of material things – he insists, in the Replies to Objections II, that the method he utilizes in the *Meditations*, which he calls "analysis," is only applicable to his study of metaphysical first principles. The method of the *Meditations*, therefore, has no application beyond the *Meditations*: once the metaphysical first principles are discovered and accepted as true, the logic of discovery developed in the *Regulae* can be employed in the study of physics. The Replies to Objections II reveals that the search for metaphysical first principles encounters difficulties which are never present in arithmetic and geometry. As a result, reflecting on arithmetic and geometry to learn the method of discovery in these subjects will never teach us how metaphysical first principles are to be discovered and accepted as true. The study of the *Regulae* can show us such matters as the hierarchical nature of knowledge, and the order to be followed when we seek to know. What the *Regulae* cannot reveal, however, is how metaphysical first principles are to be discovered and their self-evidence apprehended. Hence the need for a method in the *Meditations* which has no analog or counterpart in mathematics.

The date of the composition of the *Regulae* remains somewhat problematic (see, for example, Weber's *La Constitution du texte des "Regulae"* (Paris: Société d'editions d'enseignement superieur, 1964), and L. J. Beck, *The Method of Descartes*, ch. 1) although it was probably composed between 1619 and 1628. In a letter to Mersenne dated April 15, 1630, Descartes writes that he thinks that he has discovered how to demonstrate metaphysical truths in "a way which is more evident than the demonstrations of geometry." L. J. Beck[1] regards this as a reference to the method developed in the *Regulae*:

> The date of the composition of the *Regulae* is more controversial. Baillet, the first biographer, who saw the text written by Descartes himself, does not in fact attribute any date to their composition. . . . There is no direct reference in the letters or writings of Descartes which help to fix a date or even delimit a period of his life, except one general phrase in a letter to Mersenne of 15 April 1630 where he writes "at

least I think I have found a means of proving metaphysical truths in a more evident way than one can give a demonstration in Geometry."[2]

When commenting on the nature and scope of the method Descartes develops in the *Regulae*, Beck writes: "The object of Cartesian methodology is to extend the method used in the mathematical sciences to all other branches of knowledge, including, of course, metaphysics and the other philosophical sciences."[3]

E. M. Curley[4] also quotes the passage from the letter to Mersenne about demonstrating metaphysical truths, but he argues that this passage reveals that Descartes abandoned, or at least came to attach less importance to, the method advocated in the *Regulae*. Curley writes:

> I suggest that sometime around 1628 Descartes became convinced that the *Regulae*, though still valid at one level, did not go deeply enough into the problem of knowledge. I suggest that sometime around 1628 Descartes came to feel that pyrrhonian skepticism was a more dangerous enemy than scholasticism, and came to feel the force of skeptical arguments which cut against both his own position in the *Regulae* and that of the scholastics.[5]

If Beck's interpretation is correct, then great importance attaches to the *Regulae*, for it will be difficult to understand Descartes' method in the *Meditations* if we fail to understand the method of the *Regulae*. On the other hand, if Curley's interpretation is correct, then little, if any, light will be shed on the *Meditations* by studying the *Regulae*. Curley's interpretation also raises doubts about the value Descartes came to attach to the *Regulae*. I propose to examine each of these interpretations, and to show that a third interpretation of the relation between the *Regulae* and the *Meditations* is, in fact, the one Descartes appears to have intended.

For each of the positions cited, some supporting textual evidence can be provided. Three items should be noted in favour of Beck's reading.

1 The *Regulae* offers no indication that the method being developed will admit of areas where the method is inapplicable. The first rule, in fact, emphasizes the unity of the sciences:

> [S]ince the sciences taken all together are identical with

3

human wisdom, which always remains one and the same, however, applied to different subjects, and suffers no more differentiation proceeding from them than the light of the sun experiences from the variety of things which it illumines, there is no need for minds to be confined at all within limits; for neither does the knowing of one truth have an effect like that of the acquisition of one art and prevent us from finding out another: it rather aids us to do so. . . . [W]e must believe that all the sciences are so inter-connected, that it is much easier to study them all together than to isolate one from all the others.

(HR I, 2)[6]

Descartes emphasizes the interconnectedness of science in order to support his position that this method is universal in scope. And this tends to support Beck's interpretation.

2   Neither Beck nor Curley attempts to explain (in light of their respective interpretations of the relation of the *Regulae* to the *Meditations*) why Descartes believes that the method he has discovered for demonstrating metaphysical truths is more evident than the demonstrations of geometry. Beck, as we have seen, regards this as referring to the method in the *Regulae*. Now, there is a reading of this passage in the letter to Mersenne which would help to support Beck's position. Such a reading is the following. The *Regulae* is not concerned to take over *simpliciter* the method employed in mathematics. Descartes is quite clear that in the *Regulae* the method of mathematics must be explicated and then refined. This is the meaning behind the passage which draws a comparison between Descartes' search for a method by reflecting on the method of mathematics with the craftsman's search for proper tools.[7] Therefore, when Descartes speaks of demonstrating metaphysical truths in a way which is more evident than the demonstrations of geometry, this may be due to the fact that the mathematical method, as refined in the *Regulae*, is regarded as having improved the method employed in mathematics.

3   Textual support for Beck's position can also be found in the Preface to the *Principles of Philosophy*. Descartes there discusses "the order which should be followed in our self-instruction."[8] He recommends that we begin with the study of logic – "the logic that

4

teaches us how best to direct our reason in order to discover those truths of which we are ignorant."[9] In other words, we should begin our self-instruction with the method developed in the *Regulae* (and which is summarized in the second part of the *Discourse on Method*). It is only after we have mastered the skills required for discovering the truth that he recommends that we begin seriously to apply ourselves to the true philosophy, "the first part of which is metaphysics, which contains the principles of knowledge."[10] We are told to study logic first, because it is needed in order to study metaphysics. At least, this is a reading which tends to support Beck's position.

Curley's view that the method of the *Regulae* is not utilized in the *Meditations* gains some support (as Curley himself recognizes) from the concern which Descartes develops in the latter work with mathematics:

> Like scholasticism, the *Regulae* takes the certainty of mathematics as paradigmatic and unproblematic. It relies heavily on a faculty of intuition to supply not only the ultimate premises of its deductions but also the principles of inference themselves. And it does not even consider the possibility that someone might question this reliance. The *Regulae* differs from scholasticism principally in its rejection of formalism and in its hope that we can achieve in the nonmathematical sciences the absolute certainty which has hitherto been the privilege of mathematics. Like scholasticism, it is vulnerable to any skeptical attack which can shake our confidence in mathematics, or raise effectively the problem of first principles.[11]

In the First and Third Meditations, Descartes questions the reliability of mathematics: in both Meditations his concern with mathematics stems from God's infinite power. Now, given that the *Regulae* accepts the certainty of mathematics, and that the whole of mathematics is subjected to doubt in the *Meditations*, it appears that Descartes has utilized a method in the *Meditations* other than the mathematical-type method developed in the *Regulae*. On this interpretation, when Descartes writes to Mersenne that he has discovered how to demonstrate metaphysical truths in a way which is more evident than the demonstrations of geometry, this is an indication that the method of the *Regulae* has lost its prominence in his thinking. Unfortunately, Curley is not particularly helpful in explaining the method Descartes does utilize in the *Meditations*. On the matter of the method in the *Meditations*, he writes:

> It is this project, the project of systematically reviewing one's past beliefs and casting out those which do not conform to the highest standards of rationality, which defines Descartes' mature work. It is first announced in the *Discourse*, where it is carried out only sketchily. It is repeated again at the beginning both of the *Meditations* and of the *Principles*, where it is said to be a project which everyone should undertake once in his life. But this has no real analogue in the *Regulae*.[12]

The first edition of the *Principles of Philosophy* appeared in 1644, well after Descartes had worked on the *Regulae* and completed the *Meditations* – and, as we have already seen, Descartes recommends studying the logic of the *Regulae* before we apply ourselves to metaphysics. It is, therefore, clear that the logic developed in the *Regulae* has an important role to play in Descartes' overall philosophic scheme, and, it would appear, the importance of the *Regulae* is not diminished by the doubts raised about mathematics in the *Meditations*. Furthermore, since Descartes does not intend to abandon the method of the *Regulae* when he utilizes hyperbolic doubt in the *Meditations*, we can conclude that his remark to Mersenne, that he has discovered how to demonstrate metaphysical truths in a way which is more evident than the demonstrations of geometry, is not directed against the teaching of the *Regulae*, as Curley has explained the matter.

Since the reliability of mathematics is not established until he deals with the truth of the clear and distinct in the *Meditations*, it is evident that the discussion in the *Regulae* of mathematics as the model for learning is, at most, provisional. And, the provisional character of mathematics is never removed in the *Regulae*. Now, in light of the fact that the reliability of mathematics is established in the *Meditations*, we should ask what a mastery of the *Regulae* provides. That is, granting the provisional character of mathematics in the *Regulae*, and the philosophical method developed from mathematics in this work, we must know the epistemic status of any solution which has been arrived at through the method of philosophy taught in the *Regulae*. In this regard, Descartes' comments on the atheist in the Replies to Objections II are instructive:

> That an atheist can know clearly that the three angles of a triangle are equal to two right angles, I do not deny, I merely

affirm that, on the other hand, such knowledge on his part cannot constitute true science, because no knowledge that can be rendered doubtful should be called science. Since he is, as supposed, an atheist, he cannot be sure that he is not deceived in the things that seem most evident to him . . . and though perchance the doubt does not occur to him, nevertheless it may come up, if he examine the matter, or if another suggest it; he can never be made safe from it unless he first recognizes the existence of a God.[13]

The atheist can believe that s/he knows, but without a knowledge of God the atheist cannot know that s/he knows (Descartes' expression on this is "such knowledge on his part cannot constitute true science"). The paradigm for knowledge in the *Regulae* is mathematics; for Descartes, the distinguishing features of such knowledge are clarity and distinctness. In the Fifth Meditation, he notes of the clear and distinct in mathematics that

the nature of my mind is such that I could not prevent myself from holding them to be true so long as I conceive them clearly; and I recollect that even when I was still strongly attached to the objects of sense, I counted as the most certain those truths which I conceived clearly as regards figures, numbers, and the other matters which pertain to arithmetic and geometry, and, in general, to pure and abstract mathematics.

[p. 81]

It can now be seen that without a knowledge of God, a solution reached by utilizing the method of the *Regulae* can yield, at most, the highest mode of psychological assurance of which we are capable. The conclusion will be irresistible in light of the evidence presented; nevertheless, nothing put forth in the *Regulae* can assure us that what we perceive clearly and distinctly is true. The *Meditations* makes it clear that the mathematician is satisfied with the state of mind and level of certainty in mathematics. We learn from the *Regulae* that the philosopher can use mathematics as a model for generating a method of knowledge. Nevertheless, the provisional character of the method developed in the *Regulae* can only be removed when Descartes has successfully established that whatever is perceived clearly and distinctly is true. And this, he tells us in the synopsis to the *Meditations*, has been established in the Fourth Meditation:

. . . it is requisite that we may be assured that all things which we conceive clearly and distinctly are true in the very way in which we think them; and this could not be proved previously to the Fourth Meditation.

[p. 42]

In the Fourth Meditation it is shown that all these things which we very clearly and distinctly perceive are true.

[p. 43]

Metaphysical truths for Descartes are first principles, or as he refers to them in the Preface to the *Principles of Philosophy*, "the principles of knowledge." First principles cannot be conclusions of geometric-type demonstrations. In fact, the principles of knowledge, being first principles, cannot be conclusions of any argument. Therefore, a geometric or deductive-type demonstration is ruled out in the case of metaphysical first principles. Accordingly, Descartes correctly sees that the methodology developed in the *Regulae*, even if its reliability were assured, would not serve his purpose in the *Meditations*. According to the Third Meditation, geometric-type demonstrations will always be susceptible to doubt until we know that God exists and is not a deceiver. On the other hand, the *Meditations* reveals that knowledge of indubitable metaphysical principles can be had – in particular knowledge of the self in the *Cogito*, and knowledge of God – without the need for a divine guarantee. Accordingly, Descartes realizes that he must develop a method of demonstrating metaphysical truths which is more certain than the method of demonstrating geometric truths; metaphysics is possible only if metaphysical knowledge can be had without the divine guarantee, whereas geometric-type demonstrations can be considered knowledge only after the divine guarantee is obtained.

At this stage, it is easy to see that, given the nature and importance of metaphysical knowledge for Descartes, it could never have been his intention to apply the method developed in the *Regulae* to the *Meditations*. Both metaphysics and geometry utilize first principles. Descartes' analysis of the similarities and differences between metaphysics and geometry in regard to their respective first principles is to be found in the Replies to Objections II. He points out that the first principles of geometrical proofs "harmonize with the use of our senses, and are readily granted by all. Hence, no difficulty is involved in this case, except in the proper deduction of the consequences." [p. 102] In other words, no special method is required in order to intuit the first principles of geometry. Metaphysics, on the other hand, lacks this advantage:

[N]othing in metaphysics causes more trouble than the making the perception of its primary notions clear and distinct. For though in their own nature they are as intelligible as, or even more intelligible than those geometricians study, yet being contradicted by the many preconceptions of our senses to which we have since our earliest years been accustomed, they cannot be perfectly apprehended except by those who give strenuous attention and study to them, and withdraw their minds as far as possible from matters corporeal.

[pp. 102–3]

To apprehend the first principles of metaphysics, a different method of proof is required, which Descartes, in the Replies to Objections II, calls analysis [p. 101]. And it is this method of analysis, I submit, to which Descartes is referring in the letter to Mersenne. Notice that in his comment to Mersenne he says that he thinks he has discovered a way to demonstrate *metaphysical* truths which is more evident than the demonstrations of geometry. He is not saying that he has discovered a method for demonstrating *any* truth in a way which is more evident than geometry. It is in metaphysics that demonstrations more evident than those in geometry are required, because, as we have seen, metaphysics must provide demonstrations without the assistance of the divine guarantee, whereas in all ·other areas the divine guarantee will already be operative.

Descartes speaks of "demonstrations" in geometry, and in the letter to Mersenne, in the *Meditations*, and in the Replies to Objections II, he speaks of "demonstrations" in metaphysics. It is now clear that this term is being used equivocally. When applied to the *Regulae* and the geometric-type method developed in that work, "demonstration" is what we know as deductive reasoning. In the Replies to Objections II, this method of proof is called "synthesis."

Synthesis . . . does indeed clearly demonstrate its conclusions, and it employs a long series of definitions, postulates, axioms, theorems, and problems, so that if one of the conclusions that follows is denied, it may at once be shown to be contained in what has gone before. Thus the reader,

9

however hostile and obstinate, is compelled to render his assent.

[p. 102]

He insists that this method, "though it very suitably finds a place after analysis . . . nevertheless cannot so conveniently be applied to those metaphysical matters we are discussing." This is the case because the first principles of metaphysics are "contradicted by the many perceptions of our senses." For metaphysics, we require the method of analysis:

> Analysis shows the true way by which a thing was methodically discovered and derived . . . so that, if the reader care to follow it and give sufficient attention to everything, he understands the matter no less perfectly and makes it as much his own as if he had discovered it. But it contains nothing to incite belief in an inattentive and hostile reader; for if the very least thing brought forward escapes his notice, the necessity of the conclusions is lost.

[p. 103]

Descartes points out: "I have used in my Meditations only analysis, which is the best and truest method of teaching" [p. 102]. Analytic demonstrations are designed to guide the mind, so that all prejudice preventing us from grasping a first principle will be removed, and the first principles themselves can be intuited. An analytic demonstration, therefore, is, as it were, a process of "reasoning up" to first principles – the upward movement taking place as prejudice is removed. Accordingly, when, in the case of an analytic demonstration, Descartes speaks about drawing conclusions or concluding a first principle (for example, in the Second Meditation, he writes: "So that after having reflected well and carefully examined all things, we must come to the definite conclusions that this proposition: I am, I exist, is necessarily true each time that I pronounce it, or that I mentally conceive it"), he is not speaking of drawing a conclusion in a deductive argument. To draw a conclusion when employing analysis is tantamount to saying that I am now able to see (or better, intuit) the truth of a particular first principle.

The value of our present discussion is that it shows, at least in a general way, the type of proof of metaphysical principles we should expect to encounter in the *Meditations*, and the type of proof of first principles which we should not expect. We should not expect deductive proofs *of first principles*, although we may encounter some deductive proofs when involved with analysis. That is, an analytic demonstration could utilize a deductive proof, if this latter proof could help remove prejudice in the effort of apprehending a first principle. But the first principle itself will not be a conclusion of the deductive proof.

What, then, of the textual support used earlier in defense of Beck's and Curley's positions respectively? Our study has shown that Curley's position on the relation between the *Regulae* and the *Meditations* is fundamentally mistaken. Although Curley recognizes that the method of the *Regulae* is not the method of the *Meditations*, he fails to recognize the importance of the *Regulae* in Descartes' philosophical scheme, and, therefore, he fails to see that the *Regulae* expresses Descartes' method for philosophy, although it is not applicable to metaphysics. Curley fails to appreciate that the *Meditations*, in proving that whatever is perceived clearly and distinctly must be true, is also establishing the reliability of the *Regulae* insofar as it seeks knowledge which is clear and distinct.

Regarding the evidence cited in support of Beck's position, the following comments are relevant:

1 It is true that there is no indication in the *Regulae* that the method being developed will admit of areas where the method is inapplicable. Nevertheless, as we learned from the Replies to Objections II, the intuition of metaphysical first principles encounters difficulties because of prejudice which has no analog in the intuition of geometric first principles. Since the method developed in the *Regulae* uses a mathematical model, the removal of prejudice (as required in metaphysics) would not be addressed in the *Regulae*. In fact, it is precisely because geometry encounters no difficulties with the intuition of its first principles, that there is no (need for a) book in geometry comparable to the *Meditations*.

2 The *Regulae* emphasizes (see note 7) that the method being developed is a refinement of the method used in mathematics. We now understand that this refinement of the mathematical method is not what led Descartes to write to Mersenne about a way of demonstrating metaphysical truths which is more evident than geometric demonstrations. The refinement of the mathematical method is necessary for two reasons. First, since the mathematical method, as employed by mathematicians, is suited only to their concerns, the method must be refined if it is to have wider

application. And, second, the standards which Descartes set for the philosophical method are higher than the standards which the mathematician sets for gaining mathematical knowledge.[14] Accordingly, the mathematical method must be refined if it is to meet this higher standard.

It is important to realize that the letter to Mersenne is in no way referring to the *Regulae*. Metaphysics utilizes the method of analysis. And it is this method of demonstration which is more evident than geometric demonstrations. Geometric demonstrations reveal the logic of the proof being presented, and show how one proposition follows from others. The concern in such proofs, therefore, is with what follows from what. Analysis, on the other hand, is not concerned to show what follows from what, but is designed to lead the reader to discover, as it were first-hand, the truth of certain claims of necessary connections. Metaphysical first principles are always expressed in terms of what is necessarily connected with what – between thought and existence, between my finite existence and God's existence, between God and veracity, and between the clear and distinct and God as their cause. It is through analytic-type demonstrations that the reader is brought to see (a) that the ideas involved are necessarily connected, and (b) that, through analysis, the conviction attending our intuition "is so strong that we have no reason to doubt concerning that of the truth of which we have persuaded ourselves, [therefore] there is nothing more to enquire about; we have here all the certainty that can reasonably be desired . . . We have assumed a conviction so strong that nothing can remove it, and this persuasion is clearly the same as perfect certitude" (HR II, 41). A geometric-type demonstration always requires the divine guarantee, and never possesses perfect certitude; an analytic demonstration does not (at least in the Second and Third Meditations) require a divine guarantee, and does possess perfect certitude. And this is what Descartes had in mind in the letter to Mersenne.

3 In the course of our discussion, we have seen that Descartes urges that we study the *Regulae* before undertaking the *Meditations*, and we also saw that the concern in the *Meditations* with deception in mathematics does not in any sense refute or nullify the worth of the mathematical-type method developed in the *Regulae*. Just like the atheist who, without a knowledge of God, lacks "true science," so the philosopher will lack "true science" if

s/he solves problems using the method of the *Regulae* before gaining a knowledge of God. The *Regulae* does not provide the method which Descartes uses in the *Meditations*. The value of studying the *Regulae* is that it teaches us about the nature of knowledge, about the cognitive faculties through which knowing is possible, and about the method for gaining knowledge. The *Regulae* does not raise and address the skeptical objections introduced in the *Meditations*, and, therefore, the *Regulae* must await the proof of the truth of mathematics, and of the clear and distinct generally. I will now show how Descartes attempts to accomplish this in the *Meditations*.

If we follow Descartes from the beginning of the *Meditations* we find that he has the following to say regarding the establishment of a firm and permanent structure in the sciences. (a) From the synopsis to the First Meditation, we learn that it is essential that the mind rid itself of all prejudice, so that it can have before it only what is clear and distinct. (b) At the beginning of the Third Meditation, we are told that clarity and distinctness are the features which assured Descartes of the truth of his belief (arrived at in the Second Meditation) that he is a thing which thinks, although, with the aid of the hypothesis of a deceiving deity, he hesitates to generalize the connection between clarity and distinctness and truth. Nowhere in the *Meditations* does he give a definition of clarity and distinctness,[15] although he does state a characteristic of the clear and distinct, namely, the denial of such conceptions is "contradictory." In the case of certain conceptions, particularly mathematical ones, this contradiction is not adequate to ensure the truth of what is being conceived, and, as a result, he adds an additional requirement. (c) Descartes holds that he must establish the existence of a veracious God as his creator. But even this does not satisfy his doubts regarding the truth of the clear and distinct. In the Fourth Meditation he continues his inquiry into deception, despite the fact that he knows that God is his creator and that God is not a deceiver.[16] And in two different passages in the Synopsis to the Meditations, we are told that the principle of clarity and distinctness has not been established prior to the Fourth Meditation.[17] (4) Accordingly, Descartes requires something beyond a knowledge of God as his creator, if all clear and distinct conceptions are to be accepted as true.

I now propose to examine these four matters in order to determine how Descartes establishes the reliability of mathematics and, more generally, the truth of the principle concerning clarity and distinctness.

1 Unprejudicing the mind   The firm and permanent structure which Descartes is seeking for the sciences requires that he begin with what is certain and indubitable. As such, he must reject (and treat as false) those matters in which he finds any reason whatever for doubt. The effect of this doubt is to provide a counterbalance to his former beliefs; by this means, he can make himself indifferent to all matters with respect to which any doubt can be generated.[18] What remains will be those matters which are clear and distinct, the paradigm for which is held to be the *Cogito ergo sum*.

2 The denial of the clear and distinct is contradictory   We must now explain what Descartes means when he asserts that the denial of clear and distinct conceptions is a "contradiction", while also seeking to explain why this feature of contradictoriness is not regarded as an indubitable sign of truth in the case of some clear and distinct conceptions.

Does he mean that the denial of conceptions which are clear and distinct is logically contradictory in the sense that the denial is an assertion of the form $(P \cdot \sim P)$? From certain things which he says, it can be shown that this is not his meaning. In providing evidence for this claim, I will focus on the *Cogito*, which, as we know, is clear and distinct.

At the beginning of the Reply to the Sixth Set of Objections, he writes of the *Cogito*:

> It is indeed true that no one can be sure that he knows or that he exists, unless he knows what thought is and what exist-ence. . . . It is altogether enough for one to know it by means of that internal cognition which always precedes reflective knowledge, and which, when the object is thought and exist-ence, is innate in all men. . . . When, therefore, anyone per-ceives that he thinks and that it thence follows that he exists, although he chance never previously to have asked what thought is, nor what existence, he cannot nevertheless fail to have a knowledge of each sufficient to give him assurance on this score.
>
> (HR II, 241)

In this passage and several others which can be cited,[19] he maintains that "thought" and "existence" are among those notions "of the simplest possible kind" which must be known if the *Cogito* is to be understood and regarded as certain. Therefore, "thought" and "existence" are not identical concepts for Descartes in the way in which, for example, "bachelor" and "unmarried male" are conceptually identical. The conceptual identity of the latter two concepts accounts for the contradiction involved in the denial of "All bachelors are unmarried males." But "thought" and "existence" are not conceptually identical: therefore, although the denial of the *Cogito* may be false, even necessarily false, the denial is not self-contradictory. We conclude from this that either Descartes did not understand that his position on "thought" and "existence" should have kept him from claiming that a contradiction results if the *Cogito* is denied, or by a "contradiction" in this context he means something different from what is meant when we say that the denial of "All bachelors are unmarried males" is a contradiction. I will now establish that it is the latter disjunct which Descartes supports.

In the Replies to Objections II, immediately following his claim that some clear and distinct perceptions of the intellect, including the *Cogito*, possess a perfect certitude, Descartes writes that their perfect certitude is found in the fact that "in their case we can never doubt about believing them true" (HR II, 42). What follow are his reasons for this claim:

> For we cannot doubt them unless we think of them; but we cannot think of them without at the same time believing them to be true, the position taken up. Hence we can never doubt them without at the same time believing them to be true; i.e. we can never doubt them.
>
> (HR II, 42)

If this argument is set out in a more rigorous form – which includes providing the premise which he has omitted – what he means when he says that the denial of the *Cogito* is a contradiction will become evident. The passage quoted actually contains two arguments (Hypothetical Syllogisms):

(a) If the *Cogito* is doubted then it is thought.
   If the *Cogito* is thought then it is believed to be true.
   Therefore, if the *Cogito* is doubted then it is believed to be true.

(b) If the *Cogito* is doubted then it is believed to be true.

If the *Cogito* is believed to be true then it cannot be doubted.

Therefore, if the *Cogito* is doubted then it cannot be doubted.

According to these arguments, the contradiction is not in the *Cogito*, or more precisely, in its denial. It is the *effort* or *activity of denial* which is self-contradictory. An effort or activity would be self-contradictory if seeking to engage in it resulted in engaging in the opposite effort or activity. And Descartes maintains that this is precisely the situation with the *Cogito*: if you begin by trying to doubt it, you find that you cannot doubt it.[20]

Descartes' position regarding the contradiction involved in the effort of denying the *Cogito* can be further developed by examining his views on "necessary connections" as presented in the *Regulae*. In Rule XII, he cites as examples of simple natures which are necessarily connected "figure and extension," "motion and duration," and "7 and (4+3)." A connection between simples is necessary "when one is so implied in the concept of another in a confused sort of way that we cannot conceive either distinctly, if our thought assigns to them separateness from each other" (HR I, 41). There can, of course, be difficulty in deciding whether items can be conceived distinctly when they are regarded as separate, and to assist with this Descartes offers the following test: affirm in thought the first conception (for example, figure, motion, 7) and at the same time deny the second (for example, extension, duration, the sum of 4 and 3); in those cases where the denial of the second carries with it the inconceivability of the first, the first is necessarily connected to the second, and where the denial of the second does not carry with it the inconceivability of the first, the first is not necessarily connected to the second: "Thus figure is conjoined with extension, motion with duration or time, and so on, because it is impossible to conceive of a figure that has no extension, nor of a motion that has no duration" (HR I, 41). Descartes' notion of a necessary connection between simple natures, therefore, does not require that one thought be conceptually identical to another as is the case with "bachelor" and "unmarried male," but rather that one thought be a *sine qua non* for thinking the other.[21]

Now when two ideas are inseparable in the manner specified, it follows that when the first is thought, the second is also before the mind, although we may not be aware of this. The more prejudiced the mind, the less likely that it will be able to apprehend what is necessarily connected with what: "[M]any things are often necessarily united with one another, though most people, not noticing what their true relation is, reckon them among those that are contingently connected. As examples, I give the following proposition 'I exist, therefore God exists': also 'I know, therefore I have a mind distinct from my body', etc." (HR I, 43). Descartes insists, therefore, that to know what simple natures are necessarily connected does not require that we bring ideas together in the intellect. For, once the mind has been freed of prejudice, we need only be attentive to the simple natures before the mind to determine which are necessarily connected. In the light of this account of necessity, we can understand why necessary connections between simple natures are such that any effort to think the denial of the connection results in a contradiction of the effort. To attempt to doubt the connection requires affirming in thought the first idea, while, at the same time, denying the second one. However, since the simple natures are inseparable, we always find this to be an impossible task: once we deny the second idea, we find that we cannot think the first. Therefore, if we begin by trying to doubt these connections, we find that we cannot doubt them – either the second is thought while the first is thought, or the first cannot be thought. To think the first, therefore, requires thinking the second at the same time.

We must now explain why the hypothesis of the deceiving deity is regarded as a source of doubt in the case of mathematical statements, and not in the case of the *Cogito*.

By the end of the fourth paragraph of the Third Meditation, Descartes realizes that the clear and distinct conception of the *Cogito* makes it impossible for him to affirm that he thinks while denying that he exists, and that the same impossibility pertains to mathematical statements which are also clear and distinct. And yet, the former escapes all doubt, and the latter does not. To explain this, we must consider the fundamental difference which obtains between the *Cogito* on the one hand, and mathematical and other clear and distinct conceptions. When I think that $5 = 2 + 3$ or that motion is necessarily connected with duration, I find that I cannot think otherwise. Similarly, when I think that thought and existence are necessarily connected, I find that I cannot think otherwise. Now, to doubt, through the hypothesis of the deceiving deity, that $5 = 2 + 3$ or that motion is necessarily connected with duration, requires considering that the deceiving deity has so constituted my mind that, although I cannot think these connections other than the way I am thinking them, what I am thinking is false. But how could this be? Under what circumstances would it be false that $5 = 2 + 3$, and that motion is necessarily connected with duration? It would be false that motion is necessarily connected with duration if something could move even though time did not pass; similarly, it would be false that $5 = 2 + 3$ provided that there could be a set of 2 and a set of 3 which do not equal a set of 5. In short, Descartes' concern with clear and distinct conceptions is that his way of thinking may not represent the way these items are actually related – however their relation has been brought about – and yet he cannot help believing that they are always related as he finds he must think them. That this is precisely his concern in the Third Meditation can be seen from the fact that after he has established that what is perceived clearly and distinctly is true, he explicitly maintains that it is this problem which need no longer concern him: "But now . . . because I can draw the idea of something from my thought, it follows that all which I know clearly and distinctly as pertaining to this object does really belong to it" [pp. 81–2].

In the case of the *Cogito*, I intuit that thought and existence are necessarily connected, and, according to Descartes, I need not have – or, better, I cannot have – any doubts regarding this connection of the sort which arise in the case of mathematics. For with the *Cogito*, the connection thought is the connection thought about; it is the actual relation between the items involved which is being intuited when we think the connection between thought and existence: "What of thinking? I find here that thought is an attribute that belongs to me; it alone cannot be separated from me. I am, I exist, that is certain. But how often? Just when I think; for it might possibly be the case if I ceased entirely to think, that I should likewise cease altogether to exist" [pp. 52–3]. Therefore, Descartes' reason for distinguishing the *Cogito* from other matters which are clear and distinct and are found to be necessarily connected is that only in the case of the *Cogito* are we apprehending the items about which we are thinking, and, therefore, only in this case is the clarity and distinctness of the necessary connection between thought and existence an indubitable guarantor of the truth of this connection. For doubting here requires believing that the connection between thought and existence is not as I intuit it – even while I am intuiting it. And Descartes insists that such doubt is not possible: when the mind is freed of prejudice, what presents itself as clear and distinct is clear and distinct. The additional feature with respect to the *Cogito* is that the necessary connection intuited is the actual connection with which thought is concerned. Hence, not only can I not doubt what I am intuiting, I also cannot doubt the truth of what I am intuiting. With mathematical statements, on the other hand, to know that the connection intuited is the actual connection and, therefore, to know that the intuited connection is true, requires knowing that the way in which thought apprehends the connection between the items involved is the way the items must always be connected. And to know this, more is involved than the knowledge that the denial of mathematical statements which are clear and distinct is a contradiction in the manner explicated earlier.

Since it is the hypothesis of a deceiving deity which renders doubtful all necessary connections which are intuited, with the exception of the connection in the *Cogito*, Descartes maintains that he must inquire whether there is a God and whether He may be a deceiver.

3 Establishing the existence of God By the Third Meditation, Descartes is not troubled with whether a particular conception is clear and distinct. His concern at this stage is whether the necessary connections he intuits and apprehends clearly and distinctly invariably represent the manner in which the relata must stand to each other. Unless he can establish this, he must refrain from speaking of what is clearly and distinctly apprehended as true.

Now, in the light of these considerations, the proofs of God's existence show themselves to be unacceptable. For the essence of the proofs is to show that the objective reality of the idea of God is such that I can have this idea only if there is a Being who possesses formally all that which the idea of God possesses objectively, and, in the case of the second proof, that I, who have the idea of God, can exist only if there is a Being who possesses formally all that which the idea of God possesses objectively.[22] Each of these proofs requires, for its acceptability, the very condition which the proofs of God's existence are intended to establish, namely, that the relata – in the case of the first proof the idea of God and God, and in the case of the second the self which possesses the idea of God and God – must stand to each other as he apprehends their relation in the proofs.

To avoid this, it might be suggested that the idea of God stands to the idea of the self in a manner analogous to the way in which "existence" stands to "thinking" in the *Cogito*; if this is the case, he need not hesitate to hold as true what he perceives clearly and distinctly regarding God's relation to the self. Once again, there would be no distinction between what is thought and what is thought about, and, therefore, whatever necessary connection he apprehends would be indubitable.

There are, in fact, a number of passages which indicate that Descartes takes this position seriously. The first appears toward the end of the Third Meditation, when he asks how he acquired the idea of God:

> It only remains to me to examine into the manner in which I have acquired this idea from God; for I have not received it through the senses . . . nor is it likewise a fiction of my mind, for it is not in my power to take from or to add anything to it; and consequently the only alternative is that it is innate in me, just as the idea of myself is innate in me. And one certainly ought not to find it strange that God, in creating me, placed this idea within me to be like the mark of the workman imprinted on his work; and it is likewise not essential that the mark shall be something different from the work itself.
>
> [p. 71]

For Descartes, to have the idea of the self is to have the idea of God *in that thought*, that is to say, these two ideas are necessarily connected. And when he speaks of the idea of God in the last three paragraphs of the Third Meditation, he makes it plain that this necessary connection is apprehended intuitively:

> [I]n some way he has placed his image and similitude upon me, and . . . I perceive this similitude (in which the idea of God is contained) by means of the same faculty by which I perceive myself – that is to say, when I reflect on myself I not only know that I am something [imperfect], incomplete and dependent on another, which incessantly aspires after something which is better and greater than myself, but I also know that He on whom I depend possesses in Himself all the great things towards which I aspire and the ideas of which I find within myself, and that not indefinitely or potentially alone, but really, actually, and infinitely; and that thus He is God.
>
> [p. 71–2]

Nevertheless, even if the awareness of God is achieved through the

20

same intuition as that through which he is aware of the self, this does not, by itself, prove the truth of the necessary connection between the self and God and of the claim that God exists, for there remains the question – the same as that raised in regard to mathematics – whether what is thought accords with what is thought about. Even if this problem does not arise in the case of one of the relata – the self – it can still be raised regarding the other, God. To show that the intuition containing the awareness of the self and God is reliable and, therefore, true, it would have to be shown that the awareness of God through the intuition of the self is like the awareness of the self in this intuition – there must be no distinction between what I am thinking and that about which I am thinking. But how, in the case of God, can this be upheld? An intuition concerning God is not the same as (apprehending) God, in the way in which the intuition of the self is the same as (apprehending) the self.

I will now show how Descartes deals with this very difficult problem. The relevant passage appears in the Replies to Objections V, wherein, through an illustrative analogy, he clarifies his position that the idea of God is "like the mark of the workman imprinted on his work":

> When you ask whence I get my proof that the idea of God is, as it were, the mark of a workman imprinted on his work, and what is the mode in which it is impressed, and what is the form of that mark, it is very much as if I, coming across a picture which showed a technique that pointed to Apelles alone as the painter, were to say that the inimitable technique was, so to speak, a mark impressed by Apelles on all his pictures in order to distinguish them from others, but you replied with the questions: "what is the form of that mark?" and "what is its mode of impression?" Such an inquiry would seem to merit laughter rather than any reply.
>
> (HR II, 221)

The idea of God stands to the idea of the self in a manner analogous to the relation between a painter's technique and works of art which result from this technique. Accordingly, the idea of God is contained in the intuition of oneself as a thinking thing in a manner analogous to the way in which the observation of a painting contains within itself the technique of the artist who created the painting. Just as observing a painting aids in apprehending the

21

technique through which the painting has come to be, so by understanding myself through the *Cogito* I come to understand the only way in which I could have come to be. Therefore, when apprehending God within the intuition of the self, there is no basis for a distinction between what is intuited and what the intuition is about, in the same way that, when apprehending the technique in a painting, there is no basis for a distinction between what is apprehended and what the apprehension is about. It is in this way, then, according to Descartes, that indubitability pertains to the awareness of God in the intuition of the self.

It is important to understand that once God's "mark" in the awareness of the self is intuited, there is no need for the "proof" of God's existence: to know the self is to know God. The proofs in the Third Meditation can lead the mind to a knowledge of God in the sense of clearing the mind of prejudice so that the essential necessary connection can be intuited; but the proofs are not a substitute for this intuition and, as we have seen, they fall short of the indubitability requirement which he insists must be maintained. In the light of Descartes' doubts about clarity and distinctness, the proofs point to the fact that for a knowledge of God the apprehension of God would have to be like the apprehension of the self in that there can be no distinction between the intuition and the referent of that intuition. And once the idea of God is recognized as God's "mark" or "stamp" which is inseparable from the idea of the self, we know that God exists with the same certainty as we know that the self exists, and we require no further "proof" of God's existence.

In seeking to understand this intuition, it will be helpful to begin with a passage in which Descartes calls attention to the fact that finitude can only be understood in the light of the infinite:

> I see that there is manifestly more reality in infinite substance than in finite, and therefore that in some way I have in me the notion of the infinite earlier than the finite – to wit, the notion of God before that of myself. For how would it be possible that I should know that I doubt and desire, that is to say, that something is lacking to me, and that I am not quite perfect, unless I had within me some idea of a Being more perfect than myself, in comparison with which I should recognize the deficiencies of my nature?
>
> [p. 67]

This passage, which occurs in the course of the first proof of God's existence, is of interest here in that it reveals how a knowledge of the infinite in relation to a finite knower is being sought, namely, through the recognition that an awareness of the idea of the infinite is necessary in order to be aware of oneself as a finite being. In other words, at this stage of his analysis he finds that if he affirms that he knows himself as a finite being and at the same time denies that he has an awareness of an infinite being, then he can no longer think of himself as a finite being. As we know from the *Regulae*, this test of inconceivability is Descartes' way of determining which ideas are necessarily connected. By the Third Meditation, he finds that his finitude is inconceivable without an awareness of the infinite; accordingly, he holds that the two ideas are inseparable.

Once both proofs of God's existence have been put forth, his mind has been unprejudiced to the point where a fuller appreciation of the relation between the idea of God and the idea of the self can be had, for now the idea of God is recognized to be God's "mark" imprinted on his mind, which is apprehended through the same intuition as that through which the self is known. Descartes now realizes that not only could he not know himself as a finite being unless the thought of the infinite was inseparably connected with it, but also that he cannot exist as a finite being unless an infinitely perfect being exists as the cause of his existence. The test or analytic demonstration of the necessary connection between his existence as a finite being and the existence of God is, once again, that of inconceivability: if he thinks of himself existing as a finite being and at the same time denies that he owes his existence to an infinitely perfect being, then he can no longer think of himself existing as a finite being: "And the whole strength of the argument which I have here made use of to prove the existence of God consists in this, that I recognise that it is not possible that my nature should be what it is . . . if God did not veritably exist" [p. 72].

We find the same approach in the Second Meditation, after he has established the indubitability and truth of his existence. He goes on to ask what he is, and finds that, of all the beliefs he formerly held about his nature, only that he thinks can be affirmed indubitably: "What of thinking? I find here that thought is an attribute that belongs to me; it alone cannot be separated from me" [pp. 52–3]. That is, he demonstrates that his nature is to think by establishing that if he thinks of himself as existing and denies that he thinks, then his existence is rendered inconceivable.

Accordingly, he concludes that his nature is that of a thinking thing.

The same type of consideration leads Descartes to the next stage of his analysis. Having established that he is a thinking thing, he asks himself what it is to be a thinking thing, that is, what is inseparably connected with thinking. And he answers: "It is a thing which doubts, understands, [conceives], affirms, denies, wills, refuses, which also imagines and feels" [p. 54]. The analytic demonstration again takes the form of affirming the first relatum, and finding that it can no longer be conceived if the second relatum is denied.

The intuition through which God is known is, for Descartes, nothing more than an additional case of determining what is inseparably connected with what: in this case, that the thought of my existence as a finite being is inseparably connected with the thought of an infinitely perfect being as the cause of my existence.

Once a knowledge of God is gained through the intuition of the self, Descartes' approach to gaining knowledge of the non-deceiving nature of God is as follows. To establish that God may be a deceiver requires being able to think the notion of deception in the awareness of God. To establish that God must be a deceiver, that is, that the notion of deception is necessarily connected with the idea of God, requires finding that the effort of thinking God while denying that He is a deceiver results in the fact that God cannot be thought (Descartes' test of inseparability). And in order to maintain that God cannot be a deceiver, it must be the case that given the idea he has of God and his idea of fraud and deception, there is a necessary repugnancy between them: "all contradictoriness or impossibility is constituted by our thought, which cannot join together ideas that disagree with each other" (HR II, 46). An examination of the idea of God and fraud and deception reveals such a necessary repugnancy:

> . . . I recognize it to be impossible that He should ever deceive me; for in all fraud and deception some imperfection is to be found, and although it may appear that the power of deception is a mark of subtility or power, yet the desire to deceive without doubt testifies to malice or feebleness, and accordingly cannot be found in God.
>
> [p. 73]

Similarly, at the end of the Third Meditation, Descartes speaks of

24

God as that being "who possesses all those supreme perfections of which our mind may indeed have some idea but without understanding them all, who is liable to no errors or defect [and who has none of all those marks which denote imperfection]." He then points out: "From this it is manifest that He cannot be a deceiver since the light of nature teaches us that fraud and deception necessarily proceed from some defect" [p. 72].

Accordingly, through the necessary repugnancy which he finds between the idea of God and fraud and deception, he concludes that it cannot ever be the case that God is a deceiver. It follows from this that when, in the first three Meditations, God is spoken of as a deceiver, what is before the mind cannot be the true idea of God, for if it were the repugnancy between this idea and fraud and deception would have been apprehended.[23]

4 The last stage: establishing that what I perceive clearly and distinctly must be true That God exists and is not a deceiver is held by Descartes in the Third Meditation to be that which must be known if what is perceived clearly and distinctly can be regarded as true. It would seem, therefore, that the truth of the principle concerning clarity and distinctness has been established at the end of the Third Meditation. Nevertheless, we are told in the Synopsis to the Meditations that it is in the Fourth Meditation that this principle has been established. In our effort to understand Descartes' arguments in the Fourth Meditation, it is important to point out that in addition to a knowledge of the self in the *Cogito*, and a knowledge of God, Descartes considers a knowledge of the truth of the principle concerning clarity and distinctness to be a principle uncovered in metaphysics – the subject-matter of the *Meditations*. Therefore, the principle concerning clarity and distinctness must in the end be shown to be intuitively certain; in accordance with the method of analysis, the arguments presented are designed to unprejudice the mind and bring the attention to the point where the relevant primary notions can be intuited.

The synopsis to the *Meditations* indicates that the principle concerning clarity and distinctness has been established "at the same time as it is explained in what the nature of error or falsity consists" [p. 43]. Now, in seeking to account for error in the Fourth Meditation Descartes isolates the will and the understanding as the faculties from which error can arise: error, we are told, stems from assenting to matters which are not perceived clearly and distinctly:

Whence then come my errors? They come from the sole fact that since the will is much wider in its range and compass than the understanding, I do not restrain it within the same bounds, but extend it to things which I do not understand: and as the will is of itself indifferent to these, it easily falls into error and sin, and chooses evil for good, or the false for the true. . . . But if I abstain from giving my judgment on any thing when I do not perceive it with sufficient clearness and distinctness, it is plain that I act rightly and am not deceived.

[p. 77]

In the Third Meditation, Descartes questioned the truth of clear and distinct ideas (except for the *Cogito*) because of a concern with a deceiving deity. His concern was that perhaps he had been created by God in such a way that he cannot but think certain ideas as necessarily connected, and yet the items thought are not connected in the way he finds he must think them. Once he knows that God exists and is not a deceiver, he knows that his faculty of judgment, if used correctly, cannot lead him to error and deception. Since the doubt regarding clear and distinct ideas was generated by the concern with a deceiving deity, once he knows that God exists and is not a deceiver, he presumably knows that the correct use of the faculty of judgment is to assent only to what is clear and distinct. But if this is all that he requires to know in order to establish the truth of the principle regarding clarity and distinctness, then the truth of this principle has been established by the end of the Third Meditation. That he devotes an additional Meditation to this principle indicates that establishing its truth requires knowing more than that he was created by an all-powerful veracious God.

The passage we examined above, in which error is held to consist in assenting to what is not perceived clearly and distinctly, and truth is said to consist in assenting only to what is perceived clearly and distinctly, does follow from his analysis in the Third Meditation. That is, if his only doubt regarding a knowledge of truth and the source of error is whether God can be a deceiver, then, once he knows that God cannot deceive, he knows both that truth is found in the clear and distinct, and that error is found in the obscure and confused. However, since knowing that an all-powerful, veracious deity exists who created him is not sufficient to establish the truth of the principle of clarity and distinctness, it

26

follows that the analysis we have examined thus far in the Fourth Meditation, although it serves to clarify the faculties which can be involved in truth and error, cannot be considered a proof of the source of truth and error. His analysis shows how truth and error arise, provided the principle of clarity and distinctness is a reliable source of truth; however, the reliability of this principle has yet to be established.

But what more does Descartes insist must be known before the principle in question can be accepted as true? Since he already knows who his creator is, it cannot be his own causal origin which must be established. The intellect is God's product; but the ideas to which he finds he must assent – those which are clear and distinct – could have been given to him by the evil genius. This, I submit, is the lingering concern which carries the investigation of the truth of the principle of clarity and distinctness beyond the Third and into the Fourth Meditation: Descartes has still to know the cause of the clear and distinct.

The causal origin of the clear and distinct and its bearing on the truth of these ideas is discussed in the last paragraph of the Fourth Meditation:

> [I]t seems to me that I have not gained little by this day's Meditation, since I have discovered the source of falsity and error. And certainly there can be no other source than that which I have explained; for as often as I restrain my will within the limits of my knowledge that it forms no judgment except on matters which are clearly and distinctly represented to it by the understanding, I can never be deceived; *for every clear and distinct conception is without doubt something, and hence cannot derive its origin from what is nought, but must of necessity have God as its author – God, I say, who being supremely perfect, cannot be the cause of any error: and consequently we must conclude that such a conception is true.*
>
> [pp. 79–80]

In the Fifth Meditation, Descartes writes: "I have already fully demonstrated that all that I know clearly is true" (p. 81) and, in the passage quoted above, I have italicized that portion which contains his demonstration of the principle of clarity and distinctness.

From the passages already examined in the Replies to Objections II we know that analysis employs "demonstration", although not in the way in which synthesis does. All the differences between "demonstration" as employed by the analytic method and "demonstration" as employed by synthesis cannot be discussed here; our inquiry will be confined to explicating the "analytic demonstration" which Descartes employs in the last paragraph of the Fourth Meditation in order to establish the truth of the principle of clarity and distinctness.

From the Replies to Objections II we know that an "analytic demonstration" is designed to bring the attention to the point where all prejudices have been removed and the relevant primary notions can be intuited: Descartes insists that its special value lies in the fact that if the reader follows the demonstration and attends sufficiently to it, it will appear as though the reader has discovered the particular matter on his/her own. Our treatment of the "demonstration" employed in the Fourth Meditation must accord with these points.

To assist us with our study, I would first like to turn to a passage in the Second Meditation, namely, the one in which Descartes "demonstrates" his own existence:

> But I was persuaded that there was nothing at all in the world, that there was no heaven, no earth, that there were no minds, nor any bodies: was I not then likewise persuaded that I did not exist? Not at all; of a surety I myself did exist since I persuaded myself of something or merely because I thought of something. But there is some deceiver or other, very powerful and very cunning, whoever employs his ingenuity in deceiving me. Then without doubt I exist also if he deceives me, and let him deceive me as much as he will, he can never cause me to be nothing so long as I think that I am something. So that after having reflected well and carefully examined all things, we must come to the definite conclusion that this proposition: I am, I exist, is necessarily true each time that I pronounce it, or that I mentally conceive it.[24]

This passage contains two "demonstrations" of his existence – the first based on the notion of persuasion and the second on deception. The persuasion "demonstration" appears to be the following: Descartes affirms something which he cannot doubt, namely, that he was persuaded of something; he then attempts to affirm in thought both that he was persuaded of something and that he does not exist; by finding a repugnancy between these two thoughts (i.e. he cannot affirm in thought both that he was persuaded and that he does not exist) he concludes that his initial thought is necessarily connected with the denial of the second. A similar situation obtains in regard to his second demonstration: he affirms what he cannot doubt – that he has been deceived; he then attempts to affirm in thought both that he was deceived, and that he does not exist; by finding a repugnancy between these two thoughts, he concludes that his initial thought is necessarily connected with the denial of the second: if he is deceived, then necessarily he exists.

We can now understand why Descartes holds that an analytic demonstration, if properly attended to by the reader, will make it appear as though the reader has discovered the matter in question on his own: the "demonstration" is designed to guide the reader's attention to the relevant ideas, so that the appropriate impossible connections and necessary connections can be intuited. The repugnancies and necessities which the demonstration points out can only be appreciated by entertaining the very ideas of which the demonstration speaks, and apprehending intuitively the impossibilities and necessities. The demonstration is not a substitute for the intuition, nor for that matter can it be accepted without the intuition. As a result, the connections which the demonstration is designed to point out do not follow as conclusions from the (premises of the) demonstration. To hold otherwise is to confuse "analytic demonstration" with "synthetic demonstration" – the method of proof in metaphysics with the method of proof in geometry.

We know from Descartes' demonstration of the non-deceiving nature of God that in all fraud and deception there must be some imperfection. For a clear and distinct perception to be deceptive, therefore, insofar as its causal origin is concerned, it would have to derive from some imperfect source. Therefore, when Descartes uses the word "nought" in his demonstration of the truth of the clear and distinct ("for every clear and distinct conception is without doubt something, and hence cannot derive its origin from what is nought, but must of necessity have God as its author") we can take this to mean a cause which falls short of supreme perfection.

Descartes' "demonstration" of the truth of the principle of clarity and distinctness is analogous to his "demonstration" of his existence in the Second Meditation. The demonstration in the Second Meditation begins with some matter which he cannot doubt (that he was persuaded of something, that he has been deceived), and his demonstration in the Fourth Meditation begins with what he also cannot doubt – "that every clear and distinct conception is something [real]." From other things which Descartes says about the clear and distinct, I take it that when he says that every clear and distinct conception is something real, he means that it is apprehended as possessing a fixed or immutable nature. In the case of his existence, he then attempts to affirm in thought the matter which he cannot doubt and his non-existence; in the Fourth Meditation, we find him attempting to affirm that every clear and distinct conception is something real (that it has a fixed or immutable nature) and that it arises from some imperfect cause. In both the Second and the Fourth Meditation, he finds a repugnancy between the ideas involved – being persuaded and non-existence, being deceived and non-existence, being real and coming from an imperfect source. In each case, he then concludes (intuits) that his initial thought is necessarily connected with the denial of the second: accordingly, in the case of the Fourth Meditation, he intuits that the clear and distinct is necessarily derived from God, who Descartes knows cannot be a deceiver. This, then, is Descartes' "demonstration" of the truth of the principle of clarity and distinctness – a principle whose truth is known intuitively.

A number of consequences follow from the view of the relationship between the *Regulae* and the *Meditations* discussed here.

First, in accordance with our account, the *Meditations* performs a dual function – this work provides metaphysical first principles (the first principles of all learning) as well as a proof of the reliability of mathematics. Since the *Regulae* is based on a mathematical model, Descartes can now be confident that when the method of the *Regulae* is utilized and leads to ideas (conclusions) which are clear and distinct, the conclusions can be accepted as true.

Therefore the *Meditations*, in providing a proof of the reliability of mathematics, is also providing assurance of the reliability of the *Regulae*, when the employment of the latter leads to what is clear and distinct. Although we are instructed to study the *Regulae* before we study the *Meditations* (for the reasons set out earlier), it is only after we study the *Meditations* that the method of the *Regulae* can be used to arrive at "true science." This is a point which neither Beck nor Curley recognizes.

A second consequence which follows from our study is the exposure of a misinterpretation of Descartes' philosophy which is virtually universal – a misinterpretation which Descartes has helped to promulgate. In light of the fact that a mathematical method is developed by Descartes in the *Regulae*, it is easy to conclude that he sees all learning along the lines of a deductive system. Rule I certainly lends itself to such an interpretation. For example, he writes:

> there is nothing more prone to turn us aside from the correct way of seeking out truth than this directing of our inquiries, not towards their general end, but towards certain special investigations.

(HR I, 2)

Or again:

> Hence we must believe that all the sciences are so interconnected, that it is much easier to study them all together than to isolate one from all the others. If, therefore, anyone wishes to search out the truth of things in serious earnest, he ought not to select one special science; for all the sciences are conjoined to each other and interdependent.

(HR I, 2)

It is tempting to think that the interdependence and interconnectedness of which he speaks are logical in nature, as in a deductive or axiomatic system. However, at least insofar as the *Meditations* is related to the other branches of learning (physics, medicine, mechanics, and morals), the first principles of knowledge in the *Meditations* are not related *logically* to these other fields. It is rather that we must know the first principles of metaphysics before we can proceed in these other areas, and not that these first principles are premises in certain logical deductions. The connections between thought and existence, my existence and God's existence, etc., which are revealed in the *Meditations*, are not the first *premises* from which the physics begins.

NOTES

1 L. J. Beck, *The Method of Descartes: A Study of the Regulae* (Oxford: Clarendon Press, 1952).
2 ibid., p. 9.
3 ibid., p. 13.
4 E. M. Curley, *Descartes against the Skeptics* (Cambridge, Mass.: Harvard University Press, 1978).
5 ibid., pp. 37–8.
6 HR I, 2. References to passages not reproduced in the present volume are quoted from *The Philosophical Works of Descartes*, trans. Elizabeth S.

Haldane and G. R. T. Ross (Cambridge: Cambridge University Press, 1911) (hereafter HR).

7 "This method of ours resembles indeed those devices employed by the mechanical crafts, which do not need the aid of anything outside of them, but themselves supply the directions for making their own instruments. Thus, if a man wished to practise any one of them, e.g., the craft of a smith, and were destitute of all instruments, he would be forced to use at first a hard stone or a rough clump of iron as an anvil, take a piece of rock in place of a hammer, make pieces of wood serve as tongs, and provide himself with other such tools as necessity required. Thus equipped, he would not then at once attempt to forge swords or helmets or any manufactured article of iron to use. He would first of all fashion hammer, anvil, tongs, and the other tools useful for himself. This example teaches us that, since thus at the outset we have been able to discover only some rough precepts, apparently the innate possession of our mind, rather than the product of technical skill, we should not forthwith attempt to settle the controversies of Philosophers, or solve the puzzles of Mathematicians by their help. We must first employ them for searching out with our utmost attention all the other things that are more urgently required in the investigation of truth." (HR I, 25–6)

8 HR I, 210.

9 HR I, 211.

10 HR I, 221.

11 Curley, *Descartes against the Skeptics*, p. 36.

12 ibid., p. 44. There can be no doubt that the systematic review of one's past beliefs is part of the Cartesian enterprise in the *Meditations*. However, Descartes' method in the *Meditations* is far more complicated than this, particularly in regard to deciding which beliefs are to be retained. Descartes is somewhat to blame for the fact that commentators (like Curley) have a tendency to oversimplify his method in the *Meditations*. See, e.g., HR II, 282, and II, 61, where he replies to an objection by Hobbes.

13 HR II, 39.

14 A clear case of this is Descartes' concern with deduction as utilized by the mathematician and the philosopher. See Rules III, VII, X.

15 He does so elsewhere: see HR I, 237, Principle XLV.

16 "And no doubt respecting this matter could remain, if it were not that consequences would seem to follow that I can thus never be deceived; for if I hold all that I possess from God, and if He has not placed in me the capacity for error, it seems as though I could never fall into error. And it is true that when I think only of God [and direct my mind wholly to Him], I discover [in myself] no cause of error, of falsity; yet directly afterwards, when recurring to myself, experience shows me that I am nevertheless subject to an infinitude of errors" [p. 73].

17 "[I]t is requisite that we may be assured that all the things which we conceive clearly and distinctly are true in the very way in which we think them; and this could not be proved previously to the Fourth Meditation" [p. 42; italics omitted]. "In the Fourth Meditation, it is shown that all these things which we very clearly and distinctly per-

ceive are true and at the same time it is explained in what the nature of error and falsity consists" [p. 43; italics omitted].

18 "[T]hese ancient and commonly held opinions still revert frequently to my mind, long and familiar custom having given them the right to occupy my mind against my inclination and rendered them almost masters of my belief; nor will I ever lose the habit of deferring to them or of placing my confidence in them, so long as I consider them as they really are, i.e. opinions in some measure doubtful . . . and at the same time highly probable, so that there is much more reason to believe in than to deny them. That is why I consider that I shall not be acting amiss, if, taking of set purpose a contrary belief, I allow myself to be deceived, and for a certain time pretend that all these opinions are entirely false and imaginary, until at last, having thus balanced my former prejudices with my latter (so that they cannot divert my opinions more to one side than to the other), my judgment will no longer be dominated by bad usage or turned away from the right knowledge of the truth" [p. 49].

This same point, that to be unprejudiced means being indifferent except where what is before the mind is certain and indubitable, is also made by Descartes in the Fourth Meditation when he reviews the value of the arguments in the first meditation. See especially p. 72.

19 HR I, 222, Principle X; HR I, 324, 325.

20 We can schematize exactly what Descartes means by contrasting these statements:

(a) The [denial] of the *Cogito* is self-contradictory.
(b) The [denial of the *Cogito*] is self-contradictory.

In each sentence the accent falls on the bracketed portion. It is clear from Descartes' argument that (a) is what he intends to convey, since this withholds the claim of self-contradictoriness from the *Cogito*. It is (b) which Descartes rejects, in that it ascribes the contradiction to the denial of the *Cogito*.

21 Descartes is quick to add: "Finally we must note that very many necessary propositions become contingent when converted. Thus though from the fact that I exist I may infallibly conclude that God exists, it is not for that reason allowable to affirm that because God exists I also exist."

22 The proofs themselves need not be fully explicated to make the point I am now going to present.

23 On this point, see also *Descartes' Conversation with Burman*, trans. John Cottingham (Oxford: Clarendon Press, 1976), p. 9.

24 See p. 51. What all "analytic demonstrations" have in common is that once the mind has been freed of prejudice, it is guided by the "demonstration" to an intuition of the relevant necessary connection. I have selected the passage at p. 51 since it shows, in an unambiguous way, the nature of such "demonstrations." Hence, its illustrative value.

MEDITATIONS
ON FIRST PHILOSOPHY

LETTER OF DEDICATION

TO THE MOST WISE AND ILLUSTRIOUS THE
DEAN AND DOCTORS OF THE SACRED
FACULTY OF THEOLOGY IN PARIS.

The motive which induces me to present to you this Treatise is so
excellent, and, when you become acquainted with its design, I am
convinced that you will also have so excellent a motive for taking it
under your protection, that I feel that I cannot do better, in order to
render it in some sort acceptable to you, than in a few words to
state what I have set myself to do.

I have always considered that the two questions respecting God
and the Soul were the chief of those that ought to be demonstrated
by philosophical rather than theological argument. For although it
is quite enough for us faithful ones to accept by means of faith the
fact that the human soul does not perish with the body, and that
God exists, it certainly does not seem possible ever to persuade
infidels of any religion, indeed, we may almost say, of any moral
virtue, unless, to begin with, we prove these two facts by means of
the natural reason. And inasmuch as often in this life greater
rewards are offered for vice than for virtue, few people would
prefer the right to the useful, were they restrained neither by the
fear of God nor the expectation of another life; and although it is
absolutely true that we must believe that there is a God, because we
are so taught in the Holy Scriptures, and, on the other hand, that
we must believe the Holy Scriptures because they come from God
(the reason of this is, that, faith being a gift of God, He who gives
the grace to cause us to believe other things can likewise give

it to cause us to believe that He exists), we nevertheless could not place this argument before infidels, who might accuse us of reasoning in a circle. And, in truth, I have noticed that you, along with all the theologians, did not only affirm that the existence of God may be proved by the natural reason, but also that it may be inferred from the Holy Scriptures, that knowledge about Him is much clearer than that which we have of many created things, and, as a matter of fact, is so easy to acquire, that those who have it not are culpable in their ignorance. This indeed appears from the Wisdom of Solomon, chapter xiii., where is is said *"Howbeit they are not to be excused; for if their understanding was so great that they could discern the world and the creatures, why did they not rather find out the Lord thereof?"* and in Romans, chapter i., it is said that they are *"without excuse"*; and again in the same place, by these words *"that which may be known of God is manifest in them,"* it seems as though we were shown that all that which can be known of God may be made manifest by means which are not derived from anywhere but from ourselves, and from the simple consideration of the nature of our minds. Hence I thought it not beside my purpose to inquire how this is so, and how God may be more easily and certainly known than the things of the world.

And as regards the soul, although many have considered that it is not easy to know its nature, and some have even dared to say that human reasons have convinced us that it would perish with the body, and that faith alone could believe the contrary, nevertheless, inasmuch as the Lateran Council held under Leo X (in the eighth session) condemns these tenets, and as Leo expressly ordains Christian philosophers to refute their arguments and to employ all their powers in making known the truth, I have ventured in this treatise to undertake the same task.

More than that, I am aware that the principal reason which causes many impious persons not to desire to believe that there is a God, and that the human soul is distinct from the body, is that they declare that hitherto no one has been able to demonstrate these two facts; and although I am not of their opinion but, on the contrary, hold that the greater part of the reasons which have been brought forward concerning these two questions by so many great men are, when they are rightly understood, equal to so many demonstrations, and that it is almost impossible to invent new ones, it is yet in my opinion the case that nothing more useful can be accomplished in philosophy than once for all to seek with care for the best of these reasons, and to set them forth in so clear and exact a manner, that it will henceforth be evident to everybody that they are veritable demonstrations. And, finally, inasmuch as it was desired that I should undertake this task by many who were aware that I had cultivated a certain Method for the resolution of difficulties of every kind in the Sciences – a method which it is true is not novel, since there is nothing more ancient than the truth, but of which they were aware that I had made use successfully enough in other matters of difficulty – I have thought that it was my duty also to make trial of it in the present matter.

Now all that I could accomplish in the matter is contained in this Treatise. Not that I have here drawn together all the different reasons which might be brought forward to serve as proofs of this subject: for that never seemed to be necessary excepting when there was no one single proof that was certain. But I have treated the first and principal ones in such a manner that I can venture to bring them forward as very evident and very certain demonstrations. And more than that, I will say that these proofs are such that I do not think that there is any way open to the human mind by which it can ever succeed in discovering better. For the importance of the subject, and the glory of God to which all this relates, constrain me to speak here somewhat more freely of myself than is my habit. Nevertheless, whatever certainty and evidence I find in my reasons, I cannot persuade myself that all the world is capable of understanding them. Still, just as in Geometry there are many demonstrations that have been left to us by Archimedes, by Apollonius, by Pappus, and others, which are accepted by everyone as perfectly certain and evident (because they clearly contain nothing which, considered by itself, is not very easy to understand, and as all through that which follows has an exact connection with, and dependence on that which precedes), nevertheless, because they are somewhat lengthy, and demand a mind wholly devoted to their consideration, they are only taken in and understood by a very limited number of persons. Similarly, although I judge that those of which I here make use are equal to, or even surpass in certainty and evidence, the demonstrations of Geometry, I yet apprehend that they cannot be adequately understood by many, both because they are also a little lengthy and dependent the one on the other, and principally because they demand a mind wholly free of prejudices, and one which can be easily detached from the affairs of the senses. And, truth to say, there are not so many in the world who are fitted for metaphysical speculations as there are for those of Geometry. And more than that; there is still this difference, that in Geometry, since each one is persuaded that nothing must be advanced of which there is not a certain demonstration, those who are not entirely adept more frequently err in approving what is false, in order to give the impression that they understand it, than in refuting the true. But the case is different in philosophy where everyone believes that all is problematical, and few give themselves to the search after truth; and the greater number, in their desire to acquire a reputation for boldness of thought, arrogantly combat the most important of truths.[1]

That is why, whatever force there may be in my reasonings, seeing they belong to philosophy, I cannot hope that they will have much effect on the minds of men, unless you extend to them your protection. But the estimation in which your Company is universally held is so great, and the name of SORBONNE carries with it so much authority, that, next to the Sacred Councils, never has such deference been paid to the judgment of any Body, not only in what concerns the faith, but also in what regards human philosophy as well: everyone indeed believes that it is not possible to discover elsewhere more perspicacity and solidity, or more integrity and wisdom in pronouncing judgment. For this reason I have no doubt that if you deign to take the trouble in the first place of correcting this work (for being conscious not only of my infirmity, but also of my ignorance, I should not dare to state that it was free from errors), and then, after adding to it these things that are lacking to it, completing those which are imperfect, and yourselves taking the trouble to give a more ample explanation of those things which have need of it, or at least making me aware of the defects so that I may apply myself to remedy them[1] – when this is done and when finally the reasonings by which I prove that there is a God, and that the human soul differs from the body, shall be carried to that point of perspicuity to which I am sure they can be carried in order that they may be esteemed as perfectly exact demonstrations, if you deign to authorise your approbation and to render public testimony to their truth and certainty, I do not doubt, I say, that henceforward all the errors and false opinions which have ever existed regarding these two questions will soon be effaced from the minds of men. For the truth itself will easily cause all men of mind and

[1] The French version is followed here.

learning to subscribe to your judgment; and your authority will cause the atheists, who are usually more arrogant than learned or judicious, to rid themselves of their spirit of contradiction or lead them possibly themselves to defend the reasonings which they find being received as demonstrations by all persons of consideration, lest they appear not to understand them. And, finally, all others will easily yield to such a mass of evidence, and there will be none who dares to doubt the existence of God and the real and true distinction between the human soul and the body. It is for you now in your singular wisdom to judge of the importance of the establishment of such beliefs [you who see the disorders produced by the doubt of them].[1] But it would not become me to say more in consideration of the cause of God and religion to those who have always been the most worthy supports of the Catholic Church.

PREFACE TO THE READER

I have already slightly touched on these two questions of God and the human soul in the Discourse on the Method of rightly conducting the Reason and seeking truth in the Sciences, published in French in the year 1637. Not that I had the design of treating these with any thoroughness, but only so to speak in passing, and in order to ascertain by the judgment of the readers how I should treat them later on. For these questions have always appeared to me to be of such importance that I judged it suitable to speak of them more than once; and the road which I follow in the explanation of them is so little trodden, and so far removed from the ordinary path, that I did not judge it to be expedient to set it forth at length in French and in a Discourse which might be read by everyone, in case the feebler minds should believe that it was permitted to them to attempt to follow the same path.

But, having in this Discourse on Method begged all those who have found in my writings somewhat deserving of censure to do me the favour of acquainting me with the grounds of it, nothing worthy of remark has been objected to in them beyond two matters: to these two I wish here to reply in a few words before undertaking their more detailed discussion.

The first objection is that it does not follow from the fact that the human mind reflecting on itself does not perceive itself to be other

[1] When it is thought desirable to insert additional readings from the French version this will be indicated by the use of square brackets.

than a thing that thinks, that its nature or its essence consists only in its being a thing that thinks, in the sense that this word *only* excludes all other things which might also be supposed to pertain to the nature of the soul. To this objection I reply that it was not my intention in that place to exclude these in accordance with the order that looks to the truth of the matter (as to which I was not then dealing), but only in accordance with the order of my thought [perception]; thus my meaning was that so far as I was aware, I knew nothing clearly as belonging to my essence, excepting that I was a thing that thinks, or a thing that has in itself the faculty of thinking. But I shall show hereafter how from the fact that I know no other thing which pertains to my essence, it follows that there is no other thing which really does belong to it.

The second objection is that it does not follow from the fact that I have in myself the idea of something more perfect than I am, that this idea is more perfect than I, and much less that what is represented by this idea exists. But I reply that in this term *idea* there is here something equivocal, for it may either be taken materially, as an act of my understanding, and in this sense it cannot be said that it is more perfect than I; or it may be taken objectively, as the thing which is represented by this act, which, although we do not suppose it to exist outside of my understanding, may, none the less, be more perfect than I, because of its essence. And in following out this Treatise I shall show more fully how, from the sole fact that I have in myself the idea of a thing more perfect than myself, it follows that this thing truly exists.

In addition to these two objections I have also seen two fairly lengthy works on this subject, which, however, did not so much impugn my reasonings as my conclusions, and this by arguments drawn from the ordinary atheistic sources. But, because such arguments cannot make any impression on the minds of those who really understand my reasonings, and as the judgments of many are so feeble and irrational that they very often allow themselves to be persuaded by the opinions which they have first formed, however false and far removed from reason they may be, rather than by a true and solid but subsequently received refutation of these opinions, I do not desire to reply here to their criticisms in case of being first of all obliged to state them. I shall only say in general that all that is said by the atheist against the existence of God, always depends either on the fact that we ascribe to God affections which are human, or that we attribute so much strength and wisdom to our minds that we even have the presumption to desire to determine and understand that which God can and ought to do. In this way all that they allege will cause us no difficulty, provided only we remember that we must consider our minds as things which are finite and limited, and God as a Being who is incomprehensible and infinite.

Now that I have once for all recognised and acknowledged the opinions of men, I at once begin to treat of God and the human soul, and at the same time to treat of the whole of the First Philosophy, without however expecting any praise from the vulgar and without the hope that my book will have many readers. On the contrary, I should never advise anyone to read it excepting those who desire to meditate seriously with me, and who can detach their minds from affairs of sense, and deliver themselves entirely from every sort of prejudice. I know too well that such men exist in a very small number. But for those who, without caring to comprehend the order and connections of my reasonings, form their criticisms on detached portions arbitrarily selected, as is the custom with many, these, I say, will not obtain much profit from reading this Treatise. And although they perhaps in several parts find occasion of cavilling, they can for all their pains make no objection which is urgent or deserving of reply.

And inasmuch as I make no promise to others to satisfy them at once, and as I do not presume so much on my own powers as to believe myself capable of foreseeing all that can cause difficulty to anyone, I shall first of all set forth in these Meditations the very considerations by which I persuade myself that I have reached a certain and evident knowledge of the truth, in order to see if, by the same reasons which persuaded me, I can also persuade others. And, after that, I shall reply to the objections which have been made to me by persons of genius and learning to whom I have sent my Meditations for examination, before submitting them to the press. For they have made so many objections and these so different, that I venture to promise that it will be difficult for anyone to bring to mind criticisms of any consequence which have not been already touched upon. This is why I beg those who read these Meditations to form no judgment upon them unless they have given themselves the trouble to read all the objections as well as the replies which I have made to them.[1]

[1] Between the *Præfatio ad Lectorem* and the *Synopsis*, the Paris Edition (1st Edition) interpolates an *Index* which is not found in the Amsterdam Edition (2nd Edition). Since Descartes did not reproduce it, he was doubtless not its author. Mersenne probably composed it himself, adjusting it to the paging of the first Edition.

(Note in Adam and Tannery's Edition.)

SYNOPSIS OF THE SIX FOLLOWING MEDITATIONS

In the first Meditation I set forth the reasons for which we may, generally speaking, doubt about all things and especially about material things, at least so long as we have no other foundations for the sciences than those which we have hitherto possessed. But although the utility of a Doubt which is so general does not at first appear, it is at the same time very great, inasmuch as it delivers us from every kind of prejudice, and sets out for us a very simple way by which the mind may detach itself from the senses; and finally it makes it impossible for us ever to doubt those things which we have once discovered to be true.

In the second Meditation, mind, which making use of the liberty which pertains to it, takes for granted that all those things of whose existence it has the least doubt, are non-existent, recognises that it is however absolutely impossible that it does not itself exist. This point is likewise of the greatest moment, inasmuch as by this means a distinction is easily drawn between the things which pertain to mind – that is to say to the intellectual nature – and those which pertain to body.

But because it may be that some expect from me in this place a statement of the reasons establishing the immortality of the soul, I feel that I should here make known to them that having aimed at writing nothing in all this Treatise of which I do not possess very exact demonstrations, I am obliged to follow a similar order to that made use of by the geometers, which is to begin by putting forward as premises all those things upon which the proposition that we seek depends, before coming to any conclusion regarding it. Now the first and principal matter which is requisite for thoroughly understanding the immortality of the soul is to form the clearest possible conception of it, and one which will be entirely distinct from all the conceptions which we may have of body; and in this Meditation this has been done. In addition to this it is requisite that we may be assured that all the things which we conceive clearly and distinctly are true in the very way in which we think them; and this could not be proved previously to the Fourth Meditation. Further we must have a distinct conception of corporeal nature, which is given partly in this Second, and partly in the Fifth and Sixth Meditations. And finally we should conclude from all this, that those things which we conceive clearly and distinctly as being diverse substances, as we regard mind and body to be, are really substances essentially distinct one from the other; and this is the conclusion of the Sixth Meditation. This is further confirmed in this same Meditation by the fact that we cannot conceive of body excepting in so far as it is divisible, while the mind cannot be conceived of excepting as indivisible. For we are not able to conceive of the half of a mind as we can do of the smallest of all bodies; so that we see that not only are their natures different but even in some respects contrary to one another. I have not however dealt further with this matter in this treatise, both because what I have said is sufficient to show clearly enough that the extinction of the mind does not follow from the corruption of the body, and also to give men the hope of another life after death, as also because the premises from which the immortality of the soul may be deduced depend on an elucidation of a complete system of Physics. This would mean to establish in the first place that all substances generally – that is to say all things which cannot exist without being created by God – are in their nature incorruptible, and that they can never cease to exist unless God, in denying to them his concurrence, reduce them to nought; and secondly that body, regarded generally, is a substance, which is the reason why it also cannot perish, but that the human body, inasmuch as it differs from other bodies, is composed only of a certain configuration of members and of other similar accidents, while the human mind is not similarly composed of any accidents, but is a pure substance. For although all the accidents of mind be changed, although, for instance, it think certain things, will others, perceive others, etc., despite all this it does not emerge from these changes another mind: the human body on the other hand becomes a different thing from the sole fact that the figure or form of any of its portions is found to be changed. From this it follows that the human body may indeed easily enough perish, but the mind [or soul of man (I make no distinction between them)] is owing to its nature immortal.

In the third Meditation it seems to me that I have explained at sufficient length the principal argument of which I make use in order to prove the existence of God. But none the less, because I did not wish in that place to make use of any comparisons derived from corporeal things, so as to withdraw as much as I could the minds of readers from the senses, there may perhaps have remained many obscurities which, however, will, I hope, be entirely removed by the Replies which I have made to the Objections which have been set before me. Amongst others there is, for example, this one, "How the idea in us of a being supremely perfect possesses so much objective reality [that is to say participates by representation in so many degrees of being and perfection] that it necessarily proceeds from a cause which is absolutely perfect. This is illustrated in these Replies by the comparison of a very perfect machine, the idea of which is found in the mind of some workman. For as the objective contrivance of this idea must have some cause, i.e. either the science of the workman or that of some other from whom he has received the idea, it is similarly impossible that the idea of God which is in us should not have God himself as its cause.

In the fourth Meditation it is shown that all these things which we very clearly and distinctly perceive are true, and at the same time it is explained in what the nature of error or falsity consists. This must of necessity be known both for the confirmation of the preceding truths and for the better comprehension of those that follow. (But it must meanwhile be remarked that I do not in any way there treat of sin – that is to say of the error which is committed in the pursuit of good and evil, but only of that which arises in the deciding between the true and the false. And I do not intend to speak of matters pertaining to the Faith or the conduct of life, but only of those which concern speculative truths, and which may be known by the sole aid of the light of nature.)

In the fifth Meditation corporeal nature generally is explained, and in addition to this the existence of God is demonstrated by a new proof in which there may possibly be certain difficulties also, but the solution of these will be seen in the Replies to the Objections. And further I show in what sense it is true to say that the certainty of geometrical demonstrations is itself dependent on the knowledge of God.

Finally in the Sixth I distinguish the action of the understanding[1] from that of the imagination;[2] the marks by which this distinction is made are described. I here show that the mind of man is really distinct from the body, and at the same time that the two are so closely joined together that they form, so to speak, a single thing. All the errors which proceed from the senses are then surveyed, while the means of avoiding them are demonstrated, and finally all the reasons from which we may deduce the existence of material things are set forth. Not that I judge them to be very useful in establishing that which they prove, to wit, that there is in truth a world, that men possess bodies, and other such things which never have been doubted by anyone of sense; but because in considering these closely we come to see that they are neither so strong nor so evident as those arguments which lead us to the knowledge of our mind and of God; so that these last must be the most certain and most evident facts which can fall within the cognizance of the human mind. And this is the whole matter that I have tried to prove in these Meditations, for which reason I here omit to speak of many other questions with which I dealt incidentally in this discussion.

[1] intellectio.   [2] imaginatio.

Meditations on the First Philosophy in which the Existence of God and the Distinction Between Mind and Body are Demonstrated[1]

MEDITATION I

Of the things which may be brought within the sphere of the doubtful

It is now some years since I detected how many were the false beliefs that I had from my earliest youth admitted as true, and how doubtful was everything I had since constructed on this basis; and from that time I was convinced that I must once for all seriously undertake to rid myself of all the opinions which I had formerly accepted, and commence to build anew from the foundation, if I wanted to establish any firm and permanent structure in the sciences. But as this enterprise appeared to be a very great one, I waited until I had attained an age so mature that I could not hope that at any later date I should be better fitted to execute my design. This reason caused me to delay so long that I should feel that I was doing wrong were I to occupy in deliberation the time that yet remains to me for action. To-day, then, since very opportunely for the plan I have in view I have delivered my mind from every care [and am happily agitated by no passions] and since I have procured for myself an assured leisure in a peaceable retirement, I shall at last

---

[1] In place of this long title at the head of the page the first Edition had immediately after the Synopsis, and on the same page 7, simply "First Meditation." (Adam's Edition.)

seriously and freely address myself to the general upheaval of all my former opinions.

Now for this object it is not necessary that I should show that all of these are false – I shall perhaps never arrive at this end. But inasmuch as reason already persuades me that I ought no less carefully to withhold my assent from matters which are not entirely certain and indubitable than from those which appear to me manifestly to be false, if I am able to find in each one some reason to doubt, this will suffice to justify my rejecting the whole. And for that end it will not be requisite that I should examine each in particular, which would be an endless undertaking; for owing to the fact that the destruction of the foundations of necessity brings with it the downfall of the rest of the edifice, I shall only in the first place attack those principles upon which all my former opinions rested.

All that up to the present time I have accepted as most true and certain I have learned either from the senses or through the senses; but it is sometimes proved to me that these senses are deceptive, and it is wiser not to trust entirely to any thing by which we have once been deceived.

But it may be that although the senses sometimes deceive us concerning things which are hardly perceptible, or very far away, there are yet many others to be met with as to which we cannot reasonably have any doubt, although we recognise them by their means. For example, there is the fact that I am here, seated by the fire, attired in a dressing gown, having this paper in my hands and other similar matters. And how could I deny that these hands and this body are mine, were it not perhaps that I compare myself to certain persons, devoid of sense, whose cerebella are so troubled and clouded by the violent vapours of black bile, that they constantly assure us that they think they are kings when they are really quite poor, or that they are clothed in purple when they are really without covering, or who imagine that they have an earthenware head or are nothing but pumpkins or are made of glass. But they are mad, and I should not be any the less insane were I to follow examples so extravagant.

At the same time I must remember that I am a man, and that consequently I am in the habit of sleeping, and in my dreams representing to myself the same things or sometimes even less probable things, than do those who are insane in their waking moments. How often has it happened to me that in the night I dreamt that I found myself in this particular place, that I was dressed and seated near the fire, whilst in reality I was lying undressed in bed! At this moment it does indeed seem to me that it is with eyes awake that I am looking at this paper; that this head which I move is not asleep, that it is deliberately and of set purpose that I extend my hand and perceive it; what happens in sleep does not appear so clear nor so distinct as does all this. But in thinking over this I remind myself that on many occasions I have in sleep been deceived by similar illusions, and in dwelling carefully on this reflection I see so manifestly that there are no certain indications by which we may clearly distinguish wakefulness from sleep that I am lost in astonishment. And my astonishment is such that it is almost capable of persuading me that I now dream.

Now let us assume that we are asleep and that all these particulars, e.g. that we open our eyes, shake our head, extend our hands, and so on, are but false delusions; and let us reflect that possibly neither our hands nor our whole body are such as they appear to us to be. At the same time we must at least confess that the things which are represented to us in sleep are like painted representations which can only have been formed as the counterparts of something real and true, and that in this way those general things at least, i.e. eyes, a head, hands, and a whole body, are not imaginary things, but things really existent. For, as a matter of fact, painters, even when they study with the greatest skill to represent sirens and satyrs by forms the most strange and extraordinary, cannot give them natures which are entirely new, but merely make a certain medley of the members of different animals; or if their imagination is extravagant enough to invent something so novel that nothing similar has ever before been seen, and that then their work represents a thing purely fictitious and absolutely false, it is certain all the same that the colours of which this is composed are necessarily real. And for the same reason, although these general things, to wit, [a body], eyes, a head, hands, and such like, may be imaginary, we are bound at the same time to confess that there are at least some other objects yet more simple and more universal, which are real and true; and of these just in the same way as with certain real colours, all these images of things which dwell in our thoughts, whether true and real or false and fantastic, are formed.

To such a class of things pertains corporeal nature in general, and its extension, the figure of extended things, their quantity or magnitude and number, as also the place in which they are, the time which measures their duration, and so on.

That is possibly why our reasoning is not unjust when we conclude from this that Physics, Astronomy, Medicine and all other sciences which have as their end the consideration of composite things, are very dubious and uncertain; but that Arithmetic, Geometry and other sciences of that kind which only treat of things that are very simple and very general, without taking great trouble to ascertain whether they are actually existent or not, contain some measure of certainty and an element of the indubitable. For whether I am awake or asleep, two and three together always form five, and the square can never have more than four sides, and it does not seem possible that truths so clear and apparent can be suspected of any falsity [or uncertainty].

Nevertheless I have long had fixed in my mind the belief that an all-powerful God existed by whom I have been created such as I am. But how do I know that He has not brought it to pass that there is no earth, no heaven, no extended body, no magnitude, no place, and that nevertheless [I possess the perceptions of all these things and that] they seem to me to exist just exactly as I now see them? And, besides, as I sometimes imagine that others deceive themselves in the things which they think they know best, how do I know that I am not deceived every time that I add two and three, or count the sides of a square, or judge of things yet simpler, if anything simpler can be imagined? But possibly God has not desired that I should be thus deceived, for He is said to be supremely good. If, however, it is contrary to His goodness to have made me such that I constantly deceive myself, it would also appear to be contrary to His goodness to permit me to be sometimes deceived, and nevertheless I cannot doubt that He does permit this.

There may indeed be those who would prefer to deny the existence of a God so powerful, rather than believe that all other things are uncertain. But let us not oppose them for the present, and grant that all that is here said of a God is a fable; nevertheless in whatever way they suppose that I have arrived at the state of being that I have reached – whether they attribute it to fate or to accident, or make out that it is by a continual succession of antecedents, or by some other method – since to err and deceive oneself is a defect, it is clear that the greater will be the probability of my being so imperfect as to deceive myself ever, as is the Author to whom they assign my origin the less powerful. To these reasons I have certainly nothing to reply, but at the end I feel constrained to confess that there is nothing in all that I formerly believed to be true, of which I cannot in some measure doubt, and that not merely through want of thought or through levity, but for reasons which are very powerful and maturely considered; so that henceforth I ought not the less carefully to refrain from giving credence to these opinions than to that which is manifestly false, if I desire to arrive at any certainty [in the sciences].

But it is not sufficient to have made these remarks, we must also be careful to keep them in mind. For these ancient and commonly held opinions still revert frequently to my mind, long and familiar custom having given them the right to occupy my mind against my inclination and rendered them almost masters of my belief; nor will I ever lose the habit of deferring to them or of placing my confidence in them, so long as I consider them as they really are, i.e. opinions in some measure doubtful, as I have just shown, and at the same time highly probable, so that there is much more reason to believe in than to deny them. That is why I consider that I shall not be acting amiss, if, taking of set purpose a contrary belief, I allow myself to be deceived, and for a certain time pretend that all these opinions are entirely false and imaginary, until at last, having thus balanced my former prejudices with my latter [so that they cannot divert my opinions more to one side than to the other], my judgment will no longer be dominated by bad usage or turned away from the right knowledge of the truth. For I am assured that there can be neither peril nor error in this course, and that I cannot at present yield too much to distrust, since I am not considering the question of action, but only of knowledge.

I shall then suppose, not that God who is supremely good and the fountain of truth, but some evil genius not less powerful than deceitful, has employed his whole energies in deceiving me; I shall consider that the heavens, the earth, colours, figures, sound, and all other external things are nought but the illusions and dreams of which this genius has availed himself in order to lay traps for my credulity; I shall consider myself as having no hands, no eyes, no flesh, no blood, nor any senses, yet falsely believing myself to possess all these things; I shall remain obstinately attached to this idea, and if by this means it is not in my power to arrive at the knowledge of any truth, I may at least do what is in my power [i.e. suspend my judgment], and with firm purpose avoid giving

49

credence to any false thing, or being imposed upon by this arch deceiver, however powerful and deceptive he may be. But this task is a laborious one, and insensibly a certain lassitude leads me into the course of my ordinary life. And just as a captive who in sleep enjoys an imaginary liberty, when he begins to suspect that his liberty is but a dream, fears to awaken, and conspires with these agreeable illusions that the deception may be prolonged, so insensibly of my own accord I fall back into my former opinions, and I dread awakening from this slumber, lest the laborious wakefulness which would follow the tranquillity of this repose should have to be spent not in daylight, but in the excessive darkness of the difficulties which have just been discussed.

MEDITATION II

Of the nature of the human mind; and that it is more easily known than the body

The Meditation of yesterday filled my mind with so many doubts that it is no longer in my power to forget them. And yet I do not see in what manner I can resolve them; and, just as if I had all of a sudden fallen into very deep water, I am so disconcerted that I can neither make certain of setting my feet on the bottom, nor can I swim and so support myself on the surface. I shall nevertheless make an effort and follow anew the same path as that on which I yesterday entered, i.e. I shall proceed by setting aside all that in which the least doubt could be supposed to exist, just as if I had discovered that it was absolutely false; and I shall ever follow in this road until I have met with something which is certain, or at least, if I can do nothing else, until I have learned for certain that there is nothing in the world that is certain. Archimedes, in order that he might draw the terrestrial globe out of its place, and transport it elsewhere, demanded only that one point should be fixed and immoveable; in the same way I shall have the right to conceive high hopes if I am happy enough to discover one thing only which is certain and indubitable.

I suppose, then, that all the things that I see are false; I persuade myself that nothing has ever existed of all that my fallacious memory represents to me. I consider that I possess no senses; I imagine that body, figure, extension, movement and place are but the fictions of my mind. What, then, can be esteemed as true?

Perhaps nothing at all, unless that there is nothing in the world that is certain.

But how can I know there is not something different from those things that I have just considered, of which one cannot have the slightest doubt? Is there not some God, or some other being by whatever name we call it, who puts these reflections into my mind? That is not necessary, for is it not possible that I am capable of producing them myself? I myself, am I not at least something? But I have already denied that I had senses and body. Yet I hesitate, for what follows from that? Am I so dependent on body and senses that I cannot exist without these? But I was persuaded that there was nothing in all the world, that there was no heaven, no earth, that there were no minds, nor any bodies: was I not then likewise persuaded that I did not exist? Not at all; of a surety I myself did exist since I persuaded myself of something [or merely because I thought of something]. But there is some deceiver or other, very powerful and very cunning, who ever employs his ingenuity in deceiving me. Then without doubt I exist also if he deceives me, and let him deceive me as much as he will, he can never cause me to be nothing so long as I think that I am something. So that after having reflected well and carefully examined all things, we must come to the definite conclusion that this proposition: I am, I exist, is necessarily true each time that I pronounce it, or that I mentally conceive it.

But I do not yet know clearly enough what I am, I who am certain that I am; and hence I must be careful to see that I do not imprudently take some other object in place of myself, and thus that I do not go astray in respect of this knowledge that I hold to be the most certain and most evident of all that I have formerly learned. That is why I shall now consider anew what I believed myself to be before I embarked upon these last reflections; and of my former opinions I shall withdraw all that might even in a small degree be invalidated by the reasons which I have just brought forward, in order that there may be nothing at all left beyond what is absolutely certain and indubitable.

What then did I formerly believe myself to be? Undoubtedly I believed myself to be a man. But what is a man? Shall I say a reasonable animal? Certainly not; for then I should have to inquire what an animal is, and what is reasonable; and thus from a single question I should insensibly fall into an infinitude of others more difficult; and I should not wish to waste the little time and leisure remaining to me in trying to unravel subtleties like these. But I shall rather stop here to consider the thoughts which of themselves spring up in my mind, and which were not inspired by anything beyond my own nature alone when I applied myself to the consideration of my being. In the first place, then, I considered myself as having a face, hands, arms, and all that system of members composed of bones and flesh as seen in a corpse which I designated by the name of body. In addition to this I considered that I was nourished, that I walked, that I felt, and that I thought, and I referred all these actions to the soul: but I did not stop to consider what the soul was, or if I did stop, I imagined that it was something extremely rare and subtle like a wind, a flame, or an ether, which was spread throughout my grosser parts. As to body I had no manner of doubt about its nature, but thought I had a very clear knowledge of it; and if I had desired to explain it according to the notions that I had then formed of it, I should have described it thus: By the body I understand all that which can be defined by a certain figure: something which can be confined in a certain place, and which can fill a given space in such a way that every other body will be excluded from it; which can be perceived either by touch, or by sight, or by hearing, or by taste, or by smell: which can be moved in many ways not, in truth, by itself, but by something which is foreign to it, by which it is touched [and from which it receives impressions]: for to have the power of self-movement, as also of feeling or of thinking, I did not consider to appertain to the nature of body: on the contrary, I was rather astonished to find that faculties similar to them existed in some bodies.

But what am I, now that I suppose that there is a certain genius which is extremely powerful, and, if I may say so, malicious, who employs all his powers in deceiving me? Can I affirm that I possess the least of all those things which I have just said pertain to the nature of body? I pause to consider, I revolve all these things in my mind, and I find none of which I can say that it pertains to me. It would be tedious to stop to enumerate them. Let us pass to the attributes of soul and see if there is any one which is in me? What of nutrition or walking [the first mentioned]? But if it is so that I have no body it is also true that I can neither walk nor take nourishment. Another attribute is sensation. But one cannot feel without body, and besides I have thought I perceived many things during sleep that I recognized in my waking moments as not having been experienced at all. What of thinking? I find here that thought is an attribute that belongs to me; it alone cannot be separated from me. I am, I exist, that is certain. But how often? Just when I think; for it might possibly be the case if I ceased entirely to think, that I should likewise cease altogether to exist. I do not now admit anything which is not necessarily true: to speak accurately I am not more than a thing which thinks, that is to say a mind or a soul, or an understanding, or a reason, which are terms whose significance was formerly unknown to me. I am, however, a real thing and really exist; but what thing? I have answered: a thing which thinks.

And what more? I shall exercise my imagination [in order to see if I am not something more]. I am not a collection of members which we call the human body: I am not a subtle air distributed through these members, I am not a wind, a fire, a vapour, a breath, nor anything at all which I can imagine or conceive; because I have assumed that all these were nothing. Without changing that supposition I find that I only leave myself certain of the fact that I am somewhat. But perhaps it is true that these same things which I supposed were non–existent because they are unknown to me, are really not different from the self which I know. I am not sure about this, I shall not dispute about it now; I can only give judgment on things that are known to me. I know that I exist, and I inquire what I am, I whom I know to exist. But it is very certain that the knowledge of my existence taken in its precise significance does not depend on things whose existence is not yet known to me; consequently it does not depend on those which I can feign in imagination. And indeed the very term *feign* in imagination[1] proves to me my error, for I really do this if I image myself a something, since to imagine is nothing else than to contemplate the figure or image of a corporeal thing. But I already know for certain that I am, and that it may be that all these images, and, speaking generally, all things that relate to the nature of body are nothing but dreams [and chimeras]. For this reason I see clearly that I have as little reason to say, "I shall stimulate my imagination in order to know more distinctly what I am," than if I were to say, "I am now awake, and I perceive somewhat that is real and true: but because I do not yet perceive it distinctly enough, I shall go to sleep of express purpose, so that my dreams may represent the perception with greatest truth and evidence." And, thus, I know for certain that nothing of all that I can understand by means of my imagination belongs to this knowledge

---

[1] Or "form an image" (effingo).

which I have of myself, and that it is necessary to recall the mind from this mode of thought with the utmost diligence in order that it may be able to know its own nature with perfect distinctness.

But what then am I? A thing which thinks. What is a thing which thinks? It is a thing which doubts, understands, [conceives], affirms, denies, wills, refuses, which also imagines and feels.

Certainly it is no small matter if all these things pertain to my nature. But why should they not so pertain? Am I not that being who now doubts nearly everything, who nevertheless understands certain things, who affirms that one only is true, who denies all the others, who desires to know more, is averse from being deceived, who imagines many things, sometimes indeed despite his will, and who perceives many likewise, as by the intervention of the bodily organs? Is there nothing in all this which is as true as it is certain that I exist, even though I should always sleep and though he who has given me being employed all his ingenuity in deceiving me? Is there likewise any one of these attributes which can be distinguished from my thought, or which might be said to be separated from myself? For it is so evident of itself that it is I who doubts, who understands, and who desires, that there is no reason here to add anything to explain it. And I have certainly the power of imagining likewise; for although it may happen (as I formerly supposed) that none of the things which I imagine are true, nevertheless this power of imagining does not cease to be really in use, and it forms part of my thought. Finally, I am the same who feels, that is to say, who perceives certain things, as by the organs of sense, since in truth I see light, I hear noise, I feel heat. But it will be said that these phenomena are false and that I am dreaming. Let it be so; still it is at least quite certain that it seems to me that I see light, that I hear noise and that I feel heat. That cannot be false; properly speaking it is what is in me called feeling;[1] and used in this precise sense that is no other thing than thinking.

From this time I begin to know what I am with a little more clearness and distinction than before; but nevertheless it still seems to me, and I cannot prevent myself from thinking, that corporeal things, whose images are framed by thought, which are tested by the senses, are much more distinctly known than that obscure part of me which does not come under the imagination. Although really it is very strange to say that I know and understand more distinctly

---

[1] Sentire.

these things whose existence seems to me dubious, which are unknown to me, and which do not belong to me, than others of the truth of which I am convinced, which are known to me and which pertain to my real nature, in a word, than myself. But I see clearly how the case stands: my mind loves to wander, and cannot yet suffer itself to be retained within the just limits of truth. Very good, let us once more give it the freest rein, so that, when afterwards we seize the proper occasion for pulling up, it may the more easily be regulated and controlled.

Let us begin by considering the commonest matters, those which we believe to be the most distinctly comprehended, to wit, the bodies which we touch and see; not indeed bodies in general, for these general ideas are usually a little more confused, but let us consider one body in particular. Let us take, for example, this piece of wax: it has been taken freshly from the hive, and it has not yet lost the sweetness of the honey which it contains; it still retains somewhat of the odour of the flowers from which it has been culled; its colour, its figure, its size are apparent; it is hard, cold, easily handled, and if you strike it with the finger, it will emit a sound. Finally all the things which are requisite to cause us distinctly to recognise a body, are met with in it. But notice that while I speak and approach the fire what remained of the taste is exhaled, the smell evaporates, the colour alters, the figure is destroyed, the size increases, it becomes liquid, it heats, scarcely can one handle it, and when one strikes it, no sound is emitted. Does the same wax remain after this change? We must confess that it remains; none would judge otherwise. What then did I know so distinctly in this piece of wax? It could certainly be nothing of all that the senses brought to my notice, since all these things which fall under taste, smell, sight, touch, and hearing, are found to be changed, and yet the same wax remains.

Perhaps it was what I now think, viz. that this wax was not that sweetness of honey, nor that agreeable scent of flowers, nor that particular whiteness, nor that figure, nor that sound, but simply a body which a little while before appeared to me as perceptible under these forms, and which is now perceptible under others. But what, precisely, is it that I imagine when I form such conceptions? Let us attentively consider this, and, abstracting from all that does not belong to the wax, let us see what remains. Certainly nothing remains excepting a certain extended thing which is flexible and movable. But what is the meaning of flexible and movable? Is it not that I imagine that this piece of wax being round is capable of becoming square and of passing from a square to a triangular figure? No, certainly it is not that, since I imagine it admits of an infinitude of similar changes, and I nevertheless do not know how to compass the infinitude by my imagination, and consequently this conception which I have of the wax is not brought about by the faculty of imagination. What now is this extension? Is it not also unknown? For it becomes greater when the wax is melted, greater when it is boiled, and greater still when the heat increases; and I should not conceive [clearly] according to truth what wax is, if I did not think that even this piece that we are considering is capable of receiving more variations in extension than I have ever imagined. We must then grant that I could not even understand through the imagination what this piece of wax is, and that it is my mind[1] alone which perceives it. I say this piece of wax in particular, for as to wax in general it is yet clearer. But what is this piece of wax which cannot be understood excepting by the [understanding or] mind? It is certainly the same that I see, touch, imagine, and finally it is the same which I have always believed it to be from the beginning. But what must particularly be observed is that its perception is neither an act of vision, nor of touch, nor of imagination, and has never been such although it may have appeared formerly to be so, but only an intuition[2] of the mind, which may be imperfect and confused as it was formerly, or clear and distinct as it is at present, according as my attention is more or less directed to the elements which are found in it and of which it is composed.

Yet in the meantime I am greatly astonished when I consider [the great feebleness of mind] and its proneness to fall [insensibly] into error; for although without giving expression to my thoughts I consider all this in my own mind, words often impede me and I am almost deceived by the terms of ordinary language. For we say that we see the same wax, if it is present, and not that we simply judge that it is the same from its having the same colour and figure. From this I should conclude that I knew the wax by means of vision and not simply by the intuition of the mind; unless by chance I remember that, when looking from a window and saying I see men who pass in the street, I really do not see them, but infer that what I see is men, just as I say that I see wax. And yet what do I see from

[1] entendement F., mens L.
[2] inspectio.

the window but hats and coats which may cover automatic machines? Yet I judge these to be men. And similarly solely by the faculty of judgment which rests in my mind, I comprehend that which I believed I saw with my eyes.

A man who makes it his aim to raise his knowledge above the common should be ashamed to derive the occasion for doubting from the forms of speech invented by the vulgar; I prefer to pass on and consider whether I had a more evident and perfect conception of what the wax was when I first perceived it, and when I believed I knew it by means of the external senses or at least by the common sense[1] as it is called, that is to say by the imaginative faculty, or whether my present conception is clearer now that I have most carefully examined what it is, and in what way it can be known. It would certainly be absurd to doubt as to this. For what was there in this first perception which was distinct? What was there which might not as well have been perceived by any of the animals? But when I distinguish the wax from its external forms, and when, just as if I had taken from it its vestments, I consider it quite naked, it is certain that although some error may still be found in my judgment, I can nevertheless not perceive it thus without a human mind.

But finally what shall I say of this mind, that is, of myself, for up to this point I do not admit in myself anything but mind? What then, I who seem to perceive this piece of wax so distinctly, do I not know myself, not only with much more truth and certainty, but also with much more distinctness and clearness? For if I judge that the wax is or exists from the fact that I see it, it certainly follows much more clearly that I am or that I exist myself from the fact that I see it. For it may be that what I see is not really wax, it may also be that I do not possess eyes with which to see anything; but it cannot be that when I see, or (for I no longer take account of the distinction) when I think I see, that I myself who think am nought. So if I judge that the wax exists from the fact that I touch it, the same thing will follow, to wit, that I am; and if I judge that my imagination, or some other cause, whatever it is, persuades me that the wax exists, I shall still conclude the same. And what I have here remarked of wax may be applied to all other things which are external to me [and which are met with outside of me]. And further, if the [notion or] perception of wax has seemed to me

[1] sensus communis.

clearer and more distinct, not only after the sight or the touch, but also after many other causes have rendered it quite manifest to me, with how much more [evidence] and distinctness must it be said that I now know myself, since all the reasons which contribute to the knowledge of wax, or any other body whatever, are yet better proofs of the nature of my mind! And there are so many other things in the mind itself which may contribute to the elucidation of its nature, that those which depend on body such as these just mentioned, hardly merit being taken into account.

But finally here I am, having insensibly reverted to the point I desired, for, since it is now manifest to me that even bodies are not properly speaking known by the senses or by the faculty of imagination, but by the understanding only, and since they are not known from the fact that they are seen or touched, but only because they are understood, I see clearly that there is nothing which is easier for me to know than my mind. But because it is difficult to rid oneself so promptly of an opinion to which one was accustomed for so long, it will be well that I should halt a little at this point, so that by the length of my meditation I may more deeply imprint on my memory this new knowledge.

MEDITATION III

Of God: that He Exists

I shall now close my eyes, I shall stop my ears, I shall call away all my senses, I shall efface even from my thoughts all the images of corporeal things, or at least (for that is hardly possible) I shall esteem them as vain and false; and thus holding converse only with myself and considering my own nature, I shall try little by little to reach a better knowledge of and a more familiar acquaintanceship with myself. I am a thing that thinks, that is to say, that doubts, affirms, denies, that knows a few things, that is ignorant of many [that loves, that hates], that wills, that desires, that also imagines and perceives; for as I remarked before, although the things which I perceive and imagine are perhaps nothing at all apart from me and in themselves, I am nevertheless assured that these modes of thought that I call perceptions and imaginations, inasmuch only as they are modes of thought, certainly reside [and are met with] in me.

And in the little that I have just said, I think I have summed up all that I really know, or at least all that hitherto I was aware that I knew. In order to try to extend my knowledge further, I shall now look around more carefully and see whether I cannot still discover in myself some other things which I have not hitherto perceived. I am certain that I am a thing which thinks; but do I not then likewise know what is requisite to render me certain of a truth? Certainly in this first knowledge there is nothing that assures me of its truth, excepting the clear and distinct perception of that which I state, which would not indeed suffice to assure me that what I say is true, if it could ever happen that a thing which I conceived so clearly and distinctly could be false; and accordingly it seems to me that already I can establish as a general rule that all things which I perceive[1] very clearly and very distinctly are true.

At the same time I have before received and admitted many things to be very certain and manifest, which yet I afterwards recognised as being dubious. What then were these things? They were the earth, sky, stars and all other objects which I apprehended by means of the senses. But what did I clearly [and distinctly] perceive in them? Nothing more than that the ideas or thoughts of these things were presented to my mind. And not even now do I deny that these ideas are met with in me. But there was yet another thing which I affirmed, and which, owing to the habit which I had formed of believing it, I thought I perceived very clearly, although in truth I did not perceive it at all, to wit, that there were objects outside of me from which these ideas proceeded, and to which they were entirely similar. And it was in this that I erred, or, if perchance my judgment was correct, this was not due to any knowledge arising from my perception.

But when I took anything very simple and easy in the sphere of arithmetic or geometry into consideration, e.g. that two and three together made five, and other things of the sort, were not these present to my mind so clearly as to enable me to affirm that they were true? Certainly if I judged that since such matters could be doubted, this would not have been so for any other reason than that it came into my mind that perhaps a God might have endowed me with such a nature that I may have been deceived even concerning things which seemed to me most manifest. But every time that this preconceived opinion of the sovereign power of a God presents itself to my thought, I am constrained to confess that it is

[1] Percipio, F. nous concevons.

easy to Him, if He wishes it, to cause me to err, even in matters in which I believe myself to have the best evidence. And, on the other hand, always when I direct my attention to things which I believe myself to perceive very clearly, I am so persuaded of their truth that I let myself break out into words such as these: Let who will deceive me, He can never cause me to be nothing while I think that I am, or some day cause it to be true to say that I have never been, it being true now to say that I am, or that two and three make more or less than five, or any such thing in which I see a manifest contradiction. And, certainly, since I have no reason to believe that there is a God who is a deceiver, and as I have not yet satisfied myself that there is a God at all, the reason for doubt which depends on this opinion alone is very slight, and so to speak metaphysical. But in order to be able altogether to remove it, I must inquire whether there is a God as soon as the occasion presents itself; and if I find that there is a God, I must also inquire whether He may be a deceiver; for without a knowledge of these two truths I do not see that I can ever be certain of anything.

And in order that I may have an opportunity of inquiring into this in an orderly way [without interrupting the order of meditation which I have proposed to myself, and which is little by little to pass from the notions which I find first of all in my mind to those which I shall later on discover in it] it is requisite that I should here divide my thoughts into certain kinds, and that I should consider in which of these kinds there is, properly speaking, truth or error to be found. Of my thoughts some are, so to speak, images of the things, and to these alone is the title "idea" properly applied; examples are my thought of a man or of a chimera, of heaven, of an angel, or [even] of God. But other thoughts possess other forms as well. For example in willing, fearing, approving, denying, though I always perceive something as the subject of the action of my mind,[1] yet by this action I always add something else to the idea[2] which I have of that thing; and of the thoughts of this kind some are called volitions or affections, and others judgments.

Now as to what concerns ideas, if we consider them only in themselves and do not relate them to anything else beyond themselves, they cannot properly speaking be false; for whether I imagine a goat or a chimera, it is not less true that I imagine the one

[1] The French version is followed here as being more explicit. In it "action de mon esprit" replaces "mea cogitatio."
[2] In the Latin version "similitudinem."

than the other. We must not fear likewise that falsity can enter into will and into affections, for although I may desire evil things, or even things that never existed, it is not the less true that I desire them. Thus there remains no more than the judgments which we make, in which I must take the greatest care not to deceive myself. But the principal error and the commonest which we may meet with in them, consists in my judging that the ideas which are in me are similar or conformable to the things which are outside me; for without doubt if I considered the ideas only as certain modes of my thoughts, without trying to relate them to anything beyond, they could scarcely give me material for error.

But among these ideas, some appear to me to be innate, some adventitious, and others to be formed [or invented] by myself; for, as I have the power of understanding what is called a thing, or a truth, or a thought, it appears to me that I hold this power from no other source than my own nature. But if I now hear some sound, if I see the sun, or feel heat, I have hitherto judged that these sensations proceeded from certain things that exist outside of me; and finally it appears to me that sirens, hippogryphs, and the like, are formed out of my own mind. But again I may possibly persuade myself that all these ideas are of the nature of those which I term adventitious, or else that they are all innate, or all fictitious: for I have not yet clearly discovered their true origin.

And my principal task in this place is to consider, in respect to those ideas which appear to me to proceed from certain objects that are outside me, what are the reasons which cause me to think them similar to these objects. It seems indeed in the first place that I am taught this lesson by nature; and, secondly, I experience in myself that these ideas do not depend on my will nor therefore on myself – for they often present themselves to my mind in spite of my will. Just now, for instance, whether I will or whether I do not will, I feel heat, and thus I persuade myself that this feeling, or at least this idea of heat, is produced in me by something which is different from me, i.e. by the heat of the fire near which I sit. And nothing seems to me more obvious than to judge that this object imprints its likeness rather than anything else upon me.

Now I must discover whether these proofs are sufficiently strong and convincing. When I say that I am so instructed by nature, I merely mean a certain spontaneous inclination which impels me to believe in this connection, and not a natural light which makes me recognise that it is true. But these two things are very different; for

I cannot doubt that which the natural light causes me to believe to be true, as, for example, it has shown me that I am from the fact that I doubt, or other facts of the same kind. And I possess no other faculty whereby to distinguish truth from falsehood, which can teach me that what this light shows me to be true is not really true, and no other faculty that is equally trustworthy. But as far as [apparently] natural impulses are concerned, I have frequently remarked, when I had to make active choice between virtue and vice, that they often enough led me to the part that was worse; and this is why I do not see any reason for following them in what regards truth and error.

And as to the other reason, which is that these ideas must proceed from objects outside me, since they do not depend on my will, I do not find it any the more convincing. For just as these impulses of which I have spoken are found in me, notwithstanding that they do not always concur with my will, so perhaps there is in me some faculty fitted to produce these ideas without the assistance of any external things, even though it is not yet known by me; just as, apparently, they have hitherto always been found in me during sleep without the aid of any external objects.

And finally, though they did proceed from objects different from myself, it is not a necessary consequence that they should resemble these. On the contrary, I have noticed that in many cases there was a great difference between the object and its idea. I find, for example, two completely diverse ideas of the sun in my mind; the one derives its origin from the senses, and should be placed in the category of adventitious ideas; according to this idea the sun seems to be extremely small; but the other is derived from astronomical reasonings, i.e. is elicited from certain notions that are innate in me, or else it is formed by me in some other manner; in accordance with it the sun appears to be several times greater than the earth. These two ideas cannot, indeed, both resemble the same sun, and reason makes me believe that the one which seems to have originated directly from the sun itself, is the one which is most dissimilar to it.

All this causes me to believe that until the present time it has not been by a judgment that was certain [or premeditated], but only by a sort of blind impulse that I believed that things existed outside of, and different from me, which, by the organs of my senses, or by some other method whatever it might be, conveyed these ideas or images to me [and imprinted on me their similitudes].

But there is yet another method of inquiring whether any of the objects of which I have ideas within me exist outside of me. If ideas are only taken as certain modes of thought, I recognise amongst them no difference or inequality, and all appear to proceed from me in the same manner; but when we consider them as images, one representing one thing and the other another, it is clear that they are very different one from the other. There is no doubt that those which represent to me substances are something more, and contain so to speak more objective reality within them [that is to say, by representation participate in a higher degree of being or perfection] than those that simply represent modes or accidents; and that idea again by which I understand a supreme God, eternal, infinite, [immutable], omniscient, omnipotent, and Creator of all things which are outside of Himself, has certainly more objective reality in itself than those ideas by which finite substances are represented.

Now it is manifest by the natural light that there must at least be as much reality in the efficient and total cause as in its effect. For, pray, whence can the effect derive its reality, if not from its cause? And in what way can this cause communicate this reality to it, unless it possessed it in itself? And from this it follows, not only that something cannot proceed from nothing, but likewise that what is more perfect – that is to say, which has more reality within itself – cannot proceed from the less perfect. And this is not only evidently true of those effects which possess actual or formal reality, but also of the ideas in which we consider merely what is termed objective reality. To take an example, the stone which has not yet existed not only cannot now commence to be unless it has been produced by something which possess within itself, either formally or eminently, all that enters into the composition of the stone [i.e. it must possess the same things or other more excellent things than those which exist in the stone] and heat can only be produced in a subject in which it did not previously exist by a cause that is of an order [degree or kind] at least as perfect as heat, and so in all other cases. But further, the idea of heat, or of a stone, cannot exist in me unless it has been placed within me by some cause which possesses within it at least as much reality as that which I conceive to exist in the heat or the stone. For although this cause does not transmit anything of its actual or formal reality to my idea, we must not for that reason imagine that it is necessarily a less real cause; we must remember that [since every idea is a work of the mind] its nature is such that it demands of itself no other formal reality than that which it borrows from my thought, of which it is only a mode [i.e. a manner or way of thinking]. But in order that an idea should contain some one certain objective reality rather than another, it must without doubt derive it from some cause in which there is at least as much formal reality as this idea contains of objective reality. For if we imagine that something is found in an idea which is not found in the cause, it must then have been derived from nought; but however imperfect may be this mode of being by which a thing is objectively [or by representation] in the understanding by its idea, we cannot certainly say that this mode of being is nothing, nor, consequently, that the idea derives its origin from nothing.

Nor must I imagine that, since the reality that I consider in these ideas is only objective, it is not essential that this reality should be formally in the causes of my ideas, but that it is sufficient that it should be found objectively. For just as this mode of objective existence pertains to ideas by their proper nature, so does the mode of formal existence pertain to the causes of those ideas (this is at least true of the first and principal) by the nature peculiar to them. And although it may be the case that one idea gives birth to another idea, that cannot continue to be so indefinitely; for in the end we must reach an idea whose cause shall be so to speak an archetype, in which the whole reality [or perfection] which is so to speak objectively [or by representation] in these ideas is contained formally [and really]. Thus the light of nature causes me to know clearly that the ideas in me are like [pictures or] images which can, in truth, easily fall short of the perfection of the objects from which they have been derived, but which can never contain anything greater or more perfect.

And the longer and the more carefully that I investigate these matters, the more clearly and distinctly do I recognise their truth. But what am I to conclude from it all in the end? It is this, that if the objective reality of any one of my ideas is of such a nature as clearly to make me recognise that it is not in me either formally or eminently, and that consequently I cannot myself be the cause of it, it follows of necessity that I am not alone in the world, but that there is another being which exists, or which is the cause of this idea. On the other hand, had no such an idea existed in me, I should have had no sufficient argument to convince me of the existence of any being beyond myself; for I have made very careful investigation everywhere and up to the present time have been able to find no other ground.

But of my ideas, beyond that which represents me to myself, as to which there can here be no difficulty, there is another which represents a God, and there are others representing corporeal and inanimate things, others angels, others animals, and others again which represent to me men similar to myself.

As regards the ideas which represent to me other men or animals, or angels, I can however easily conceive that they might be formed by an admixture of the other ideas which I have of myself, of corporeal things, and of God, even although there were apart from me neither men nor animals, nor angels, in all the world.

And in regard to the ideas of corporeal objects, I do not recognise in them anything so great or so excellent that they might not have possibly proceeded from myself; for if I consider them more closely, and examine them individually, as I yesterday examined the idea of wax, I find that there is very little in them which I perceive clearly and distinctly. Magnitude or extension in length, breadth, or depth, I do so perceive; also figure which results from a termination of this extension, the situation which bodies of different figure preserve in relation to one another, and movement or change of situation; to which we may also add substance, duration and number. As to other things such as light, colours, sounds, scents, tastes, heat, cold and the other tactile qualities, they are thought by me with so much obscurity and confusion that I do not even know if they are true or false, i.e. whether the ideas which I form of these qualities are actually the ideas of real objects or not [or whether they only represent chimeras which cannot exist in fact]. For although I have before remarked that it is only in judgments that falsity, properly speaking, or formal falsity, can be met with, a certain material falsity may nevertheless be found in ideas, i.e. when these ideas represent what is nothing as though it were something. For example, the ideas which I have of cold and heat are so far from clear and distinct that by their means I cannot tell whether cold is merely a privation of heat, or heat a privation of cold, or whether both are real qualities, or are not such. And inasmuch as [since ideas resemble images] there cannot be any ideas which do not appear to represent some things, if it is correct to say that cold is merely a privation of heat, the idea which represents it to me as something real and positive will not be improperly termed false, and the same holds good of other similar ideas.

To these it is certainly not necessary that I should attribute any author other than myself. For if they are false, i.e. if they represent things which do not exist, the light of nature shows me that they issue from nought, that is to say, that they are only in me in so far as something is lacking to the perfection of my nature. But if they are true, nevertheless because they exhibit so little reality to me that I cannot even clearly distinguish the thing represented from non-being, I do not see any reason why they should not be produced by myself.

As to the clear and distinct idea which I have of corporeal things, some of them seem as though I might have derived them from the idea which I possess of myself, as those which I have of substance, duration, number, and such like. For [even] when I think that a stone is a substance, or at least a thing capable of existing of itself, and that I am a substance also, although I conceive that I am a thing that thinks and not one that is extended, and that the stone on the other hand is an extended thing which does not think, and that thus there is a notable difference between the two conceptions – they seem, nevertheless, to agree in this, that both represent substances. In the same way, when I perceive that I now exist and further recollect that I have in former times existed, and when I remember that I have various thoughts of which I can recognise the number, I acquire ideas of duration and number which I can afterwards transfer to any object that I please. But as to all the other qualities of which the ideas of corporeal things are composed, to wit, extension, figure, situation and motion, it is true that they are not formally in me, since I am only a thing that thinks; but because they are merely certain modes of substance [and so to speak the vestments under which corporeal substance appears to us] and because I myself am also a substance, it would seem that they might be contained in me eminently.

Hence there remains only the idea of God, concerning which we must consider whether it is something which cannot have proceeded from me myself. By the name God I understand a substance that is infinite [eternal, immutable], independent, all-knowing, all-powerful, and by which I myself and everything else, if anything else does exist, have been created. Now all these characteristics are such that the more diligently I attend to them, the less do they appear capable of proceeding from me alone; hence, from what has been already said, we must conclude that God necessarily exists.

For although the idea of substance is within me owing to the fact that I am substance, nevertheless I should not have the idea of an infinite substance – since I am finite – if it had not proceeded from some substance which was veritably infinite.

Nor should I imagine that I do not perceive the infinite by a true idea, but only by the negation of the finite, just as I perceive repose and darkness by the negation of movement and of light; for, on the contrary, I see that there is manifestly more reality in infinite substance than in finite, and therefore that in some way I have in me the notion of the infinite earlier than the finite – to wit, the notion of God before that of myself. For how would it be possible that I should know that I doubt and desire, that is to say, that something is lacking to me, and that I am not quite perfect, unless I had within me some idea of a Being more perfect than myself, in comparison with which I should recognise the deficiencies of my nature?

And we cannot say that this idea of God is perhaps materially false and that consequently I can derive it from nought [i.e. that possibly it exists in me because I am imperfect], as I have just said is the case with ideas of heat, cold and other such things; for, on the contrary, as this idea is very clear and distinct and contains within it more objective reality than any other, there can be none which is of itself more true, nor any in which there can be less suspicion of falsehood. The idea, I say, of this Being who is absolutely perfect and infinite, is entirely true; for although, perhaps, we can imagine that such a Being does not exist, we cannot nevertheless imagine that His idea represents nothing real to me, as I have said of the idea of cold. This idea is also very clear and distinct; since all that I conceive clearly and distinctly of the real and the true, and of what conveys some perfection, is in its entirety contained in this idea. And this does not cease to be true although I do not comprehend the infinite, or though in God there is an infinitude of things which I cannot comprehend, nor possibly even reach in any way by thought; for it is of the nature of the infinite that my nature, which is finite and limited, should not comprehend it; and it is sufficient that I should understand this, and that I should judge that all things which I clearly perceive and in which I know that there is some perfection, and possibly likewise an infinitude of properties of which I am ignorant, are in God formally or eminently, so that the idea which I have of Him may become the most true, most clear, and most distinct of all the ideas that are in my mind.

But possibly I am something more than I suppose myself to be, and perhaps all those perfections which I attribute to God are in some way potentially in me, although they do not yet disclose themselves, or issue in action. As a matter of fact I am already sensible that my knowledge increases [and perfects itself] little by little, and I see nothing which can prevent it from increasing more and more into infinitude; nor do I see, after it has thus been increased [or perfected], anything to prevent my being able to acquire by its means all the other perfections of the Divine nature; nor finally why the power I have of acquiring these perfections, if it really exists in me, shall not suffice to produce the ideas of them.

At the same time I recognise that this cannot be. For, in the first place, although it were true that every day my knowledge acquired new degrees of perfection, and that there were in my nature many things potentially which are not yet there actually, nevertheless these excellences do not pertain to [or make the smallest approach to] the idea which I have of God in whom there is nothing merely potential [but in whom all is present really and actually]; for it is an infallible token of imperfection in my knowledge that it increases little by little. And further, although my knowledge grows more and more, nevertheless I do not for that reason believe that it can ever be actually infinite, since it can never reach a point so high that it will be unable to attain to any greater increase. But I understand God to be actually infinite, so that He can add nothing to His supreme perfection. And finally I perceive that the objective being of an idea cannot be produced by a being that exists potentially only, which properly speaking is nothing, but only by a being which is formal or actual.

To speak the truth, I see nothing in all that I have just said which by the light of nature is not manifest to anyone who desires to think attentively on the subject; but when I slightly relax my attention, my mind, finding its vision somewhat obscured and so to speak blinded by the images of sensible objects, I do not easily recollect the reason why the idea that I possess of a being more perfect than I, must necessarily have been placed in me by a being which is really more perfect; and this is why I wish here to go on to inquire whether I, who have this idea, can exist if no such being exists.

And I ask, from whom do I then derive my existence? Perhaps

from myself or from my parents, or from some other source less perfect than God; for we can imagine nothing more perfect than God, or even as perfect as He is.

But [were I independent of every other and] were I myself the author of my being, I should doubt nothing and I should desire nothing, and finally no perfection would be lacking to me; for I should have bestowed on myself every perfection of which I possessed any idea and should thus be God. And it must not be imagined that those things that are lacking to me are perhaps more difficult of attainment than those which I already possess; for, on the contrary, it is quite evident that it was a matter of much greater difficulty to bring to pass that I, that is to say, a thing or a substance that thinks, should emerge out of nothing, than it would be to attain to the knowledge of many things of which I am ignorant, and which are only the accidents of this thinking substance. But it is clear that if I had of myself possessed this greater perfection of which I have just spoken [that is to say, if I had been the author of my own existence], I should not at least have denied myself the things which are the more easy to acquire [to wit, many branches of knowledge of which my nature is destitute]; nor should I have deprived myself of any of the things contained in the idea which I form of God, because there are none of them which seem to me specially difficult to acquire: and if there were any that were more difficult to acquire, they would certainly appear to me to be such (supposing I myself were the origin of the other things which I possess) since I should discover in them that my powers were limited.

But though I assume that perhaps I have always existed just as I am at present, neither can I escape the force of this reasoning, and imagine that the conclusion to be drawn from this is, that I need not seek for any author of my existence. For all the course of my life may be divided into an infinite number of parts, none of which is in any way dependent on the other; and thus from the fact that I was in existence a short time ago it does not follow that I must be in existence now, unless some cause at this instant, so to speak, produces me anew, that is to say, conserves me. It is as a matter of fact perfectly clear and evident to all those who consider with attention the nature of time, that, in order to be conserved in each moment in which it endures, a substance has need of the same power and action as would be necessary to produce and create it anew, supposing it did not yet exist, so that the light of nature shows us clearly that the distinction between creation and conservation is solely a distinction of the reason.

All that I thus require here is that I should interrogate myself, if I wish to know whether I possess a power which is capable of bringing it to pass that I who now am shall still be in the future; for since I am nothing but a thinking thing, or at least since thus far it is only this portion of myself which is precisely in question at present, if such a power did reside in me, I should certainly be conscious of it. But I am conscious of nothing of the kind, and by this I know clearly that I depend on some being different from myself.

Possibly, however, this being on which I depend is not that which I call God, and I am created either by my parents or by some other cause less perfect than God. This cannot be, because, as I have just said, it is perfectly evident that there must be at least as much reality in the cause as in the effect; and thus since I am a thinking thing, and possess an idea of God within me, whatever in the end be the cause assigned to my existence, it must be allowed that it is likewise a thinking thing and that it possesses in itself the idea of all the perfections which I attribute to God. We may again inquire whether this cause derives its origin from itself or from some other thing. For if from itself, it follows by the reasons before brought forward, that this cause must itself be God; for since it possesses the virtue of self-existence, it must also without doubt have the power of actually possessing all the perfections of which it has the idea, that is, all those which I conceive as existing in God. But if it derives its existence from some other cause than itself, we shall again ask, for the same reason, whether this second cause exists by itself or through another, until from one step to another, we finally arrive at an ultimate cause, which will be God.

And it is perfectly manifest that in this there can be no regression into infinity, since what is in question is not so much the cause which formerly created me, as that which conserves me at the present time.

Nor can we suppose that several causes may have concurred in my production, and that from one I have received the idea of one of the perfections which I attribute to God, and from another the idea of some other, so that all these perfections indeed exist somewhere in the universe, but not as complete in one unity which is God. On the contrary, the unity, the simplicity or the inseparability of all things which are in God is one of the principal perfections which I conceive to be in Him. And certainly the idea of this unity of all

Divine perfections cannot have been placed in me by any cause from which I have not likewise received the ideas of all the other perfections; for this cause could not make me able to comprehend them as joined together in an inseparable unity without having at the same time caused me in some measure to know what they are [and in some way to recognise each one of them].

Finally, so far as my parents [from whom it appears I have sprung] are concerned, although all that I have ever been able to believe of them were true, that does not make it follow that it is they who conserve me, nor are they even the authors of my being in any sense, in so far as I am a thinking being; since what they did was merely to implant certain dispositions in that matter in which the self – i.e. the mind, which alone I at present identify with myself – is by me deemed to exist. And thus there can be no difficulty in their regard, but we must of necessity conclude from the fact alone that I exist, or that the idea of a Being supremely perfect – that is of God – is in me, that the proof of God's existence is grounded on the highest evidence.

It only remains to me to examine into the manner in which I have acquired this idea from God; for I have not received it through the senses, and it is never presented to me unexpectedly, as is usual with the ideas of sensible things when these things present themselves, or seem to present themselves, to the external organs of my senses; nor is it likewise a fiction of my mind, for it is not in my power to take from or to add anything to it; and consequently the only alternative is that it is innate in me, just as the idea of myself is innate in me.

And one certainly ought not to find it strange that God, in creating me, placed this idea within me to be like the mark of the workman imprinted on his work; and it is likewise not essential that the mark shall be something different from the work itself. For from the sole fact that God created me it is most probable that in some way he has placed his image and similitude upon me, and that I perceive this similitude (in which the idea of God is contained) by means of the same faculty by which I perceive myself – that is to say, when I reflect on myself I not only know that I am something [imperfect], incomplete and dependent on another, which incessantly aspires after something which is better and greater than myself, but I also know that He on whom I depend possesses in Himself all the great things towards which I aspire [and the ideas of which I find within myself], and that not indefinitely or potentially alone, but really, actually and infinitely; and that thus He is God. And the whole strength of the argument which I have here made use of to prove the existence of God consists in this, that I recognise that it is not possible that my nature should be what it is, and indeed that I should have in myself the idea of a God, if God did not veritably exist – a God, I say, whose idea is in me, i.e. who possesses all those supreme perfections of which our mind may indeed have some idea but without understanding them all, who is liable to no errors or defect [and who has none of all those marks which denote imperfection]. From this it is manifest that He cannot be a deceiver, since the light of nature teaches us that fraud and deception necessarily proceed from some defect.

But before I examine this matter with more care, and pass on to the consideration of other truths which may be derived from it, it seems to me right to pause for a while in order to contemplate God Himself, to ponder at leisure His marvellous attributes, to consider, and admire, and adore, the beauty of this light so resplendent, at least as far as the strength of my mind, which is in some measure dazzled by the sight, will allow me to do so. For just as faith teaches us that the supreme felicity of the other life consists only in this contemplation of the Divine Majesty, so we continue to learn by experience that a similar meditation, though incomparably less perfect, causes us to enjoy the greatest satisfaction of which we are capable in this life.

MEDITATION IV

Of the true and the false

I have been well accustomed these past days to detach my mind from my senses, and I have accurately observed that there are very few things that one knows with certainty respecting corporeal objects, that there are many more which are known to us respecting the human mind, and yet more still regarding God Himself; so that I shall now without any difficulty abstract my thoughts from the consideration of [sensible or] imaginable objects, and carry them to those which, being withdrawn from all contact with matter, are purely intelligible. And certainly the idea which I possess of the human mind inasmuch as it is a thinking thing, and not extended in length, width and depth, nor participating in anything pertaining to body, is incomparably more distinct than is the idea of any corporeal thing. And when I consider that I doubt, that is to say, that I am an incomplete and dependent being, the idea of a being that is complete and independent, that is of God, presents itself to my mind with so much distinctness and clearness – and from the fact alone that this idea is found in me, or that I who possess this idea exist, I conclude so certainly that God exists, and that my existence depends entirely on Him in every moment of my life – that I do not think that the human mind is capable of knowing anything with more evidence and certitude. And it seems to me that I now have before me a road which will lead us from the contemplation of the true God (in whom all the treasures of science and wisdom are contained) to the knowledge of the other objects of the universe.

For, first of all, I recognise it to be impossible that He should ever deceive me; for in all fraud and deception some imperfection is to be found, and although it may appear that the power of deception is a mark of subtilty or power, yet the desire to deceive without doubt testifies to malice or feebleness, and accordingly cannot be found in God.

In the next place I experienced in myself a certain capacity for judging which I have doubtless received from God, like all the other things that I possess; and as He could not desire to deceive me, it is clear that He has not given me a faculty that will lead me to err if I use it aright.

And no doubt respecting this matter could remain, if it were not that the consequence would seem to follow that I can thus never be deceived; for if I hold all that I possess from God, and if He has not placed in me the capacity for error, it seems as though I could never fall into error. And it is true that when I think only of God [and direct my mind wholly to Him][1] I discover [in myself] no cause of error, or falsity; yet directly afterwards, when recurring to myself, experience shows me that I am nevertheless subject to an infinitude of errors, as to which, when we come to investigate them more closely, I notice that not only is there a real and positive idea of God or of a Being of supreme perfection present to my mind, but also, so to speak, a certain negative idea of nothing, that is, of that which is infinitely removed from any kind of perfection; and that I am in a sense something intermediate between God and nought, i.e. placed in such a manner between the supreme Being

---

[1] Not in the French version.

and non-being, that there is in truth nothing in me that can lead to error in so far as a sovereign Being has formed me; but that, as I in some degree participate likewise in nought or in non-being, i.e. in so far as I am not myself the supreme Being, and as I find myself subject to an infinitude of imperfections, I ought not to be astonished if I should fall into error. Thus do I recognise that error, in so far as it is such, is not a real thing depending on God, but simply a defect; and therefore, in order to fall into it, that I have no need to possess a special faculty given me by God for this very purpose, but that I fall into error from the fact that the power given me by God for the purpose of distinguishing truth from error is not infinite.

Nevertheless this does not quite satisfy me; for error is not a pure negation [i.e. is not the simple defect or want of some perfection which ought not to be mine], but it is a lack of some knowledge which it seems that I ought to possess. And on considering the nature of God it does not appear to me possible that He should have given me a faculty which is not perfect of its kind, that is, which is wanting in some perfection due to it. For if it is true that the more skilful the artizan, the more perfect is the work of his hands, what can have been produced by this supreme Creator of all things that is not in all its parts perfect? And certainly there is no doubt that God could have created me so that I could never have been subject to error; it is also certain that He ever wills what is best; is it then better that I should be subject to err than that I should not?

In considering this more attentively, it occurs to me in the first place that I should not be astonished if my intelligence is not capable of comprehending why God acts as He does; and that there is thus no reason to doubt of His existence from the fact that I may perhaps find many other things besides this as to which I am able to understand neither for what reason nor how God has produced them. For, in the first place, knowing that my nature is extremely feeble and limited, and that the nature of God is on the contrary immense, incomprehensible, and infinite, I have no further difficulty in recognising that there is an infinitude of matters in His power, the causes of which transcend my knowledge; and this reason suffices to convince me that the species of cause termed final, finds no useful employment in physical [or natural] things; for it does not appear to me that I can without temerity seek to investigate the [inscrutable] ends of God.

It further occurs to me that we should not consider one single creature separately, when we inquire as to whether the works of God are perfect, but should regard all his creations together. For the same thing which might possibly seem very imperfect with some semblance of reason if regarded by itself, is found to be very perfect if regarded as part of the whole universe; and although, since I resolved to doubt all things, I as yet have only known certainly my own existence and that of God, nevertheless since I have recognised the infinite power of God, I cannot deny that He may have produced many other things, or at least that He has the power of producing them, so that I may obtain a place as a part of a great universe.

Whereupon, regarding myself more closely, and considering what are my errors (for they alone testify to there being any imperfection in me), I answer that they depend on a combination of two causes, to wit, on the faculty of knowledge that rests in me, and on the power of choice or of free will – that is to say, of the understanding and at the same time of the will. For by the understanding alone I [neither assert nor deny anything, but] apprehend[1] the ideas of things as to which I can form a judgment. But no error is properly speaking found in it, provided the word error is taken in its proper signification; and though there is possibly an infinitude of things in the world of which I have no idea in my understanding, we cannot for all that say that it is deprived of these ideas [as we might say of something which is required by its nature], but simply it does not possess these; because in truth there is no reason to prove that God should have given me a greater faculty of knowledge than He has given me; and however skilful a workman I represent Him to be, I should not for all that consider that He was bound to have placed in each of His works all the perfections which He may have been able to place in some. I likewise cannot complain that God has not given me a free choice or a will which is sufficient, ample and perfect, since as a matter of fact I am conscious of a will so extended as to be subject to no limits. And what seems to me very remarkable in this regard is that of all the qualities which I possess there is no one so perfect and so comprehensive that I do not very clearly recognise that it might be yet greater and more perfect. For, to take an example, if I consider the faculty of comprehension which I possess, I find that it is of very small extent and extremely limited, and at the same time I find the

---

[1] percipio.

idea of another faculty much more ample and even infinite, and seeing that I can form the idea of it, I recognise from this very fact that it pertains to the nature of God. If in the same way I examine the memory, the imagination, or some other faculty, I do not find any which is not small and circumscribed, while in God it is immense [or infinite]. It is free-will alone or liberty of choice which I find to be so great in me that I can conceive no other idea to be more great; it is indeed the case that it is for the most part this will that causes me to know that in some manner I bear the image and similitude of God. For although the power of will is incomparably greater in God than in me, both by reason of the knowledge and the power which, conjoined with it, render it stronger and more efficacious, and by reason of its object, inasmuch as in God it extends to a great many things; it nevertheless does not seem to me greater if I consider it formally and precisely in itself: for the faculty of will consists alone in our having the power of choosing to do a thing or choosing not to do it (that is, to affirm or deny, to pursue or to shun it), or rather it consists alone in the fact that in order to affirm or deny, pursue or shun those things placed before us by the understanding, we act so that we are unconscious that any outside force constrains us in doing so. For in order that I should be free it is not necessary that I should be indifferent as to the choice of one or the other of two contraries; but contrariwise the more I lean to the one – whether I recognise clearly that the reasons of the good and true are to be found in it, or whether God so disposes my inward thought – the more freely do I choose and embrace it. And undoubtedly both divine grace and natural knowledge, far from diminishing my liberty, rather increase it and strengthen it. Hence this indifference which I feel, when I am not swayed to one side rather than to the other by lack of reason, is the lowest grade of liberty, and rather evinces a lack or negation in knowledge than a perfection of will: for if I always recognised clearly what was true and good, I should never have trouble in deliberating as to what judgment or choice I should make, and then I should be entirely free without ever being indifferent.

From all this I recognise that the power of will which I have received from God is not of itself the source of my errors – for it is very ample and very perfect of its kind – any more than is the power of understanding; for since I understand nothing but by the power which God has given me for understanding, there is no doubt that all that I understand, I understand as I ought, and it is not possible that I err in this. Whence then come my errors? They come from the sole fact that since the will is much wider in its range and compass than the understanding, I do not restrain it within the same bounds, but extend it also to things which I do not under-stand: and as the will is of itself indifferent to these, it easily falls into error and sin, and chooses the evil for the good, or the false for the true.

For example, when I lately examined whether anything existed in the world, and found that from the very fact that I considered this question it followed very clearly that I myself existed, I could not prevent myself from believing that a thing I so clearly con-ceived was true: not that I found myself compelled to do so by some external cause, but simply because from great clearness in my mind there followed a great inclination of my will; and I believed this with so much the greater freedom or spontaneity as I possessed the less indifference towards it. Now, on the contrary, I not only know that I exist, inasmuch as I am a thinking thing, but a certain representation of corporeal nature is also presented to my mind; and it comes to pass that I doubt whether this thinking nature which is in me, or rather by which I am what I am, differs from this corporeal nature, or whether both are not simply the same thing; and I here suppose that I do not yet know any reason to persuade me to adopt the one belief rather than the other. From this it follows that I am entirely indifferent as to which of the two I affirm or deny, or even whether I abstain from forming any judgment in the matter.

And this indifference does not only extend to matters as to which the understanding has no knowledge, but also in general to all those which are not apprehended with perfect clearness at the moment when the will is deliberating upon them: for, however probable are the conjectures which render me disposed to form a judgment respecting anything, the simple knowledge that I have that those are conjectures alone and not certain and indubitable reasons, suf-fices to occasion me to judge the contrary. Of this I have had great experience of late when I set aside as false all that I had formerly held to be absolutely true, for the sole reason that I remarked that it might in some measure be doubted.

But if I abstain from giving my judgment on any thing when I do not perceive it with sufficient clearness and distinctness, it is plain that I act rightly and am not deceived. But if I determine to deny or affirm, I no longer make use as I should of my free will, and if I affirm what is not true, it is evident that I deceive myself; even though I judge according to truth, this comes about only by chance, and I do not escape the blame of misusing my freedom; for the light of nature teaches us that the knowledge of the understanding should always precede the determination of the will. And it is in the misuse of the free will that the privation which constitutes the characteristic nature of error is met with. Privation, I say, is found in the act, in so far as it proceeds from me, but it is not found in the faculty which I have received from God, nor even in the act in so far as it depends on Him.

For I have certainly no cause to complain that God has not given me an intelligence which is more powerful, or a natural light which is stronger than that which I have received from Him, since it is proper to the finite understanding not to comprehend a multitude of things, and it is proper to a created understanding to be finite; on the contrary, I have every reason to render thanks to God who owes me nothing and who has given me all the perfections I possess, and I should be far from charging Him with injustice, and with having deprived me of, or wrongfully withheld from me, these perfections which He has not bestowed upon me.

I have further no reason to complain that He has given me a will more ample than my understanding, for since the will consists only of one single element, and is so to speak indivisible, it appears that its nature is such that nothing can be abstracted from it [without destroying it]; and certainly, the more comprehensive it is found to be, the more reason I have to render gratitude to the giver.

And, finally, I must also not complain that God concurs with me in forming the acts of the will, that is the judgment in which I go astray, because these acts are entirely true and good, inasmuch as they depend on God; and in a certain sense more perfection accrues to my nature from the fact that I can form them, than if I could not do so. As to the privation in which alone the formal reason of error or sin consists, it has no need of any concurrence from God, since it is not a thing [or an existence], and since it is not related to God as to a cause, but should be termed merely a negation [according to the significance given to these words in the Schools]. For in fact it is not an imperfection in God that He has given me the liberty to give or withhold my assent from certain things as to which He has not placed a clear and distinct knowledge in my understanding; but it is without doubt an imperfection in me not to make a good use of my freedom, and to give my judgment readily on matters which I only understand obscurely. I nevertheless perceive that God could easily have created me so that I never should err, although I still remained free, and endowed with a limited knowledge, viz. by giving to my understanding a clear and distinct intelligence of all things as to which I should ever have to deliberate; or simply by His engraving deeply in my memory the resolution never to form a judgment on anything without having a clear and distinct understanding of it, so that I could never forget it. And it is easy for me to understand that, in so far as I consider myself alone, and as if there were only myself in the world, I should have been much more perfect than I am, if God had created me so that I could never err. Nevertheless I cannot deny that in some sense it is a greater perfection in the whole universe that certain parts should not be exempt from error as others are than that all parts should be exactly similar. And I have no right to complain if God, having placed me in the world, has not called upon me to play a part that excels all others in distinction and perfection.

And further I have reason to be glad on the ground that if He has not given me the power of never going astray by the first means pointed out above, which depends on a clear and evident knowledge of all the things regarding which I can deliberate, He has at least left within my power the other means, which is firmly to adhere to the resolution never to give judgment on matters whose truth is not clearly known to me; for although I notice a certain weakness in my nature in that I cannot continually concentrate my mind on one single thought, I can yet, by attentive and frequently repeated meditation, impress it so forcibly on my memory that I shall never fail to recollect it whenever I have need of it, and thus acquire the habit of never going astray.

And inasmuch as it is in this that the greatest and principal perfection of man consists, it seems to me that I have not gained little by this day's Meditation, since I have discovered the source of falsity and error. And certainly there can be no other source than that which I have explained; for as often as I so restrain my will within the limits of my knowledge that it forms no judgment except on matters which are clearly and distinctly represented to it by the understanding, I can never be deceived; for every clear and distinct conception[1] is without doubt something, and hence cannot derive its origin from what is nought, but must of necessity have

---

[1] perceptio.

God as its author – God, I say, who being supremely perfect, cannot be the cause of any error; and consequently we must conclude that such a conception [or such a judgment] is true. Nor have I only learned to-day what I should avoid in order that I may not err, but also how I should act in order to arrive at a knowledge of the truth; for without doubt I shall arrive at this end if I devote my attention sufficiently to those things which I perfectly understand; and if I separate from these that which I only understand confusedly and with obscurity. To these I shall henceforth diligently give heed.

MEDITATION V

Of the essence of material things, and, again, of God, that He exists

Many other matters respecting the attributes of God and my own nature or mind remain for consideration; but I shall possibly on another occasion resume the investigation of these. Now (after first noting what must be done or avoided, in order to arrive at a knowledge of the truth) my principal task is to endeavour to emerge from the state of doubt into which I have these last days fallen, and to see whether nothing certain can be known regarding material things.

But before examining whether any such objects as I conceive exist outside of me, I must consider the ideas of them in so far as they are in my thought, and see which of them are distinct and which confused.

In the first place, I am able distinctly to imagine that quantity which philosophers commonly call continuous, or the extension in length, breadth, or depth, that is in this quantity, or rather in the object to which it is attributed. Further, I can number in it many different parts, and attribute to each of its parts many sorts of size, figure, situation and local movement, and, finally, I can assign to each of these movements all degrees of duration.

And not only do I know these things with distinctness when I consider them in general, but, likewise [however little I apply my attention to the matter], I discover an infinitude of particulars respecting numbers, figures, movements, and other such things, whose truth is so manifest, and so well accords with my nature, that when I begin to discover them, it seems to me that I learn nothing new, or recollect what I formerly knew – that is to say, that

I for the first time perceive things which were already present to my mind, although I had not as yet applied my mind to them.

And what I here find to be most important is that I discover in myself an infinitude of ideas of certain things which cannot be esteemed as pure negations, although they may possibly have no existence outside of my thought, and which are not framed by me, although it is within my power either to think or not to think them, but which possess natures which are true and immutable. For example, when I imagine a triangle, although there may nowhere in the world be such a figure outside my thought, or ever have been, there is nevertheless in this figure a certain determinate nature, form, or essence, which is immutable and eternal, which I have not invented, and which in no wise depends on my mind, as appears from the fact that diverse properties of that triangle can be demonstrated, viz. that its three angles are equal to two right angles, that the greatest side is subtended by the greatest angle, and the like, which now, whether I wish it or do not wish it, I recognise very clearly as pertaining to it, although I never thought of the matter at all when I imagined a triangle for the first time, and which therefore cannot be said to have been invented by me.

Nor does the objection hold good that possibly this idea of a triangle has reached my mind through the medium of my senses, since I have sometimes seen bodies triangular in shape; because I can form in my mind an infinitude of other figures regarding which we cannot have the least conception of their ever having been objects of sense, and I can nevertheless demonstrate various properties pertaining to their nature as well as to that of the triangle, and these must certainly all be true since I conceive them clearly. Hence they are something, and not pure negation; for it is perfectly clear that all that is true is something, and I have already fully demonstrated that all that I know clearly is true. And even although I had not demonstrated this, the nature of my mind is such that I could not prevent myself from holding them to be true so long as I conceive them clearly; and I recollect that even when I was still strongly attached to the objects of sense, I counted as the most certain those truths which I conceived clearly as regards figures, numbers, and the other matters which pertain to arithmetic and geometry, and, in general, to pure and abstract mathematics.

But now, if just because I can draw the idea of something from my thought, it follows that all which I know clearly and distinctly as pertaining to this object does really belong to it, may I not derive from this an argument demonstrating the existence of God? It is certain that I no less find the idea of God, that is to say, the idea of a supremely perfect Being, in me, than that of any figure or number whatever it is; and I do not know any less clearly and distinctly that an [actual and] eternal existence pertains to this nature than I know that all that which I am able to demonstrate of some figure or number truly pertains to the nature of this figure or number, and therefore, although all that I concluded in the preceding Meditations were found to be false, the existence of God would pass with me as at least as certain as I have ever held the truths of mathematics (which concern only numbers and figures) to be.

This indeed is not at first manifest, since it would seem to present some appearance of being a sophism. For being accustomed in all other things to make a distinction between existence and essence, I easily persuade myself that the existence can be separated from the essence of God, and that we can thus conceive God as not actually existing. But, nevertheless, when I think of it with more attention, I clearly see that existence can no more be separated from the essence of God than can its having its three angles equal to two right angles be separated from the essence of a [rectilinear] triangle, or the idea of a mountain from the idea of a valley; and so there is not any less repugnance to our conceiving a God (that is, a Being supremely perfect) to whom existence is lacking (that is to say, to whom a certain perfection is lacking), than to conceive of a mountain which has no valley.

But although I cannot really conceive of a God without existence any more than a mountain without a valley, still from the fact that I conceive of a mountain with a valley, it does not follow that there is such a mountain in the world; similarly although I conceive of God as possessing existence, it would seem that it does not follow that there is a God which exists; for my thought does not impose any necessity upon things, and just as I may imagine a winged horse, although no horse with wings exists, so I could perhaps attribute existence to God, although no God existed.

But a sophism is concealed in this objection; for from the fact that I cannot conceive a mountain without a valley, it does not follow that there is any mountain or any valley in existence, but only that the mountain and the valley, whether they exist or do not exist, cannot in any way be separated one from the other. While from the fact that I cannot conceive God without existence, it follows that existence is inseparable from Him, and hence that He really exists; not that my thought can bring this to pass, or impose any necessity on things, but, on the contrary, because the necessity which lies in the thing itself, i.e. the necessity of the existence of God determines me to think in this way. For it is not within my power to think of God without existence (that is of a supremely perfect Being devoid of a supreme perfection) though it is in my power to imagine a horse either with wings or without wings.

And we must not here object that it is in truth necessary for me to assert that God exists after having presupposed that He possesses every sort of perfection, since existence is one of these, but that as a matter of fact my original supposition was not necessary, just as it is not necessary to consider that all quadrilateral figures can be inscribed in the circle; for supposing I thought this, I should be constrained to admit that the rhombus might be inscribed in the circle since it is a quadrilateral figure, which, however, is manifestly false. [We must not, I say, make any such allegations because] although it is not necessary that I should at any time entertain the notion of God, nevertheless whenever it happens that I think of a first and a sovereign Being, and, so to speak, derive the idea of Him from the storehouse of my mind, it is necessary that I should attribute to Him every sort of perfection, although I do not get so far as to enumerate them all, or to apply my mind to each one in particular. And this necessity suffices to make me conclude (after having recognised that existence is a perfection) that this first and sovereign Being really exists; just as though it is not necessary for me ever to imagine any triangle, yet, whenever I wish to consider a rectilinear figure composed only of three angles, it is absolutely essential that I should attribute to it all those properties which serve to bring about the conclusion that its three angles are not greater than two right angles, even although I may not then be considering this point in particular. But when I consider which figures are capable of being inscribed in the circle, it is in no wise necessary that I should think that all quadrilateral figures are of this number; on the contrary, I cannot even pretend that this is the case, so long as I do not desire to accept anything which I cannot conceive clearly and distinctly. And in consequence there is a great difference between the false suppositions such as this, and the true ideas born within me, the first and principal of which is that of God. For really I discern in many ways that this idea is not something factitious, and depending solely on my thought, but that it is the image of a true and immutable nature; first of all, because I cannot conceive anything but God himself to whose essence existence [necessarily] pertains; in the second place because it is not possible for me to conceive two or more Gods in this same position; and, granted that there is one such God who now exists, I see clearly that it is necessary that He should have existed from all eternity, and that He must exist eternally; and finally, because I know an infinitude of other properties in God, none of which I can either diminish or change.

For the rest, whatever proof or argument I avail myself of, we must always return to the point that it is only those things which we conceive clearly and distinctly that have the power of persuading me entirely. And although amongst the matters which I conceive of in this way, some indeed are manifestly obvious to all, while others only manifest themselves to those who consider them closely and examine them attentively; still, after they have once been discovered, the latter are not esteemed as any less certain than the former. For example, in the case of every right-angled triangle, although it does not so manifestly appear that the square of the base is equal to the squares of the two other sides as that this base is opposite to the greatest angle; still, when this has once been apprehended, we are just as certain of its truth as of the truth of the other. And as regards God, if my mind were not pre-occupied with prejudices, and if my thought did not find itself on all hands diverted by the continual pressure of sensible things, there would be nothing which I could know more immediately and more easily than Him. For is there anything more manifest than that there is a God, that is to say, a Supreme Being, to whose essence alone existence pertains?[1]

And although for a firm grasp of this truth I have need of a strenuous application of mind, at present I not only feel myself to be as assured of it as of all that I hold as most certain, but I also remark that the certainty of all other things depends on it so absolutely, that without this knowledge it is impossible ever to know anything perfectly.

For although I am of such a nature that as long as[2] I understand anything very clearly and distinctly, I am naturally impelled to believe it to be true, yet because I am also of such a nature that I

---

[1] "In the idea of whom alone necessary or eternal existence is comprised." French version.

[2] "From the moment that." French version.

cannot have my mind constantly fixed on the same object in order to perceive it clearly, and as I often recollect having formed a past judgment without at the same time properly recollecting the reasons that led me to make it, it may happen meanwhile that other reasons present themselves to me, which would easily cause me to change my opinion, if I were ignorant of the facts of the existence of God, and thus I should have no true and certain knowledge, but only vague and vacillating opinions. Thus, for example, when I consider the nature of a [rectilinear] triangle, I who have some little knowledge of the principles of geometry recognise quite clearly that the three angles are equal to two right angles, and it is not possible for me not to believe this so long as I apply my mind to its demonstration; but so soon as I abstain from attending to the proof, although I still recollect having clearly comprehended it, it may easily occur that I come to doubt its truth, if I am ignorant of there being a God. For I can persuade myself of having been so constituted by nature that I can easily deceive myself even in those matters which I believe myself to apprehend with the greatest evidence and certainty, especially when I recollect that I have frequently judged matters to be true and certain which other reasons have afterwards impelled me to judge to be altogether false.

But after I have recognised that there is a God – because at the same time I have also recognised that all things depend upon Him, and that He is not a deceiver, and from that have inferred that what I perceive clearly and distinctly cannot fail to be true – although I no longer pay attention to the reasons for which I have judged this to be true, provided that I recollect having clearly and distinctly perceived it no contrary reason can be brought forward which could ever cause me to doubt of its truth; and thus I have a true and certain knowledge of it. And this same knowledge extends likewise to all other things which I recollect having formerly demonstrated, such as the truths of geometry and the like; for what can be alleged against them to cause me to place them in doubt? Will it be said that my nature is such as to cause me to be frequently deceived? But I already know that I cannot be deceived in the judgment whose grounds I know clearly. Will it be said that I formerly held many things to be true and certain which I have afterwards recognised to be false? But I had not had any clear and distinct knowledge of these things, and not as yet knowing the rule whereby I assure myself of the truth, I had been impelled to give my assent from reasons which I have since recognised to be less strong than I had at the time imagined them to be. What further objection can then be raised? That possibly I am dreaming (an objection I myself made a little while ago), or that all the thoughts which I now have are no more true than the phantasies of my dreams? But even though I slept the case would be the same, for all that is clearly present to my mind is absolutely true.

And so I very clearly recognise that the certainty and truth of all knowledge depends alone on the knowledge of the true God, in so much that, before I knew Him, I could not have a perfect knowledge of any other thing. And now that I know Him I have the means of acquiring a perfect knowledge of an infinitude of things, not only of those which relate to God Himself and other intellectual matters, but also of those which pertain to corporeal nature in so far as it is the object of pure mathematics [which have no concern with whether it exists or not].

MEDITATION VI

Of the existence of material things, and of the real distinction between the soul and body of man

Nothing further now remains but to inquire whether material things exist. And certainly I at least know that these may exist in so far as they are considered as the objects of pure mathematics, since in this aspect I perceive them clearly and distinctly. For there is no doubt that God possesses the power to produce everything that I am capable of perceiving with distinctness, and I have never deemed that anything was impossible for Him, unless I found a contradiction in attempting to conceive it clearly. Further, the faculty of imagination which I possess, and of which, experience tells me, I make use when I apply myself to the consideration of material things, is capable of persuading me of their existence; for when I attentively consider what imagination is, I find that it is nothing but a certain application of the faculty of knowledge to the body which is immediately present to it, and which therefore exists.

And to render this quite clear, I remark in the first place the difference that exists between the imagination and pure intellection [or conception[1]]. For example, when I imagine a triangle, I do not conceive it only as a figure comprehended by three lines, but I also apprehend[2] these three lines as present by the power and inward vision of my mind,[3] and this is what I call imagining. But if I desire to think of a chiliagon, I certainly conceive truly that it is a figure composed of a thousand sides, just as easily as I conceive of a triangle that it is a figure of three sides only; but I cannot in any way imagine the thousand sides of a chiliagon [as I do the three sides of a triangle], nor do I, so to speak, regard them as present [with the eyes of my mind]. And although in accordance with the habit I have formed of always employing the aid of my imagination when I think of corporeal things, it may happen that in imagining a chiliagon I confusedly represent to myself some figure, yet it is very evident that this figure is not a chiliagon, since it in no way differs from that which I represent to myself when I think of a myriagon or any other many-sided figure; nor does it serve my purpose in discovering the properties which go to form the distinction between a chiliagon and other polygons. But if the question turns upon a pentagon, it is quite true that I can conceive its figure as well as that of a chiliagon without the help of my imagination; but I can also imagine it by applying the attention of my mind to each of its five sides, and at the same time to the space which they enclose. And thus I clearly recognise that I have need of a particular effort of mind in order to effect the act of imagination, such as I do not require in order to understand, and this particular effort of mind clearly manifests the difference which exists between imagination and pure intellection.[4]

I remark besides that this power of imagination which is in one, inasmuch as it differs from the power of understanding, is in no wise a necessary element in my nature, or in [my essence, that is to say, in] the essence of my mind; for although I did not possess it I should doubtless ever remain the same as I now am, from which it appears that we might conclude that it depends on something which differs from me. And I easily conceive that if some body exists with which my mind is conjoined and united in such a way that it can apply itself to consider it when it pleases, it may be that

---

[1] "Conception," French version; "intellectionem," Latin version.
[2] intueor.
[3] acie mentis.
[4] intellectionem.

by this means it can imagine corporeal objects; so that this mode of thinking differs from pure intellection only inasmuch as mind in its intellectual activity in some manner turns on itself, and considers some of the ideas which it possesses in itself; while in imagining it turns towards the body, and there beholds in it something conformable to the idea which it has either conceived of itself or perceived by the senses. I easily understand, I say, that the imagination could be thus constituted if it is true that body exists; and because I can discover no other convenient mode of explaining it, I conjecture with probability that body does exist; but this is only with probability, and although I examine all things with care, I nevertheless do not find that from this distinct idea of corporeal nature, which I have in my imagination, I can derive any argument from which there will necessarily be deduced the existence of body.

But I am in the habit of imagining many other things besides this corporeal nature which is the object of pure mathematics, to wit, the colours, sounds, scents, pain, and other such things, although less distinctly. And inasmuch as I perceive these things much better through the senses, by the medium of which, and by the memory, they seem to have reached my imagination, I believe that, in order to examine them more conveniently, it is right that I should at the same time investigate the nature of sense perception, and that I should see if from the ideas which I apprehend by this mode of thought, which I call feeling, I cannot derive some certain proof of the existence of corporeal objects.

And first of all I shall recall to my memory those matters which I hitherto held to be true, as having perceived them through the senses, and the foundations on which my belief has rested; in the next place I shall examine the reasons which have since obliged me to place them in doubt; in the last place I shall consider which of them I must now believe.

First of all, then, I perceived that I had a head, hands, feet, and all other members of which this body – which I considered as a part, or possibly even as the whole, of myself – is composed. Further I was sensible that this body was placed amidst many others, from which it was capable of being affected in many different ways, beneficial and hurtful, and I remarked that a certain feeling of pleasure accompanied those that were beneficial, and pain those which were harmful. And in addition to this pleasure and pain, I also experienced hunger, thirst, and other similar appetites, as also certain corporeal inclinations towards joy, sadness, anger, and other similar passions. And outside myself, in addition to extension, figure, and motions of bodies, I remarked in them hardness, heat, and all other tactile qualities, and, further, light and colour, and scents and sounds, the variety of which gave me the means of distinguishing the sky, the earth, the sea, and generally all the other bodies, one from the other. And certainly, considering the ideas of all these qualities which presented themselves to my mind, and which alone I perceived properly or immediately, it was not without reason that I believed myself to perceive objects quite different from my thought, to wit, bodies from which those ideas proceeded; for I found by experience that these ideas presented themselves to me without my consent being requisite, so that I could not perceive any object, however desirous I might be, unless it were present to the organs of sense; and it was not in my power not to perceive it, when it was present. And because the ideas which I received through the senses were much more lively, more clear, and even, in their own way, more distinct than any of those which I could of myself frame in meditation, or than those I found impressed on my memory, it appeared as though they could not have proceeded from my mind, so that they must necessarily have been produced in me by some other things. And having no knowledge of those objects excepting the knowledge which the ideas themselves gave me, nothing was more likely to occur to my mind than that the objects were similar to the ideas which were caused. And because I likewise remembered that I had formerly made use of my senses rather than my reason, and recognised that the ideas which I formed of myself were not so distinct as those which I perceived through the senses, and that they were most frequently even composed of portions of these last, I persuaded myself easily that I had no idea in my mind which had not formerly come to me through the senses. Nor was it without some reason that I believed that this body (which by a certain special right I call my own) belonged to me more properly and more strictly than any other; for in fact I could never be separated from it as from other bodies; I experienced in it and on account of it all my appetites and affections, and finally I was touched by the feeling of pain and the titillation of pleasure in its parts, and not in the parts of other bodies which were separated from it. But when I inquired, why, from some, I know not what, painful sensation, there follows sadness of mind, and from the pleasurable sensation there arises joy, or why this mysterious pinching of the stomach which I call hunger causes me to desire to eat, and dryness of throat causes a desire to drink, and so on, I could give no reason excepting that nature taught me so; for there is certainly no affinity (that I at least can understand) between the craving of the stomach and the desire to eat, any more than between the perception of whatever causes pain and the thought of sadness which arises from this perception. And in the same way it appeared to me that I had learned from nature all the other judgments which I formed regarding the objects of my senses, since I remarked that these judgments were formed in me before I had the leisure to weigh and consider any reasons which might oblige me to make them.

But afterwards many experiences little by little destroyed all the faith which I had rested in my senses; for I from time to time observed that those towers which from afar appeared to me to be round, more closely observed seemed square, and that colossal statues raised on the summit of these towers, appeared as quite tiny statues when viewed from the bottom; and so in an infinitude of other cases I found error in judgments founded on the external senses. And not only in those founded on the external senses, but even in those founded on the internal as well; for is there anything more intimate or more internal than pain? And yet I have learned from some persons whose arms or legs have been cut off, that they sometimes seemed to feel pain in the part which had been amputated, which made me think that I could not be quite certain that it was a certain member which pained me, even although I felt pain in it. And to those grounds of doubt I have lately added two others, which are very general; the first is that I never have believed myself to feel anything in waking moments which I cannot also sometimes believe myself to feel when I sleep, and as I do not think that these things which I seem to feel in sleep, proceed from objects outside of me, I do not see any reason why I should have this belief regarding objects which I seem to perceive while awake. The other was that being still ignorant, or rather supposing myself to be ignorant, of the author of my being, I saw nothing to prevent me from having been so constituted by nature that I might be deceived even in matters which seemed to me to be most certain. And as to the grounds on which I was formerly persuaded of the truth of sensible objects, I had not much trouble in replying to them. For since nature seemed to cause me to lean towards many things from which reason repelled me, I did not believe that I should trust much to the teachings of nature. And although the ideas which I receive by the senses do not depend on my will, I did not think that one should for that reason conclude that they proceeded from things different from myself, since possibly some faculty might be discovered in me – though hitherto unknown to me – which produced them.

But now that I begin to know myself better, and to discover more clearly the author of my being, I do not in truth think that I should rashly admit all the matters which the senses seem to teach us, but, on the other hand, I do not think that I should doubt them all universally.

And first of all, because I know that all things which I apprehend clearly and distinctly can be created by God as I apprehend them, it suffices that I am able to apprehend one thing apart from another clearly and distinctly in order to be certain that the one is different from the other, since they may be made to exist in separation at least by the omnipotence of God; and it does not signify by what power this separation is made in order to compel me to judge them to be different: and, therefore, just because I know certainly that I exist, and that meanwhile I do not remark that any other thing necessarily pertains to my nature or essence, excepting that I am a thinking thing, I rightly conclude that my essence consists solely in the fact that I am a thinking thing [or a substance whose whole essence or nature is to think]. And although possibly (or rather certainly, as I shall say in a moment) I possess a body with which I am very intimately conjoined, yet because, on the one side, I have a clear and distinct idea of myself inasmuch as I am only a thinking and unextended thing, and as, on the other, I possess a distinct idea of body, inasmuch as it is only an extended and unthinking thing, it is certain that this I [that is to say, my soul by which I am what I am], is entirely and absolutely distinct from my body, and can exist without it.

I further find in myself faculties employing modes of thinking peculiar to themselves, to wit, the faculties of imagination and feeling, without which I can easily conceive myself clearly and distinctly as a complete being; while, on the other hand, they cannot be so conceived apart from me, that is without an intelligent substance in which they reside, for [in the notion we have of these faculties, or, to use the language of the Schools] in their formal concept, some kind of intellection is comprised, from which I infer that they are distinct from me as its modes are from a thing. I observe also in me some other faculties such as that of change of position, the assumption of different figures and such like, which cannot be conceived, any more than can the preceding, apart from some substance to which they are attached, and consequently cannot exist without it; but it is very clear that these faculties, if it be true that they exist, must be attached to some corporeal or extended substance, and not to an intelligent substance, since in the clear and distinct conception of these there is some sort of extension found to be present, but no intellection at all.

There is certainly further in me a certain passive faculty of perception, that is, of receiving and recognising the ideas of sensible things, but this would be useless to me [and I could in no way avail myself of it], if there were not either in me or in some other thing another active faculty capable of forming and producing these ideas. But this active faculty cannot exist in me [inasmuch as I am a thing that thinks] seeing that it does not presuppose thought, and also that those ideas are often produced in me without my contributing in any way to the same, and often even against my will; it is thus necessarily the case that the faculty resides in some substance different from me in which all the reality which is objectively in the ideas that are produced by this faculty is formally or eminently contained, as I remarked before. And this substance is either a body, that is, a corporeal nature in which there is contained formally [and really] all that which is objectively [and by representation] in those ideas, or it is God Himself, or some other creature more noble than body in which that same is contained eminently. But, since God is no deceiver, it is very manifest that He does not communicate to me these ideas immediately and by Himself, nor yet by the intervention of some creature in which their reality is not formally, but only eminently, contained. For since He has given me no faculty to recognise that this is the case, but, on the other hand, a very great inclination to believe [that they are sent to me or] that they are conveyed to me by corporeal objects, I do not see how He could be defended from the accusation of deceit if these ideas were produced by causes other than corporeal objects. Hence we must allow that corporeal things exist. However, they are perhaps not exactly what we perceive by the senses, since this comprehension by the senses is in many instances very obscure and confused; but we must at least admit that all things which I conceive in them clearly and distinctly, that is to say, all things which, speaking generally, are comprehended in the object of pure mathematics, are truly to be recognised as external objects.

As to other things, however, which are either particular only, as, for example, that the sun is of such and such a figure, etc., or which are less clearly and distinctly conceived, such as light, sound, pain and the like, it is certain that although they are very dubious and uncertain, yet on the sole ground that God is not a deceiver, and that consequently He has not permitted any falsity to exist in my opinion which He has not likewise given me the faculty of correcting, I may assuredly hope to conclude that I have within me the means of arriving at the truth even here. And first of all there is no doubt that in all things which nature teaches me there is some truth contained; for by nature, considered in general, I now understand no other thing than either God Himself or else the order and disposition which God has established in created things; and by my nature in particular I understand no other thing than the complexus of all the things which God has given me.

But there is nothing which this nature teaches me more expressly [nor more sensibly] than that I have a body which is adversely affected when I feel pain, which has need of food or drink when I experience the feelings of hunger and thirst, and so on; nor can I doubt there being some truth in all this.

Nature also teaches me by these sensations of pain, hunger, thirst, etc., that I am not only lodged in my body as a pilot in a vessel, but that I am very closely united to it, and so to speak so intermingled with it that I seem to compose with it one whole. For if that were not the case, when my body is hurt, I, who am merely a thinking thing, should not feel pain, for I should perceive this wound by the understanding only, just as the sailor perceives by sight when something is damaged in his vessel; and when my body has need of drink or food, I should clearly understand the fact without being warned of it by confused feelings of hunger and thirst. For all these sensations of hunger, thirst, pain, etc. are in truth none other than certain confused modes of thought which are produced by the union and apparent intermingling of mind and body.

Moreover, nature teaches me that many other bodies exist around mine, of which some are to be avoided, and others sought after. And certainly from the fact that I am sensible of different sorts of colours, sounds, scents, tastes, heat, hardness, etc., I very easily conclude that there are in the bodies from which all these diverse sense-perceptions proceed certain variations which answer to them, although possibly these are not really at all similar to them. And also from the fact that amongst these different sense-perceptions some are very agreeable to me and others disagreeable, it is quite certain that my body (or rather myself in my entirety, inasmuch as I am formed of body and soul) may receive different impressions agreeable and disagreeable from the other bodies which surround it.

But there are many other things which nature seems to have taught me, but which at the same time I have never really received from her, but which have been brought about in my mind by a certain habit which I have of forming inconsiderate judgments on things; and thus it may easily happen that these judgments contain some error. Take, for example, the opinion which I hold that all space in which there is nothing that affects [or makes an impression on] my senses is void; that in a body which is warm there is something entirely similar to the idea of heat which is in me; that in a white or green body there is the same whiteness or greenness that I perceive; that in a bitter or sweet body there is the same taste, and so on in other instances; that the stars, the towers, and all other distant bodies are of the same figure and size as they appear from far off to our eyes, etc. But in order that in this there should be nothing which I do not conceive distinctly, I should define exactly what I really understand when I say that I am taught somewhat by nature. For here I take nature in a more limited signification than when I term it the sum of all the things given me by God, since in this sum many things are comprehended which only pertain to mind (and to these I do not refer in speaking of nature) such as the notion which I have of the fact that what has once been done cannot ever be undone and an infinitude of such things which I know by the light of nature [without the help of the body]; and seeing that it comprehends many other matters besides which only pertain to body, and are no longer here contained under the name of nature, such as the quality of weight which it possesses and the like, with which I also do not deal; for in talking of nature I only treat of those things given by God to me as a being composed of mind and body. But the nature here described truly teaches me to flee from things which cause the sensation of pain, and seek after the things which communicate to me the sentiment of pleasure and so forth; but I do not see that beyond this it teaches me that from those diverse sense-perceptions we should ever form any conclusion regarding things outside of us, without having [carefully and maturely] mentally examined them beforehand. For it seems to me that it is mind alone, and not mind and body in conjunction, that is requisite to a knowledge of the truth in regard to such things. Thus, although a star makes no larger an impression on my eye than the flame of a little candle there is yet in me no real or positive propensity impelling me to believe that it is not greater than that flame; but I have judged it to be so from my earliest years, without any rational foundation. And although in approaching fire I feel heat, and in approaching it a little too near I even feel pain, there is at the same time no reason in this which could persuade me that there is in the fire something resembling this heat any more than there is in it something resembling the pain; all that I have any reason to believe from this is, that there is something in it, whatever it may be, which excites in me these sensations of heat or of pain. So also, although there are spaces in which I find nothing which excites my senses, I must not from that conclude that these spaces contain no body; for I see in this, as in other similar things, that I have been in the habit of perverting the order of nature, because these perceptions of sense having been placed within me by nature merely for the purpose of signifying to my mind what things are beneficial or hurtful to the composite whole of which it forms a part, and being up to that point sufficiently clear and distinct, I yet avail myself of them as though they were absolute rules by which I might immediately determine the essence of the bodies which are outside me, as to which, in fact, they can teach me nothing but what is most obscure and confused.

But I have already sufficiently considered how, notwithstanding the supreme goodness of God, falsity enters into the judgments I make. Only here a new difficulty is presented – one respecting those things the pursuit or avoidance of which is taught me by nature, and also respecting the internal sensations which I possess, and in which I seem to have sometimes detected error [and thus to be directly deceived by my own nature]. To take an example, the agreeable taste of some food in which poison has been intermingled may induce me to partake of the poison, and thus deceive me. It is true, at the same time, that in this case nature may be excused, for it only induces me to desire food in which I find a pleasant taste, and not to desire the poison which is unknown to it; and thus I can infer nothing from this fact, except that my nature is not omniscient, at which there is certainly no reason to be astonished, since man, being finite in nature, can only have knowledge the perfectness of which is limited.

But we not unfrequently deceive ourselves even in those things to which we are directly impelled by nature, as happens with those who when they are sick desire to drink or eat things hurtful to them. It will perhaps be said here that the cause of their deceptiveness is that their nature is corrupt, but that does not remove the difficulty, because a sick man is none the less truly God's creature than he who is in health; and it is therefore as repugnant to God's goodness for the one to have a deceitful nature as it is for the other. And as a clock composed of wheels and counter-weights no less exactly observes the laws of nature when it is badly made, and does not show the time properly, than when it entirely satisfies the wishes of its maker, and as, if I consider the body of a man as being a sort of machine so built up and composed of nerves, muscles, veins, blood and skin, that though there were no mind in it at all, it would not cease to have the same motions as at present, exception being made of those movements which are due to the direction of the will, and in consequence depend upon the mind [as opposed to those which operate by the disposition of its organs], I easily recognise that it would be as natural to this body, supposing it to be, for example, dropsical, to suffer the parchedness of the throat which usually signifies to the mind the feeling of thirst, and to be disposed by this parched feeling to move the nerves and other parts in the way requisite for drinking, and thus to augment its malady and do harm to itself, as it is natural to it, when it has no indisposition, to be impelled to drink for its good by a similar cause. And although, considering the use to which the clock has been destined by its maker, I may say that it deflects from the order of its nature when it does not indicate the hours correctly; and as, in the same way, considering the machine of the human body as having been formed by God in order to have in itself all the movements usually manifested there, I have reason for thinking that it does not follow the order of nature when, if the throat is dry, drinking does harm to the conservation of health, nevertheless I recognise at the same time that this last mode of explaining nature is very different from the other. For this is but a purely verbal characterisation depending entirely on my thought, which compares a sick man and a badly constructed clock with the idea which I have of a healthy man and a well made clock, and it is hence extrinsic to the things to which it is applied; but according to the other interpretation of the term nature I understand something which is truly found in things and which is therefore not without some truth.

But certainly although in regard to the dropsical body it is only so to speak to apply an extrinsic term when we say that its nature is corrupted, inasmuch as apart from the need to drink, the throat is parched; yet in regard to the composite whole, that is to say, to the mind or soul united to this body, it is not a purely verbal predicate, but a real error of nature, for it to have thirst when drinking would be hurtful to it. And thus it still remains to inquire how the goodness of God does not prevent the nature of man so regarded from being fallacious.

In order to begin this examination, then, I here say, in the first place, that there is a great difference between mind and body, inasmuch as body is by nature always divisible, and the mind is entirely indivisible. For, as a matter of fact, when I consider the mind, that is to say, myself inasmuch as I am only a thinking thing, I cannot distinguish in myself any parts, but apprehend myself to be clearly one and entire; and although the whole mind seems to be united to the whole body, yet if a foot, or an arm, or some other part, is separated from my body, I am aware that nothing has been taken away from my mind. And the faculties of willing, feeling, conceiving, etc. cannot be properly speaking said to be its parts, for it is one and the same mind which employs itself in willing and in feeling and understanding. But it is quite otherwise with corporeal or extended objects, for there is not one of these imaginable by me which my mind cannot easily divide into parts, and which consequently I do not recognise as being divisible; this would be sufficient to teach me that the mind or soul of man is entirely different from the body, if I had not already learned it from other sources.

I further notice that the mind does not receive the impressions from all parts of the body immediately, but only from the brain, or perhaps even from one of its smallest parts, to wit, from that in which the common sense[1] is said to reside, which, whenever it is disposed in the same particular way, conveys the same thing to the mind, although meanwhile the other portions of the body may be differently disposed, as is testified by innumerable experiments which it is unnecessary here to recount.

[1] sensus communis.

I notice, also, that the nature of body is such that none of its parts can be moved by another part a little way off which cannot also be moved in the same way by each one of the parts which are between the two, although this more remote part does not act at all. As, for example, in the cord *ABCD* [which is in tension] if we pull the last part *D*, the first part *A* will not be moved in any way differently from what would be the case if one of the intervening parts *B* or *C* were pulled, and the last part *D* were to remain unmoved. And in the same way, when I feel pain in my foot, my knowledge of physics teaches me that this sensation is communicated by means of nerves dispersed through the foot, which, being extended like cords from there to the brain, when they are contracted in the foot, at the same time contract the inmost portions of the brain which is their extremity and place of origin, and then excite a certain movement which nature has established in order to cause the mind to be affected by a sensation of pain represented as existing in the foot. But because these nerves must pass through the tibia, the thigh, the loins, the back and the neck, in order to reach from the leg to the brain, it may happen that although their extremities which are in the foot are not affected, but only certain ones of their intervening parts [which pass by the loins or the neck], this action will excite the same movement in the brain that might have been excited there by a hurt received in the foot, in consequence of which the mind will necessarily feel in the foot the same pain as if it had received a hurt. And the same holds good of all the other perceptions of our senses.

I notice finally that since each of the movements which are in the portion of the brain by which the mind is immediately affected brings about one particular sensation only, we cannot under the circumstances imagine anything more likely than that this movement, amongst all the sensations which it is capable of impressing on it, causes mind to be affected by that one which is best fitted and most generally useful for the conservation of the human body when it is in health. But experience makes us aware that all the feelings with which nature inspires us are such as I have just spoken of; and there is therefore nothing in them which does not give testimony to the power and goodness of the God [who has produced them].[1] Thus, for example, when the nerves which are in the feet are violently or more than usually moved, their movement,

[1] Latin version only.

passing through the medulla of the spine[1] to the inmost parts of the brain, gives a sign to the mind which makes it feel somewhat, to wit, pain, as though in the foot, by which the mind is excited to do its utmost to remove the cause of the evil as dangerous and hurtful to the foot. It is true that God could have constituted the nature of man in such a way that this same movement in the brain would have conveyed something quite different to the mind; for example, it might have produced consciousness of itself either in so far as it is in the brain, or as it is in the foot, or as it is in some other place between the foot and the brain, or it might finally have produced consciousness of anything else whatsoever; but none of all this world have contributed so well to the conservation of the body. Similarly, when we desire to drink, a certain dryness of the throat is produced which moves its nerves, and by their means the internal portions of the brain; and this movement causes in the mind the sensation of thirst, because in this case there is nothing more useful to us than to become aware that we have need to drink for the conservation of our health; and the same holds good in other instances.

From this it is quite clear that, notwithstanding the supreme goodness of God, the nature of man, inasmuch as it is composed of mind and body, cannot be otherwise than sometimes a source of deception. For if there is any cause which excites, not in the foot but in some part of the nerves which are extended between the foot and the brain, or even in the brain itself, the same movement which usually is produced when the foot is detrimentally affected, pain will be experienced as though it were in the foot, and the sense will thus naturally be deceived; for since the same movement in the brain is capable of causing but one sensation in the mind, and this sensation is much more frequently excited by a cause which hurts the foot than by another existing in some other quarter, it is reasonable that it should convey to the mind pain in the foot rather than in any other part of the body. And although the parchedness of the throat does not always proceed, as it usually does, from the fact that drinking is necessary for the health of the body, but sometimes comes from quite a different cause, as is the case with dropsical patients, it is yet much better that it should mislead on this occasion than if, on the other hand, it were always to deceive us when the body is in good health; and so on in similar cases.

[1] spini dorsae medullam.

And certainly this consideration is of great service to me, not only in enabling me to recognise all the errors to which my nature is subject, but also in enabling me to avoid them or to correct them more easily. For knowing that all my senses more frequently indicate to me truth than falsehood respecting the things which concern that which is beneficial to the body, and being able almost always to avail myself of many of them in order to examine one particular thing, and, besides that, being able to make use of my memory in order to connect the present with the past, and of my understanding which already has discovered all the causes of my errors, I ought no longer to fear that falsity may be found in matters every day presented to me by my senses. And I ought to set aside all the doubts of these past days as hyperbolical and ridiculous, particularly that very common uncertainty respecting sleep, which I could not distinguish from the waking state; for at present I find a very notable difference between the two, inasmuch as our memory can never connect our dreams one with the other, or with the whole course of our lives, as it unites events which happen to us while we are awake. And, as a matter of fact, if someone, while I was awake, quite suddenly appeared to me and disappeared as fast as do the images which I see in sleep, so that I could not know from whence the form came nor whither it went, it would not be without reason that I should deem it a spectre or a phantom formed by my brain [and similar to those which I form in sleep], rather than a real man. But when I perceive things as to which I know distinctly both the place from which they proceed, and that in which they are, and the time at which they appeared to me; and when, without any interruption, I can connect the perceptions which I have of them with the whole course of my life, I am perfectly assured that these perceptions occur while I am waking and not during sleep. And I ought in no wise to doubt the truth of such matters, if, after having called up all my senses, my memory, and my understanding, to examine them, nothing is brought to evidence by any one of them which is repugnant to what is set forth by the others. For because God is in no wise a deceiver, it follows that I am not deceived in this. But because the exigencies of action often oblige us to make up our minds before having leisure to examine matters carefully, we must confess that the life of man is very frequently subject to error in respect to individual objects, and we must in the end acknowledge the infirmity of our nature.

EXCERPT FROM
REPLIES TO OBJECTIONS II

Further, in the matter of the counsel you give me about *propounding my arguments in geometrical fashion, in order that the reader may perceive them as it were with a single glance,*[1] it is worth while setting forth here the extent to which I have followed this method and that to which I intend in future to follow it. Now there are two things that I distinguish in the geometrical mode of writing, viz. the order and the method of proof.

The order consists merely in putting forward those things first that should be known without the aid of what comes subsequently, and arranging all other matters so that their proof depends solely on what precedes them. I certainly tried to follow this order as accurately as possible in my Meditations; and it was through keeping to this that I treated of the distinction between the mind and the body, not in the second Meditation, but finally in the sixth, and deliberately and consciously omitted much, because it required an explanation of much else besides.

Further, the method of proof is two-fold, one being analytic, the other synthetic.

Analysis shows the true way by which a thing was methodically discovered and derived, as it were effect from cause,[2] so that, if the reader care to follow it and give sufficient attention to everything, he understands the matter no less perfectly and makes it as much his own as if he had himself discovered it. But it contains nothing to incite belief in an inattentive or hostile reader; for if the very least thing brought forward escapes his notice, the necessity of the conclusions is lost; and on many matters which, nevertheless,

---

[1] Cf. Obj. II. sub fin.
[2] tanquam a priori.

should be specially noted, it often scarcely touches, because they are clear to anyone who gives sufficient attention to them.

GEOMETRY METHOD — Synthesis contrariwise employs an opposite procedure, one in which the search goes as it were from effect to cause[1] (though often here the proof itself is from cause to effect to a greater extent than in the former case). It does indeed clearly demonstrate its conclusions, *SELF EVIDENT Truth* and it employs a long series of definitions, postulates, axioms, theorems and problems, so that if one of the conclusions that follow is denied, it may at once be shown to be contained in what has gone before. Thus the reader, however hostile and obstinate, is *ANALYSIS* compelled to render his assent. Yet this method is not so satisfactory as the other and does not equally well content the eager learner, because it does not show the way in which the matter taught was discovered.

It was this synthesis alone that the ancient Geometers employed in their writings, not because they were wholly ignorant of the analytic method, but, in my opinion, because they set so high a value on it that they wished to keep it to themselves as an important secret.

But I have used in my Meditations only analysis, which is the best and truest method of teaching. On the other hand synthesis, doubtless the method you here ask me to use, though it very suitably finds a place after analysis in the domain of geometry, nevertheless cannot so conveniently be applied to these metaphysical matters we are discussing. *MEDITATIONS — ANALYSIS GEOMETRY — SYNTHESIS*

HIERARCHICAL For there is this difference between the two cases, viz. that the primary notions that are the presuppositions of geometrical proofs harmonize with the use of our senses, and are readily *EXCEPTED* granted by all. Hence, no difficulty is involved in this case, except in the proper deduction of the consequences. But this may be performed by people of all sorts, even by the inattentive, if only they remember what has gone before; and the minute subdivisions of propositions is designed for the purpose of rendering citation easy and thus making people recollect even against their will.

QUOTE On the contrary, nothing in metaphysics causes more trouble than the making the perception of its primary notions clear and distinct. For, though in their own nature they are as intelligible as, or even more intelligible than those the geometricians study, yet being contradicted by the many preconceptions of our senses to

[1] tanquam a posteriori quaesitam.

102

which we have since our earliest years been accustomed, they cannot be perfectly apprehended except by those who give strenuous attention and study to them, and <u>withdraw their minds</u> <u>as far as possible from matters corporeal</u>. Hence if they alone were brought forward it would be easy for anyone with a zeal for contradiction to deny them.

[margin note: WITHDRAWL - DEPENDENT ON SENSES]

This is why my writing took the form of Meditations rather than that of Philosophical Disputations or the theorems and problems of a geometer; so that hence I might by this very fact testify that I had no dealings except with those who will not shrink from joining me in giving the matter attentive care and meditation. For from the very fact that anyone girds himself up for an attack upon the truth, he makes himself less capable of perceiving the truth itself, since he withdraws his mind from the consideration of those reasons that tend to convince him of it, in order to discover others that have the opposite effect.

But perhaps some one will here raise the objection, that, while indeed a man ought not to seek for hostile arguments when he knows that it is the truth that is set before him, yet, so long as this is in doubt, it is right that he should fully explore all the arguments on either side, in order to find out which are the stronger. According to this objection it is unfair of me to want to have the truth of my contentions admitted before they have been fully scrutinised, while prohibiting any consideration of those reasonings that oppose them.

This would certainly be a just criticism if any of the matters in which I desire attention and absence of hostility in my reader were capable of withdrawing him from the consideration of any others in which there was the least hope of finding greater truth than in mine. But consider that in what I bring forward you find the most extreme doubt about all matters, and that there is nothing I more strongly urge than that every single thing should be most carefully examined and that nothing should be admitted but what has been rendered so clear and distinct to our scrutiny that we cannot withhold our assent from it. Consider too that, on the other hand, there is nothing else from which I wish to divert the minds of my readers, save beliefs which they have never properly examined and which are derived from no sound reasoning, but from the senses alone. Therefore I hardly think that anyone will believe that there is much risk in confining his attention to my statement of the case; the danger will be no more than that of turning his gaze away from it towards other things which in some measure conflict with it and only darken counsel (i.e. to the prejudices of the senses).

Hence, in the first place, I rightly require singular attention on the part of my readers and have specially selected the style of writing which I thought would best secure it and which, I am convinced, will bring my readers more profit than they would acquire if I had used the synthetic method, one which would have made them appear to have learned more than they really had. But besides this I deem it quite fair to ignore wholly and to despise as of no account the criticisms of those who refuse to accompany me in my Meditations and cling to their preconceived opinions.

But I know how difficult it will be, even for one who does attend and seriously attempt to discover the truth, to have before his mind the entire bulk of what is contained in my Meditations, and at the same time to have distinct knowledge of each part of the argument; and yet, in my opinion, one who is to reap the full benefit from my work must know it both as a whole and in detail.

DESCARTES' USE OF "DEMONSTRATION" AND "DEDUCTION"

Desmond M. Clarke

Descartes notoriously claims that his physics is constructed with the clarity of a mathematical demonstration. For example, the final article of Book II of the *Principles* (in which he had discussed the basic laws of nature) contains the following description of the proposed development of Cartesian physics in the remainder of the treatise: "I claim . . . to admit that nothing concerning them (the divisions, shapes and motions of particles) is true which cannot be so evidently deduced (*deducatur*) from those common notions, whose truth we cannot doubt, that it could be considered a mathematical demonstration (*demonstratione*)" (ATVIII-1, 79).[1] The last page of the *Principles* (in the French version) reminds the reader that he has indeed accomplished what he planned: "I think that one should also recognize that I have proved (*prouvé*) all the things I wrote by means of a mathematical demonstration (*par demonstration Mathematique*), at least the more general" (ATIX-2, 325).

If one approaches texts like these with our present understanding of mathematic proof, it is difficult to make any sense of Descartes' remarks. For the two books of the *Principles* which intervene between the quoted comments are a tissue of hypotheses, guesses, experimental findings, models and analogies for natural phenomena, descriptions of *explananda*, etc.; in short, anything but mathematical proofs. One standard resolution of this anomaly is to suggest that Descartes vainly attempted to reduce physics to mathematics and that his failure was inevitable from the outset. Unable to accept the obvious discrepancy between the ideal of a mathematical physics and the complex of untested or poorly confirmed hypotheses which he constructs in the *Principles*,

Descartes is said to stubbornly misdescribe the results of his scientific investigations.[2]

Another equally plausible interpretation of Descartes' position is suggested in what follows. If Descartes says that he is going to provide a mathematical demonstration of his physics and if, when he concludes the work, he claims to have realized his objective, then probably what he means by "mathematical demonstration" is the kind of inquiry which is contained between the initial plan and the consequent characterization of his achievement. To investigate this possibility it is necessary to look more closely at Descartes' language and at the contexts in which he discusses demonstrations or proofs. The two key terms for this inquiry, both used in the first quotation above, are "demonstration" and "deduction." In Sections I and II below, I examine alternative readings of each term in Cartesian usage, beginning with the first. The available evidence shows that neither term, in Descartes' language, has the more precise sense which it has since acquired in philosophical literature. In the third section I examine Descartes' supposed adoption of pure mathematics as an ideal method for all investigations, and suggest that Descartes simply reflects the standard classification of physics as a branch of applied mathematics. I conclude that Descartes' use of such words as "deduction," "demonstration" and "mathematical" is best understood in terms of the ordinary usage of his time. A "mathematical demonstration," in the context of the *Principles*, is nothing more than a clearly articulated and appropriately corroborated argument.

I

Descartes uses the Latin *demonstrare* and the French word *démontrer* with approximately the same degree of ambiguity as the English verb "to show." Further specification of the meaning of "demonstration" depends on explicit comments by the author, on a closer scrutiny of the context or on a comparison of the French and Latin versions of the same text. The following comments use all three approaches whenever they are available.

In Part VI of the *Discourse* there is a well-known passage in which Descartes speaks of demonstrating (*démontrer*) the principles of his science by the conclusions which are derived from them and *vice-versa*. This is not a circular procedure, he contends, because

since experience makes most of these effects very certain, the causes from which I deduce (*déduire*) them serve less to prove them (*prouver*) than to explain (*expliquer*) them; but, on the contrary, it is the causes which are proved (*prouver*) by the effects.

(AT VI, 76)

This indicates that although the effects are deduced from the causes, the latter are proved by the former. It is evident to the contemporary reader that Descartes meant that the causes explain the effects, and the effects confirm the (hypothetical) causes. This clarification of his methodology was apparently insufficient for his readers, and he returns to the same problem again in a letter to Morin, July 13, 1638: "There is a great difference between proving (*prouver*) and explaining (*expliquer*) . . . one can use the word demonstrate (*démontrer*) to signify one or the other, at least if one takes the word in its ordinary usage" (AM II, 311).

Descartes seems to have been clear on the distinction between an explanation and a corroborating argument. Both procedures are similar in that, assuming certain antecedents, one derives consequences from them by means of what Descartes calls a "deduction." The logical structure of this kind of inference will be examined in more detail below. For Descartes, the argument from antecedent to consequent or *vice-versa* may be called a "demonstration."

There is a wide variety of Cartesian texts which illustrate Descartes' ambiguous use of the word "demonstration." The "confirmation" sense of "demonstration" is often expressed by the word *prouver*. Thus, in the *Passions of the Soul* he suggests that the brain can cause muscular reactions without any involvement of the soul, and he "proves" this hypothesis by our experience of reflex actions ("ce que je prouveray seulement icy par un example": XI, 338). A similar example is found in the *Description of the Human Body* (XI, 226), and in the *Principles*, IX-2, 146 and 270 ("j'ay prouvé"). In none of these proofs does one find anything more than corroborating evidence for an hypothesis. One of the Latin equivalents of *prouver*, *probare*, is closer to our sense of confirmation and this is found in the *Principles* (AT VIII-1, 81), the *Discourse* (AT VI, 582), and in Descartes' notes on anatomy (AT XI, 587): "Adeo ut probem."

This apparent uniformity in the use of "prove" is complicated by other examples where it is difficult to decide whether Descartes means "to confirm" or "to explain." This is particularly noticeable when, in the development of a physical theory, Descartes mentions phenomena which are compatible with the theory in question. It is only in the vaguest sense that one could claim that such a theory explains the phenomenon, or that the observation of the phenomenon confirms the theory. It looks as if Descartes simply incorporates a reference to some observed results into the development of a wide ranging hypothesis, and then refers, in retrospect, to a "proof." For example, in the *Meteorology*, the roundness of raindrops is said to have been proved (*prouvé*: AT VI, 325. Cf. ibid., 280), and in two instances in the *Principles* (AT IX-2, 146, 298) what is "proved" in the French version is said to be shown (*ostensum*) in the Latin original (AT VIII-1, 133, 303).[3]

Any of the above uses of *prouver* could be substituted by *demontrer*. Thus, in the notes on anatomy, a different corroborating argument (for an explanation of why our breath is sometimes warm) is introduced by *demonstratur* (AT XI, 625), and in the discussion of the basic laws of physics two instances of *demonstrare* (AT VIII-1, 65, 66) are translated into French by the phrase "connaître la verité de" (AT IX-2, 87). In some cases the Latin *demonstrare* is rendered into French by *prouver* (e.g., AT VIII-1, 105 and IX-2, 128). The other kind of demonstration, namely a deductively constructed explanation of some natural phenomenon, is also frequently alluded to in Cartesian texts. For example, the discussion of physiology in the *Discourse* is acknowledged to fall short of the method of "démontrant les effets par les causes" (AT VI, 45), and Descartes writes to M. le Comte of demonstrating (*esse demonstratam*) the differences in rotational velocity of celestial matter from hypotheses (AM VII, 150).

Thus, Descartes evidently has a wide selection of words available for referring to what we distinguish as explanations or confirmations, and he obviously uses "demonstrate" as a description of both procedures. This in itself is not a problem. The cause of a contemporary reader's concern is the suggestion that all these demonstrations are, in some sense, deductive or mathematical. For example, Descartes speaks in the *Principles* of explaining certain effects from hypothetical causes or principles, and whereas the French version uses the word *démontrer* (AT IX-2, 126), the Latin uses *deduci* (AT VIII-1, 102). There are frequent references to deducing effects from hypothetical causes: AT VIII-1, 99 (*deducentur*), ibid., 103 (*deduci possit*); and where one would expect to find *demonstrare* doing double duty for both "explain" and "confirm," one sometimes finds *deducere*. For example, Descartes speaks of deducing causes from effects and effects from causes: "cupimus enim rationes effectuum a causis, non autem e contra causarum ab effectibus deducere" (AT VIII-1, 81). If explanations and confirmatory arguments take the form of deductions, then any clarification of the concept of a deduction will correspondingly elucidate Descartes' understanding of physical theories as mathematical demonstrations. For this purpose, the *Regulae* is of primary value.

II

In the *Regulae*, Descartes reduces the sources of human knowledge to experience and deduction (AT X, 364–5). Since experience is sometimes liable to error, scientific knowledge is acquired only by intuition and deduction (where intuition is a form of experience): "All the activities of our intellect, by which we can arrive at a knowledge of things without fear of error, are considered here. Only two are acceptable, namely, intuition and deduction" (AT X, 368; cf. 372, 400). Rather than gratuitously supply Descartes with our own understanding of deduction and then exclude various kinds of arguments from his scientific method on that basis, it is preferable to examine some of the scientific procedures he recommends in the *Regulae* and interpret his use of "deduction" in this light. For whatever he proposes as part of his scientific method must either be an intuition or a deduction (or some combination of both).

There is a second reason for a cautious interpretation of Descartes' use of "deduction" in the *Regulae*. The first Book was intended by the author as a general summary of his method, and was necessarily vague as a result (cf., AT X, 399, 429–30). He planned to apply the general methodological principles of Book I to the specific problems of mathematics in Book II and to physics in Book III. Since the work is incomplete, one can only extrapolate from hints in the early sections to what Descartes would have written about deduction in the physical sciences in Book III.

Deduction is not identical with syllogistic reasoning.[4] One could legitimately translate Descartes' comment in this regard as the claim that Cartesian deduction is not limited to the patterns of deductive inference which are validated by formal logicians. For Descartes, deduction has two forms, which are distinguished by their relative complexity. In its simplest form, deduction is an instance of what might be called immediate inference, or an insight into the relationship between the truth values of two propositions. Once the number of propositions involved in a deduction increases, the mental process of deriving a conclusion from the evidence becomes more complex. For this reason, the activity of moving from a series of discrete propositions to a "conclusion" which is warranted by them is called an induction or enumeration by Descartes ("cui enumerationis, sive inductionis nomen dedimus": AT X, 408). This is the second type of deduction. From this explication of "induction" it is evident that a scientific explanation of some phenomenon normally takes the form of a Cartesian induction.

A more detailed discussion of enumerative deduction in the physical sciences was planned for Book III of the *Regulae*.[5] In the absence of this evidence, one is limited to the examples used in the extant portion of the work. Consider the following example from Rule XII. If someone wishes to explain magnetism ("si petatur quae sit magnetis natura": AT X, 427), he should proceed in three stages to his so-called deductive conclusion:

Step 1: Assuming that whatever can be known about a magnet is known in terms of simple natures, the investigator should first collect all the empirical information available concerning magnetic stones (X, 427).

Step 2: He will then try to "deduce" what combination of simple natures is sufficient to produce all those properties of magnets which are empirically known. "Ex quibus deinde deducere conatur" (AT X, 427). If the word "deduce" in this context is understood in the vague sense of giving reasons for one's choice of hypotheses, then Descartes' proposed deduction matches his discussion of magnetism in the *Principles* (AT VIII-1, 284 and 310–11).

Step 3: The scientist realizes that when he has completed his task, he has done everything possible, within the limits of human understanding and the empirical information available, to discover the nature of magnetism.

Descartes returns to the example of magnetism in Rule XIII to illustrate the possibility of reducing an indeterminate or imperfect problem to a determinate one. Again there are three stages in the process, from listing everything we know about magnets as a result of Gilbert's work to acknowledging that the final explanation of magnetism is limited by the empirical information available. The initial survey of available observations involves an adequate *enumeratio* (AT X, 432). The second step is again an attempt to deduce the nature of magnets from the observational evidence available ("quid de natura magnetis sit inferendum": AT X, 431). The process of deriving a theory or explanation from the inductively gathered evidence is also referred to as concluding (*concluditur*: AT X, 389) the truth from observations. The precise nature of this deduction is deferred for further analysis to Book III (cf. AT X, 432).

A more detailed discussion of Descartes' logic of discovery and explanation is found in his suggested resolution of a problem in optics in Rule VIII. The search for the anaclastic line for a given medium involves an analysis of the problem into the elements which contribute to a solution (i.e. the appropriate simple natures) and the construction of a solution in terms of these elements. Deduction is involved in two steps here. The investigator should attempt to "deduce" the explanation of illumination from his understanding of natural powers. If this fails, he should enumerate all the natural powers he understands and then the nature of illumination will at least be known by analogy ("saltem per imitationem": AT X, 395) with other natural powers. The analogical argument suggested here, and the demonstration of the optical properties of light which is based on it, were the source of objections when Descartes implemented this plan in the beginning of the *Dioptrique*.[6] He replied to Mersenne, in May, 1638: "What I claim to have demonstrated (*démontré*) concerning refraction . . . depends only on my assumption that light is an action, or a power (vertu, potentia), which follows the same laws as local motion . . ." (AM, II, 266). In this case, an argument from analogy provides the basis for an hypothesis, and the explanation which results from this is called a demonstration.

These examples of the method of the *Regulae* applied in physics suggest that Descartes uses the word "induction" (or enumeration) in significantly different ways. One use of the term is close to the standard meaning of induction as a generalization based on a sample of a given class. Descartes extends this usage to arguments by analogy. If one cannot examine a representative sample of a certain type of phenomenon, one might examine some instances of a similar type and conclude to a general claim about this analogous class. One then applies the results of this induction to the type of phenomenon which could not be directly examined.[7] This is a combination of induction and argument by analogy, which is still called *enumeratio* by Descartes. Finally, Descartes considers any deductive argument which involves a series of deductive stages as an induction, because the mind must marshal all the relevant evidence together to adequately warrant the final conclusion. Since all of these mental processes must fit into one of the categories of experience or deduction, it is clear that the word "deduction" refers to any reasoning process by means of which we argue from whatever evidence is available for the credibility of a given conclusion. The direction and complexity of such arguments explains why such diverse procedures as induction, retroductive inference, hypothetico–deductive explanations, arguments from models or analogies, or any hybrid mixture of these, can be called a deduction by Descartes. The question remains: why are such arguments called mathematical demonstrations?

III

Descartes is often said to be so enamored of the rigor of mathematical deductions that he tries to force physics into the limits of purely mathematical or formal proofs. The simplicity of this interpretation is not warranted by the text of Descartes.

In the first place, Descartes rather quickly lost interest in pure mathematics once he began his studies in physics. This lack of interest was a constant theme of his correspondence from 1630 on. He writes to Mersenne (April 15, 1630): "I am so fed up with mathematics and I take such little account of it now that I could hardly take the trouble to resolve them (problems) myself" (AM I, 131). The same attitude comes across in later correspondence: "such questions have no usefulness" (AM I, 210); "I avoid all opportunities to engage in mathematics as much as possible" (ibid., 246); "you realize that it is more than fifteen years since I vowed to neglect Geometry, ..." (AM II, 222 – written on March 31, 1638); "To tell you the truth, I am so tired of abstract mathematics that I can no longer work at it" (AM III, 182–3).[8] The *Discourse* reflects Descartes' disillusionment with abstract studies in terms of the distinction of pure and applied mathematics.[9] When his correspondents express surprise at the change of heart (for example, M. Desargues), Descartes replies:

I have only decided to abandon abstract mathematics . . . and the reason for this is because I will have so much more time to cultivate a different type of geometry, which is concerned with explaining natural phenomena. For if he cares to consider what I wrote about salt, the snow, and the rainbow, he will quickly realize that all my physics is nothing else but geometry.

(AM II, 362–3)

The last line here is partly an attempt to placate an importunate correspondent. It is just as much a reflection of the standard distinction between pure and applied mathematics, the latter of which included music, astronomy, and optics.[10] Descartes speaks of two kinds of geometry (rather than of mathematics), where geometry is understood "as a science which, in general, teaches one to know the measures of all bodies" (*Geometry* VI, 389). In other words, any exact science is part of applied mathematics.

Corresponding to Descartes' primary interest in physics, one finds clear expressions of the fact that demonstrations in physics do not guarantee the truth-values of one's conclusions as they do in purely formal deductions. Descartes wrote to Mersenne in 1638:

You ask me if I claim that what I wrote about refraction is a demonstration. And I believe it is, at least insofar as it is possible to give one in this matter . . . and insofar as any other question of mechanics, or optics, or astronomy, or any matter which is not purely geometrical or arithmetical, has even been demonstrated. But to expect geometrical demonstrations in a matter which depends on physics, is to wish that I do the impossible.

(AM II, 266)

Demonstrations in the physical sciences, Descartes continues, are satisfactory if one's initial assumptions are not manifestly incompatible with experience, and if one's arguments are not invalid.[11] It is significant that, in describing exactly the same methodology in the *Principles*, Descartes qualifies the deductive phase of this procedure as mathematical.[12]

This clarification of the status of demonstration in physics corresponds to the distinction between perfect and imperfect problems in the *Regulae*. A perfect problem is such that the solution depends on what is already known in such a way that the former is "completely determined by the latter" (AT X, 461).[13] Problems of this kind are "for the most part abstract and occur almost exclusively in Arithmetic or Geometry" (AT X, 429–30). Since the physicist's investigations are not normally determinate in this way, Descartes suggests that it is possible to reduce indeterminate problems to a pseudodeterminate (or more tractable) status by limiting the information on the basis of which a solution is to be worked out. "Once we have decided to consider this or that group of observations about the magnet, there is no difficulty in ignoring all the others" (AT X, 431). The selection of relevant information is necessary because a complete account of all available evidence is impossible.[14] However, as a result, we can never provide more than a tentative answer to questions in the physical sciences.

Since Descartes considers physics to be a part of applied mathematics, the type of demonstration (or argument) which is ideal for this discipline could be called a mathematical demonstration. There is no danger of confusion in this nomenclature once it is clearly realized that the necessarily hypothetical character of physical theories implies a significant difference between the demonstrations of pure and applied mathematics. Descartes seems to have been not unaware of this point.

IV

The so-called method of Descartes is a rather general and necessarily vague account of basic rules for any systematic inquiry, whether in metaphysics, physics, or mathematics. The ideal of clear and distinct ideas is a metaphor for making the necessary distinctions and providing appropriate and adequate evidence for whatever claims one makes, in whatever discipline. As applied to physics, this was equivalent to demanding a step-by-step analysis of any *explanandum*, and a well-founded explanation with careful attention to the corroborating force of the available evidence. The understanding of such evidence presupposes what Descartes calls an intuition. Once the individual items of relevant information are understood, the task remains of developing an hypothesis (or finding a cause) which could explain any given phenomenon.

The collation of relevant information, the construction, testing, and confirmation (or disconfirmation) of an explanation, involve the scientist in various kinds of reasoning processes. Descartes evidently recommends such procedures in the *Regulae* and *Discourse*, and he implements these plans in the scientific essays.

Since none of these complex reasoning processes qualifies as an intuition, they should be classified (according to the *Regulae*) as deductions.

The explication of the concept of a deduction in the *Regulae*, and the multiplicity of contexts in which Descartes refers to demonstrations or deductions, indicate that the word "deduction" covers a wide range of inferential procedures, such as induction, arguments by analogy, deductive inferences in formal disciplines such as logic or mathematics, hypothetico–deductive explanations, retro–deductive inferences, or any argument the structure and evidentiary value of which is clear. The word "deduction" refers to the logical structure of such varied arguments. The result of a "deduction" is what Descartes calls a demonstration, although the word "demonstrate" is also used in contexts where it simply means "to show clearly" (for example, by providing unambiguous observational evidence). Thus, scientific demonstrations are carefully constructed arguments (deductions) which serve either to explain a given phenomenon or to confirm the plausibility of one's hypothetical explanations.

It is anachronistic to expect a clear line of demarcation, in Descartes' methodology, between purely formal proofs and the logic of scientific theories. Such clarity was not available in the seventeenth century. What one finds instead is an emerging realization of the hypothetical character of physical sciences – a development to which Descartes contributes significantly. Consequently, it is not inconsistent to find Descartes explain the distinction between mathematical and physical demonstrations, and at the same time refer to the contents of the *Principles* as mathematical demonstrations. For the vocabulary of Cartesian science reflects the standard classification of the time in describing physics as a branch of applied mathematics. When Descartes calls his scientific explanations a "mathematical deduction," this can be translated as a physical theory with appropriate arguments and adequately assessed evidence.

NOTES

1 References to Descartes' correspondence are to the *Correspondance*, ed. C. Adam and G. Milhaud (Paris, 1936–63). Prefixed by AM, the volume and page numbers are given in roman and arabic numerals respectively. All other references to Descartes' works are to the Adam and Tannery edition of the *Oeuvres*, new edn (Paris: Vrin, 1964). The volume and page numbers are in roman and arabic numerals respectively. The translations throughout are my own.

DESMOND M. CLARKE

2 Cf., for example, John Herman Randall, Jr, *The Career of Philosophy* (New York and London, 1962), p. 384; Geneviève Rodis-Lewis, *Descartes et le rationalisme* (Paris, 1966), p. 15; Louis Chauvois, *Descartes: Sa méthode et ses erreurs en physiologie* (Paris, 1966); Jean-Louis Allard, *Le Mathématisme de Descartes* (Ottawa, 1963), p. 49; John Passmore, "William Harvey and the Philosophy of Science," *Australian Journal of Philosophy* 36 (1958):89; E. J. Dijksterhuis, *The Mechanization of the World Picture*, trans. D. Dikshoorn (Oxford, 1961), p. 404.

3 Descartes' use of *prouver* in contexts where a weaker verb would seem to be more appropriate is not explained by the poverty of his vocabulary. In discussions of corroborating evidence for different hypotheses one finds a great variety of words such as: *montrer* (VI, 87); *verifier* (VI, 91); *certum reddit* (VIII-1, 61); *accorde avec l'expérience* (IX-2, 158); *confirmare* (VIII-1, 301); *confirmer* (IX-2, 121); *justifier* (IX-2, 17); *favoriser cette opinion* (XI, 10); *probabiliter conjicio* (VII, 73); *testatur* (VIII-1, 205), and many more. When discussing the claim that there is no vacuum in nature, Descartes writes: "Les expériences dont j'ay parlé, ne sont point suffisantes pour le prouver, quoy qu'elles le soient assez, pour persuader que les espaces . . . sont remplis de la mesme matière" (XI, 20–1).

4 Cf. X, 405–6.

5 ". . . how these things should be done will be more clearly apparent from the third book of this treatise" (X, 432).

6 The first discourse of the *Optics* explicitly assumes a hypothetical approach towards explaining various optical phenomena. Descartes is content to begin with various *suppositions* (VI, 83) and to deduce consequences from them which are compatible with our observations. Thus, the treatise begins with three models of light, or what Descartes calls *comparaisons* (VI, 83, 86, 89, 93).

7 Cf. Descartes' letter to Plempius, October 3, 1637: "There is nothing more in keeping with reason than that we should make judgments about those things which we do not perceive, because of their extremely small size, by analogy and comparison with those which we see" (AM II, 16). For the disanalogy in models, see Descartes to Mersenne, July 27, 1638 (AM, II, 363).

8 See also Descartes to Mersenne, September 12, 1638 (AM III, 63); Descartes to Mersenne, April 1, 1640 (AM IV, 49); and Descartes to Dozem, March 25, 1642 (AM V, 181). Cf. P. Golliet, "Le problème de la méthode chez Descartes," *Revue des sciences humaines* 61 (1951): 62.

9 See VI, 17–18.

10 See VI, 19–20, and E. Gilson, *Discours de la méthode: Texte et commentaire*, 2nd edn (Paris, 1947), pp. 216–17. For Descartes' distinction of geometry and mechanics, cf. VI, 389 and 392. Pierre Boutroux, *L'Imagination et les mathématiques chez Descartes* (Paris, 1900, p. 34), discusses Descartes' attitude towards pure mathematics.

11 Cf. Descartes' letter to an unknown correspondent (AM VII, 184), where he discusses the explanation of unusual phenomena: "in those matters about which one has little experiential information, it is

enough to imagine a cause which could produce the effect in question, even though it might just as well have been produced by a different cause and one does not know which is the correct one."

12 "And surely, if we only use those principles which seem to be most evident, if we deduce nothing from them unless by mathematical arguments (*per Mathematicas consequentias*), and if we find that those things which we have thus deduced from them correspond accurately with all the phenomena of nature, then we would seem to insult God if we suspect that the causes, which we have thus discovered, are false . . ." (VIII-1, 99). Cf. ibid., 101.

13 Descartes expands on this in Rule XII. A perfect problem is such that the terms in which it is stated are well understood, the procedure for finding a solution is a deductive one, and the solution is easily recognizable once it is found (X, 429).

14 Cf. X, 390–1. Descartes tries to compensate for this necessary limitation by making the selection of relevant information methodical. Descartes elsewhere requires a sufficient enumeration of everything which is known about some problem as a prerequisite for the deductive stage of his method. However, "by a sufficient enumeration or induction we only understand one from which the truth is more certainly derived than from any other kind of proof apart from simple intuition" (X, 389).

A DISCOURSE
ON DESCARTES' METHOD

Jaakko Hintikka

Descartes believed that ancient mathematicians had suppressed their chief method of discovery "with a certain pernicious crafti- ness, just as we know many inventors have suppressed their dis- coveries, being very much afraid that to publish this method . . . would make it seem worthless" (*Regulae*: HR I, 12; AT X, 376). But was this self-confessed secretive man any more candid himself? The actual rules listed in the second part of the *Discourse* are but pale shadows of the *Regulae*, which Descartes never completed and which were never published during his lifetime. But even from the *Regulae*, the import of Descartes' method is not immediately clear or distinct. What *is* Descartes' method, which was so dramatically revealed to him in his famous dream and which he valued so highly? What does it amount to in his actual scientific or philo- sophical work?

In this paper I shall argue for a familiar and apparently unexciting answer to this question about Descartes' own method: I shall suggest that it can be profitably considered as a variant of the method of analysis which was used in Greek mathematics and whose discovery was ascribed by some sources to Plato. There does not seem to be anything surprising or novel in this suggestion. Indeed, it turns out that it is largely just this analytical method that Descartes accused (as we saw) the Greek mathematicians of having hidden. (This is shown by Descartes' Replies to Objections II, see p. 102). The epithet "analytic" commonly associated with Descartes' own geometry referred originally to his use and system- atization of the Greek method of analysis rather than to the use of "analytic" tools in any of the several modern senses of the word, e.g. by reference to "higher" analysis, by reference to "analytic," i.e. algebraic and equational methods, or by reference to "analytic" functions. Descartes himself acknowledged that in *Meditations on the First Philosophy* he had used "only analysis, which is the best and truest method of teaching" [p. 102]. In his Replies to Objections (to the *Meditations*) as well as in these objections themselves, Descartes and his adversaries several times refer as a matter of course to his "analysis" (see HR II, 234, 256–7, 324, 352.)

Moreover, Descartes' reliance on the method of analysis seems to be only a special case of a much more widespread use of this method by all the leading philosopher-scientists of the early modern period. Galileo's method has often been described as consisting of "resolution and composition," and in the famous Query 23/31 in the second English edition of his *Opticks*, Newton emphatically formulates his own method by reference to apparently the same method:

> As in Mathematicks, so in Natural Philosophy, the Investigation of difficult Things by the Method of Analysis, ought ever to precede the Method of Composition. This Analysis consists in Making Experiments and Observations, and drawing general Conclusions from them by Induction, and admitting no Objections against the Conclusions, but such as are taken from Experiments, or other certain Truths. For Hypotheses are not to be regarded in experimental Philosophy. . . . By this way of Analysis we may proceed from Compounds to Ingredients, and from Motions to Forces producing them; and in general, from Effects to their Causes. . . . This is the Method of Analysis: And the Synthesis consists in assuming the Causes discover'd, and establish'd as Principles, and by them explaining the Phaenomena proceeding from them, and proving the Explanations.

We shall have occasion to return to this Newtonian statement later. It is clear that Newton thinks of his own work in the *Opticks* and in his investigations into other difficult things as having proceeded by the method of analysis.

In view of all this direct and indirect evidence, why has this diagnosis of Descartes' method as a variant of the old method of analysis been so frequently rejected or at least underemphasized recently? The basic reason seems to be that the nature of the method of analysis as it was preached and practiced by Greek mathematicians has not been understood clearly enough. Among other things, the difficulties that there are in the practice of the method and in attempts to describe it in precise philosophical and logical terms have not been appreciated sufficiently keenly. As a consequence, the difference between the geometrical method of analysis and certain other techniques which have been given similar labels has not been kept in mind by philosophers and historians, nor have they been able to master the perplexing multiplicity of different directions into which the old geometrical method was developed in the early modern period. As a consequence, the recognition of the analytic character of Descartes' method has not served to illuminate his thought in the way it could do. An extreme example of the desperation to which scholars have been driven by these failures is perhaps Gerd Buchdahl's attempt to distinguish several allegedly entirely different senses of "analysis" in Descartes.[1]

Yet one can easily sympathize with the frustration of many scholars and philosophers with the simple identification of Descartes' method with the analytic one. For it is not always the clear, positive aspects of the legendary Greek method that help us to understand Descartes' methological struggles, but often rather the ambiguities and difficulties with which this method was inflicted.

What do we actually know of the Greek method? Not very much, yet enough to disprove the paranoid theory of intentional secrecy on the part of the Greeks held by Descartes and his contemporaries. The only extensive, explicit description of the method is found in Pappus. It goes as follows:

> Now analysis is the way from what is sought – as if it were admitted – through its concomitants, in their order, to something admitted in synthesis. For in analysis we suppose that which is sought to be already done, and we inquire from what it results, and again what is the antecedent of the latter, until we on our backward way light upon something already known and being first in order. . . . In synthesis, on the other hand, we suppose that which was reached last in analysis to be already done, and arranging in their natural order as consequents the former antecedents and linking them one with another, we in the end arrive at the construction of the thing sought. And this we call synthesis.[2]

Pappus goes on to distinguish two kinds of analysis, theoretical and problematical. In the former, we search for a proof of a theorem, in the latter for a construction to solve a problem. He then characterizes briefly these two kinds of analysis.

What are the interpretational difficulties connected with this description of the method of analysis and synthesis? How was this method developed so as to yield the methods of Descartes and Newton? I have previously discussed, with Unto Remes, the interpretation of the ancient method. Here I can only summarize some of the main points, trying to relate them to Descartes.[3]

1   It may appear that Pappus is describing a kind of hypothetico-deductive method in mathematical heuristics. According to this construal of method, one assumes in following it the desired theorem (or assumes the desired construction to have already been accomplished) and studies step by step the logical consequences of this assumption. However, the only consistent (or almost consistent) interpretation of Pappus' statement is to take him to say that analysis consists in looking for premises from which the desired result can be deduced.[4]

This fact is far from obvious, however, and in many later discussions there is considerable confusion on this point. Nor is Pappus himself completely free from confusion, as his statement concerning the different possible outcomes of theoretical and problematical analysis shows. If analysis consists in looking for suitable premises, eventually reaching an established truth suffices to prove the desired result. If analysis consists of a sequence of inferences, reaching an impossibility disproves it. Both of these cannot hold, however, contrary to what Pappus seems to say, unless analysis consists of a series of equivalences. But this can be excluded by collateral evidence. And even in the best of circumstances, the convertibility of all the steps of analysis can only be established afterwards in the synthesis.

This uncertainty concerning the direction of analysis in Pappus reappears in many later descriptions and applications of the method of analysis.

2   A further complication is that Pappus' logical and philosophical description of analysis agrees neither with his own mathematical practice nor with Greek mathematical practice in general. In that practice, a geometer assumed the conjunction of earlier theorems, an instantiated form of the antecedent of the general implication that a geometrical theorem is, and a correspondingly instantiated

conclusion of the implication, and examined the joint consequences of these three.

Then there is, of course, no certainty that the process can be inverted or otherwise transformed into a proof of the desired theorem. This explains an important part of Pappus' description as well as the corresponding feature of ancient mathematicians' practice, namely, the fact that in ancient mathematics analysis was typically followed by a synthesis, that is, an ordinary deductive proof of the theorem. Indeed, we perhaps ought to speak of the method of analysis and synthesis rather than just of the method of analysis. Descartes himself registers in passing the fact that in geometry synthesis finds a place after analysis.

Descartes apparently thinks of analysis as consisting of deductive inferences. This is strongly suggested by a comparison of Descartes' description of his *Meditations* as proceeding analytically with his statement in the *Regulae* (HR I, 43; AT X, 421–2) that the connection expressed in "I exist, therefore God exists" is a necessary one, and likewise for "I think, therefore I have a mind distinct from the body." He also indicates, in the same place, that the converse implications do not hold. Hence, the steps of analysis cannot be merely converted in order to obtain the synthesis, according to Descartes.

It is especially tempting to view Descartes' procedure in the *Meditations* as analysis in the light of the widespread view (which we have seen formulated by Newton) that in an analysis one moves "from effects to their causes." Descartes proceeds from the certainty of his existence as uncovered in the *cogito* insight to the idea that his essence is thinking. How and why? Highly interesting light is thrown on this step by Descartes' identification of the essence of any one thing with a kind of efficient cause of its being, albeit in an extended sense of the word (HR II, 110). (A little later, HR II, 112, Descartes runs together the formal cause of a thing and its essential nature.) This squares particularly well with my "performative" interpretation of the *cogito*, according to which Descartes in his insight as it were produces the grounds of his certainty of his own existence by an act of thinking.[5]

Likewise, Descartes argues in the *Meditations* from our ideas of God and perfection to the first cause of all these ideas, that is, to God's existence.

I do think that this idea of analysis as consisting of logical inferences is part and parcel of what Descartes means by saying that in the *Meditations* he employed analysis. However, at the same time we can see that Descartes was far from being clear about the logic of his own method. When he presents a sketch of his arguments transformed into a synthetic (deductive) form (HR II, 52–9), the direction of his main lines of thought is the same as in the original *Meditations*, and not the inverse of the latter, as we were led to expect. For instance, God's existence is again proved from "the mere fact that the idea of God exists in us." Hence, Descartes' ideas of the relation between analysis and synthesis are obviously very unclear. He can scarcely hold that synthesis is obtainable by reversing the direction of the several steps of analysis, as Pappus asserted. It is not surprising that this uncertainty concerning the direction of analysis as compared with the direction of logical inference should surface in Descartes, as it happens, in the form of the famous problem of the so-called "Cartesian Circle."

Furthermore, Descartes' description of his procedure in the empirical sciences is at variance with his method in his metaphysical meditations. For in the former the starting-points, the effects, are said to be "deduced" from their causes (HR I, 129), thus reversing the direction of Descartes' alleged logical implications as compared with the *Meditations*. A little earlier, Descartes also speaks of causes and effects as being "reciprocally demonstrated," thus affirming the kind of convertibility he denied in the *Regulae* in philosophical (and theological) contexts. Nor are these remarks casual comments *en passant*. They are a part of Descartes' defense against allegations of arguing in a circle. All told, Descartes can scarcely escape an indictment on charges of confusion as far as the direction of analysis is concerned.

3   A mere reversal of the order of one's steps when one moves from analysis to synthesis will not work anyway in the simple-minded way Pappus seems to think. The reason for this lies in the need of what are often called auxiliary constructions in geometrical analysis. In order to prove a geometrical theorem, it does not usually suffice to operate with those geometrical objects which are depicted in the figure illustrating the theorem. New geometric objects will have to be "constructed," that is, introduced to the argument, if it is to succeed. Elsewhere I have shown that the reliance on such auxiliary individuals can be thought of as the main nontrivial ingredient not only in geometrical proofs but in deductive arguments in general.[6] As Leibniz aptly put it, the "greatest

art" in geometry frequently consists in finding the best constructions. A deductive theory is undecidable precisely when these
generalized "auxiliary constructions" are recursively unpredictable.

It follows that in an analysis these auxiliary constructions must
be thought of as having been carried out before the rest of the
argument, for otherwise we could not find the desired proof by
means of the analysis. But by the same token the constructions
cannot be carried out last in the corresponding synthesis. Hence,
more must be involved in synthesis than merely traversing in the
opposite order the same steps as were taken in the preceding
analysis.

Concerning this point there was no clarity among the pre-
Cartesian theorists of the analytic method. Descartes likewise pays
little attention to the problem. In Greek geometrical practice, the
initial analysis proper ("analysis" in the narrower sense of the
word) was followed by a "resolution" in which the feasibility of the
requisite auxiliary constructions was established.[7]

4   Clearly we have not yet found the main link between the
classical method of analysis and Descartes' method. In order to see
this connection, we have to ask what is probably the single most
important question concerning the ancient geometrical analysis.
This is the question "What is geometrical analysis analysis *of*? What
is it that is being analyzed, i.e., taken apart, in this process?"
Pappus' text might suggest that what is being anatomized is the
deductive leap from "the given," presumably axioms and earlier
theorems, to the theorem to be proved (and analogously in the case
of problems instead of theorems). This is a mistaken view, and it
would in effect assimilate the geometrical method of analysis to
other kinds of analysis, notably to the Aristotelian idea of reducing
syllogistic arguments to a number of minimal steps of inference.
This is the sense of analysis which has given Aristotle's *Prior* and
Posterior Analytics their name. Most of the medieval discussion of
resolution and composition belongs to this Aristotelian tradition
rather than to the geometric one. Hence, it is misleading to see
anticipations of the analytic method of the early modern scientists
in medieval or renaissance references to resolution and composition. Several scholars as impressive as Ernst Cassirer and John H.
Randall have, for instance, claimed to find anticipations of Galileo's
method of resolution and composition in Giacomo Zabarella and
other Paduan Aristotelians. In reality, however, the Paduan ideas of

resolution and composition were rooted in the Aristotelian tradition and hence basically foreign to Galileo's use of geometrical analysis as a paradigm of scientific method in general.[8] This is one of the many places where we must separate the (in the last analysis) Aristotelian questions of the direction of the scientific procedure and of the analysis of syllogisms into finer ones from questions concerning the (in the last analysis) geometrical questions of the interdependencies of the ingredients of a physical or mathematical configuration.

5   An illuminating answer to the question of what is analyzed in analysis is obtained from a study of the actual practice of ancient Greek mathematicians in applying the method of analysis. As I helped to show before, what was being analyzed in the Greek method was essentially a geometrical configuration illustrated by a figure.[9] The several steps of analysis were steps from a geometrical object to another one, or perhaps from a number of objects to a number of others. Likewise, the beginning and the end of an analysis, that is to say, "the given" and "what is sought" (cf. the quotation from Pappus above), were typically (in the former case, well-nigh exclusively) geometrical *objects* (possibly with a determined position, determined orientation, or otherwise determined characteristics), not geometrical *truths*. Steps from a geometrical object to another were mediated by their interdependence within the framework of the rest of the configuration. By studying such interdependencies, an analyst was almost literally "analyzing" the configuration ("figure") in question in the commonsense meaning of taking it apart.

Incidentally, we can now see an intuitive reason why auxiliary constructions are typically indispensable in geometrical analysis. Their vital role is made understandable by the idea of analysis as a series of steps from one geometrical object to another. Auxiliary constructs are unavoidable intermediate links in these chains of dependencies that are ultimately hoped to connect the unknown with the known.

This idea of analysis as an analysis of configuration, not proofs, is the most important aspect of the old method that Descartes and his contemporaries were generalizing and developing further. As was indicated, in analyzing a geometrical figure in the appropriate sense, the main questions pertain to the interrelations of the different geometrical objects in the figure. In the practice of ancient

Greek geometers like Euclid, these interrelations are typically (but not exclusively) simple equivalences between the different lines and angles in the figure. With a greater use of algebraic methods by Descartes' immediate predecessors, these interdependencies gradually grew more flexible, till in Descartes' analytical geometry any polynomial dependency could be represented geometrically. In his geometry, in fact, Descartes strongly emphasized this algebraic representability of a wide variety of different kinds of geometrical interdependencies.

It is the same liberated idea of geometrical analysis as turning on a wide variety of algebraic dependencies between different geometrical magnitudes that easily led to generalizations of the ancient method of analysis. In the same way as a geometrical analyst studied the different algebraically expressible dependencies between the several parts of a geometrical figure, in the same way a physicist or other natural scientist studied the mathematically expressible dependencies between the different factors of a physical configuration, for instance forces, masses, and motions. Hence, a natural scientist who examined these interdependencies could also be thought of as practicing analysis. This is precisely what we saw Newton describing in the passage quoted above. The generalization is not restricted to him, but appears also in several of his predecessors, contemporaries, and followers. It is my thesis that Descartes' method can be viewed as a result of this sort of extension of the method of analysis from geometrical configurations to all complexes of interdependent elements.

Of course, there is a difference between the two cases in that the actual physical dependencies can only be ascertained by experimentation and observation while the geometrical dependencies are consequences of our explicit assumptions concerning geometrical objects. But this difference was not perceived as being fundamental. In the same way as a physicist uncovers functional relationships experimentally by varying certain factors in an experimental setup, so a geometer could be thought of as varying certain parts of his configuration, viz. his figure, in his mind. The general geometrization of the world undoubtedly also contributed to the force of this analogy.

I would go so far as to think of this generalized conception of analysis as analysis of configurations, not of proofs, as a highly interesting and highly topical methodological model, even today. Most philosophers of science have overlooked it, no one has analyzed it satisfactorily, and yet in some disciplines, especially in theoretical linguistics, it could provide a highly salutary correction to current methodological excesses. It is a more flexible paradigm than those fashionable ones which rely on straightforward generalization ("inductive generalization") from data. Instead of such a simple schema:

observation of particular data →
inductive leap to a general law

Newton's double (or triple) method requires a more sophisticated schema:

"analysis" of a complex phenomenon into ingredients →
experimental or observational discovery of dependencies between different ingredients →
inductive generalization of these dependencies to all similar cases →
deductive application of the generalization to other cases.

The last, synthetic step can often be thought of as assembling a new, more complex situation from the same kind of interacting ingredients as were included in the original experimental situation.

In the tradition of analysis, Descartes belongs in an important respect together with Pappus and Newton rather than with Aristotle or Grosseteste. This respect is the very idea on which we have just been commenting, viz. the conception of analysis as an analysis of configurations rather than of proofs, in other words, analysis as a systematic study of functional dependencies between known and unknown factors. It is worth registering Descartes' way of expressing himself on this point. He did not have at his disposal any general concept of function (functional dependence). Hence, he had to resort to speaking of "comparisons." His point is nonetheless clear. Descartes, in fact, goes as far as to say that "absolutely every item of knowledge which [one] does not acquire through the simple and pure intuition of a single object in isolation is obtained through the comparison of two or more with each other" (AT X, 440).

Thus we can now perceive the most important respect in which Descartes' characteristic mode of philosophical argumentation can be said to turn on the analytical method. Take, for instance, the famous strategy of radical doubt. Is there anything more to this strategy of asking whether anything (call it x) retains its certainty in the teeth of total doubt than in the method of an algebraist who

takes an equation one side of which contains an unknown quantity
x and who then manipulates the equation in such a way that only
the unknown remains on that side as, e.g., in the transition from
$(x + a)^2 \times \sqrt{b}$, to $x = b - a$ through an application of the same
"elimination operation" $\sqrt{z} - a$ to both sides of the original
equation? In order to see my point, consider the characteristic
strategy that underlies typical Cartesian arguments from the doubt
that prompted Descartes' famous *Cogito* insight to his determination of what the essence of a piece of wax is by considering
what stays constant when it is subjected to various manipulations.
In such typical arguments, Descartes is studying the interdependencies of different factors in an ontological or epistemological situation by letting certain factors vary systematically. (In some cases,
e.g., in the case of the doubt, the variation is pushed by him to the
limit, to an extreme case.)

The same diagnosis of Descartes' method can be expressed by
saying that the three allegedly different types of analysis which
Gerd Buchdahl has distinguished in Descartes are in reality one and
the same method, and that the peculiar flavor of Descartes' method
consists precisely in this identification.

The three types of analysis Buchdahl separates from each other
are the following:

(a) analysis as a technique of operating algebraically with unknowns, in the hope of finding equations that contain them, and
then solving these equations for the unknowns;

(b) analysis as a literal or metaphoric "taking apart" of an actual
physical or geometrical complex of phenomena;

(c) the Pappian hypothetico–deductive procedure of "assuming
what is to be proved as though it were known."

Of these, the algebraic technique (a) can be thought of, as we
already saw, as a mere further technical development of the
Pappian idea (c). Actually, a little more than this is involved in
the identification of types (a) and (c) of analysis. This additional
element is the insight mentioned earlier that, in the proof that we
are looking for in an analysis of type (c), we need certain auxiliary
constructions without which the proof cannot be carried out.
Conversely, when these auxiliary constructions have been found,
the proof is obvious. Hence, the problem one is faced with in a
"theoretical" analysis of the kind (c) is basically the same as in
a "problematical" analysis of the type (a), viz. finding (and con-

structing) the magnitudes needed for the solution of the problem in question, whether it is the problem of proving a proposed theorem or something else.

All this is intrinsic to the logic of the situation. Ancient mathematicians seem to have been dimly aware of the same features of the conceptual situation, at least in their working practice. What is especially relevant here, a recognition of this link between analysis of kind (a) and of kind (c), is part and parcel of Descartes' methodology. Not only does he speak of his geometry of lines needed for the solution of any given problem. In this *Regulae*, he makes it crystal clear that according to his view *every* problem can be construed as a search for certain "unknowns," and more specifically construed on the algebraic model (i).

This explains the identification of (a) and (c). As far as the identification of (b) with the other kinds of analysis is concerned, it was explained above how already in Greek mathematicians like Pappus the actual course of analysis is better described as an analysis of figures or configurations than as an analysis of deductive connections. Thus, Buchdahl overlooks precisely those ideas which connect the allegedly different kinds of analysis with each other in Descartes.

This way of looking at Descartes' method deserves further documentation and further explanation. Descartes' main statement of his method of geometry is as follows:

> If, then, we wish to solve any problem, we first suppose the solution to be already effected and give names to all the lines that seem needful for its construction – to those that are unknown as well as to those that are known. Then, making no distinction between known and unknown lines, we must unravel the difficulty in any way that shows most naturally the relations between these lines, until we find it possible to express a single quantity in two ways. This will constitute an equation . . . We must find as many such equations as there are supposed to be unknown lines.
>
> (*La Geométrie*, AT VI, 372)

Then Descartes goes on to describe the ways of solving sets of equations. He has already earlier correlated the algebraic operations needed in the solution of equations with certain geometrical operations. Hence, the algebraic solution of an equation will yield a construction of the desired line.

Here we can see how Descartes' method is related to Pappus'. The basic idea is precisely the same. Both start from the assumption that the problem has already been solved. This involves the assumption that the unknowns are at hand, that they can be symbolized ("named"), and treated as if they were known. What has happened between Pappus and Descartes is that algebraic methods have been introduced to systematize the whole procedure. One of the crucial steps here is the systematic use of symbols for the unknowns. Once they have been introduced, the main cash value of the Pappian injunction to deal with "what is sought as if it were admitted" is to feel free to apply to them all the same algebraic operations that can be applied to symbols for known quantities. (In this way, the Pappian injunction became very much like an invitation to apply algebra to geometry.) The stepwise search backward for connections with the given in Pappus becomes in Descartes a search of suitable equations to connect the unknowns with the known lines. The actual solution of an equation or a set of equations will correspond to the synthesis in Pappus.

From this algebrization of Pappus' procedure several differences between Descartes and the Greeks ensue. One of them is a partly accidental shift of interest from the problem of finding the right auxiliary constructions to the problem of solving the resulting equations. In the quoted passage, Descartes in effect brushes aside the whole problem of auxiliary constructions by speaking casually of "all the lines that seem needful for its construction."

It is of some interest to see what the counterpart of Descartes' glib assumption in his geometry is in the realm of physical science. The geometrical assumption that all auxiliary individuals have been introduced corresponds to the assumption that all the relevant factors in (say) a physical configuration have been taken into account. It is hard not to see traces of Descartes' bad methodological conscience on this score in his frequent expressions of concern about the "completeness" of our "enumerations" or about making sure that "nothing has been left out" (see, e.g., *Regulae*, Rule VII).

Another thing that we can now see is that Descartes has freed himself of the old preoccupation with the direction of analysis. Since we need several different equations to solve a problem with more than one unknown, we have to connect the unknowns and the given in several different ways.

So much for Descartes' method in geometry. A number of

Descartes' general methodological ideas likewise become clearer when we realize that he is thinking in terms of a network of functional dependencies between the known and the unknown, not in terms of a linear sequence of inferences. That this geometrical procedure was really Descartes' general methodological paradigm is perhaps best shown by a comparison with his *Regulae*. In explaining what a perfectly understood problem is like, Descartes writes:

> First, in any problem it is necessary that something is unknown, for otherwise it would be pointless to search for it; second, this unknown must be designated in some manner, for otherwise we would not be led to the discovery of that thing rather than any other; and third, it cannot be so designated except in terms of something else which is already known.
>
> (AT X, 430)

Moreover, Descartes adds: "All this is also true of imperfectly understood problems." What is characteristic of imperfectly understood problems is that in them the given does not yet determine the unknowns. Descartes' program includes showing "how all imperfect problems can be reduced to perfect ones" (*Regulae*, AT X, 431).

Likewise, in Rule XII of the *Regulae*, Descartes writes: "Lastly, we must make use of every assistance of the intellect . . . also for correctly comparing what is being sought with what is known . . . and for finding those things which ought to be compared with each other . . . This rule comprehends everything which has been said before" (cf. also the passage in *Regulae*, partly quoted above: AT X, 440). Thus Descartes' whole method turns on connecting the unknowns with the known via functional dependencies.

Of course, the algebrization of geometry which we find in Descartes does not change completely the problems involved in the generalizations of the method of analysis. Rightly understood, the original Greek method already turned on establishing connections between the known and the unknown geometrical objects. Perhaps the most characteristic feature of Descartes' method is the way he thinks of the dependencies to be established. In his general methodological practice, he follows the mathematical paradigm and thinks of the basic interrelations as being intuitively perceived, from which it follows that our search for them has the nature of conceptual clarification which prepares the ground for the operations of intuition. Much of the *Regulae* is devoted to explaining how this is to be accomplished. In this respect, Descartes remained rather similar to Aristotle, to whom the basic premises of a science are likewise seen intuitively and are likewise partially conceptual.

Another aspect of this comparison may also be helpful. Descartes' preoccupation in geometry with equations and their solution carries over to his general methodology. Even in his general philosophical methodology, his attitude is that of a mathematician who is setting up equations and solving them. This attitude is one of the factors which lend a strong flavor of logical or conceptual analysis to Descartes' method, as used both in philosophy and in science.

It is this conceptual (a priori) character of Cartesian science and not his characteristic variant of the idea of analysis that creates the similarities between Descartes and Aristotle.

This characteristic feature of Cartesian analysis as a kind of *conceptual* analysis would deserve further comments, as it is not always easy to pinpoint by reference to explicit pronouncements. One of the more easily discernible manifestations of this characteristic is Descartes' adherence to the so-called "principle of plenitude." I have briefly considered the role of this principle as a symptom of the Aristotelian idea of scientific truths as conceptual truths in two earlier papers.[10]

The conceptual-analysis character of Cartesian analysis betrays an especially sharp contrast between Descartes and Newton. For according to Newton we find the basic dependencies which can often be expressed equationally by *experimental* analysis. When a geometer notes a dependency between the different ingredients of a geometrical figure, we can perhaps metaphorically think of him as varying (perhaps "in his thinking") the different ingredients so as to see how the others change accordingly. By contrast, Newton thinks that in typical cases of experimental analysis the dependencies are established by an actual variation of some of the relevant parameters. Newton's analysis, unlike Descartes', thus "consists in making Experiments and Observations, and in drawing general conclusions from them by Induction."

It is not impossible that this contrast between Newton and Descartes is connected with Newton's idea that geometry itself is founded on mechanical practice (see Newton's preface to the first edition of the *Principia*). This enabled him to consider any old analysis carried out in his mechanics to be completely on all fours with geometrical analysis. What is even more important, it made it possible for Newton to consider any use of geometrical intuition as a mere tacit appeal to our mechanical experience. Whichever of these differences between Descartes and Newton is in the last analysis the basic one, the contrast could scarcely be sharper.

The conceptual character of Descartes' method also helps to lend it a wide scope far beyond the purview of Newton's experimental analysis. It was thus instrumental in enabling Descartes to think that he had in his possession a single method, as fully applicable in his metaphysical meditations as in the methodological exercises that were appended to the *Discourse*. We do not appreciate Descartes' characteristic way of thinking until we realize that in his philosophical system, too, he is studying certain functional dependencies. For instance, in his metaphysical *Meditations* Descartes is thus studying (according to his own lights) certain interdependencies of different ingredients of our ontology. Using intuitively clear connections between those factors he hoped to argue backward to the metaphysical structure of the world and to its determinants, including God's existence.

It is Descartes' use of his analytic method (in the sense of a procedure that focuses on the study of functional dependencies) in his philosophy that makes his philosophical thought so novel and so modern. It is at the same time what makes Descartes' philosophy hard to understand and to reconstruct if one relies only on propositional methods: for instance, methods that turn on relations of logical consequence between propositions. Perhaps we can thus have a glimpse of one of the reasons why Descartes has exerted the fascination on subsequent philosophers that he has done, and also why the usual logico-deductive methods have contributed relatively little to our understanding of his characteristic way of thinking and arguing.

NOTES

1 Gerd Buchdahl, *Metaphysics and the Philosophy of Science* (Oxford: Blackwell, 1969), pp. 118–41.
2 *Pappi Alexandrini Collectionis Quae Supersunt I–III*, ed. Fr Hultsch (Berlin: Weideman, 1876–7), 2:634.
3 Jaakko Hintikka and Unto Remes, *The Method of Analysis* (Dordrecht: D. Reidel, 1974), and "Ancient geometrical analysis and modern

logic," in Robert S. Cohen *et al.*, eds, *Essays in Memory of Imre Lakatos* (Dordrecht: D. Reidel, 1975), pp. 253–76.

4 Hintikka and Remes, *The Method of Analysis*, ch. 2.

5 Jaakko Hintikka, "*Cogito, ergo sum*: inference or performance?", *Philosophical Review* 71 (1962): 3–32.

6 Jaakko Hintikka, *Logic, Language-Games and Information* (Oxford: Clarendon, Press, 1973).

7 Hintikka and Remes, *The Method of Analysis*, ch. 6.

8 This is convincingly shown in Nicholas Jardine, "Galileo's road to truth and the demonstrative regress," *Studies in the History and Philosophy of Science* 7 (1976): 277–318.

9 Hintikka and Remes, *The Method of Analysis*, chs 4 and 7.

10 Jaakko Hintikka, "Leibniz on plenitude, relations, and the 'reign of law'," in Harry G. Frankfurt, ed., *Leibniz* (Garden City, NY: Doubleday, 1972), and "Gaps in the Great Chain of Being," *Proceedings and Addresses of the APA* 49 (1976): 22–38.

A POINT OF ORDER:
ANALYSIS, SYNTHESIS, AND
DESCARTES' *PRINCIPLES*

Daniel Garber and Lesley Cohen

The serious student of Descartes' philosophy must deal with the
fact that Descartes' metaphysics is presented in a number of
different ways in a number of different works. While the
Meditations ought to be regarded as the authoritative text, it is
important to account for the sometimes significantly different
versions of the philosophy that Descartes presents in the
Discourse, the *Principles of Philosophy*, the *Search After Truth*, and in
numerous remarks scattered throughout the correspondence. In
this note we shall examine one attempt to explain the principal
differences between two of these works: the *Meditations* and the
Principles. It is often claimed that these differences can be
explained by the fact that the *Meditations* are written in accordance
with the analytic method, whereas the *Principles* are written in
accordance with the synthetic method. We shall argue against two
somewhat different versions of this thesis. Although we have no
counter-thesis of comparable power or simplicity to offer, we
shall suggest some ways of understanding the relations between
these two central works that better reflect the texts and what
appear to be Descartes' intentions.

The main source for our understanding of Descartes' distinction
between analysis and synthesis is the difficult though often cited
passage at the end of the Replies to Objections II (AT VII, 155–6) [p.
101–3].[1] In the Replies to Objections II, Descartes is requested to
present his argument *in more geometrico*, with the full apparatus of
definitions, postulates, and axioms (AT VII, 128). Descartes complies
with this request in the *Geometrical Appendix* which follows his Replies
to Objections II, where he provides a geometrical exposition of some of
his arguments. But first Descartes gives a general discussion of the

135

geometrical method of presentation. This discussion begins with a distinction between two aspects (*res*) of the geometrical mode of writing (*modus scribendi*): *ordo* and *ratio demonstrandi*. *Ordo*, Descartes says, is simply the arrangement of material in such a way that that which is presented earlier can be known without having to appeal to that which follows. The terms "analysis" and "synthesis" are introduced when Descartes attempts to distinguish between two different kinds of *rationes demonstrandi* that one could follow, presumably without violating *ordo*. Analysis is presented as the *ratio* which shows "the true way by which a thing was methodically and, as it were, *a priori* discovered (*methodice & tanquam a priori inventa est*)" (AT VII, 155) [p. 101]. Descartes' account of synthesis is [p. 101] somewhat more complicated. He explains:

> Synthesis on the contrary, clearly demonstrates its conclusions in an opposite way, proceding as it were *a posteriori* (*tanquam a posteriori quaesitam*) (although the proof is here more often *a priori* than in the preceding case), and makes use of a long series of definitions, postulates, axioms, theorems, and problems.
>
> (AT VII, 156) [p. 102]

In the Replies to Objections II Descartes explicitly relates this distinction between analysis and synthesis to his procedure in the *Meditations*. There he states: "In my *Meditations* I followed only analysis, which is the true and best way for teaching (*via . . . ad docendum*)" (AT VII, 156) [p. 102]. However, the Replies to Objections II itself provides no direct evidence as to how the *Principles* fit into the distinction drawn there. Although Descartes does present an example of synthetic argumentation in the *Geometrical Appendix* to the Replies to Objections II, he does not mention the as yet uncompleted *Principles* in that connection. The only passage in the Cartesian corpus in which there is a direct statement that the *Principles* are synthetic occurs in the *Conversation with Burman*. Burman raises a question relating to the two kinds of proofs for the existence of God offered in the *Meditations*. In the course of his answer, Descartes points out that in the *Principles*, unlike in the *Meditations*, the *a priori* argument precedes the *a posteriori* arguments. The explanation Burman reports is this:

The way and order of discovery (*via et ordo inveniendi*) is one thing, that of teaching (*docendi*) another; in the *Principles* he teaches, and procedes synthetically.

(AT V, 153)[2]

There is some doubt about the reliability of this passage, as with all of the *Conversation with Burman*, particularly insofar as teaching is associated with synthetic method here rather than with analytic method as it is in the unquestionably genuine Replies to Objections II.[3] But it does provide at least *prima-facie* evidence that Descartes thought that the *Principles* are synthetic, and that he saw this as explaining at least some of the differences between that work and the analytic *Meditations*.

These observations, however, are of little use in understanding the differences between the two works in question until some further content is given to the rather obscure distinction between analysis and synthesis that Descartes offers in the Replies to Objections II. One account of this distinction is offered by Martial Gueroult in his numerous influential writings on Descartes.[4] According to Gueroult, the distinction between analysis and synthesis is properly understood as a distinction between two *orders* of presentation, namely, the order of knowledge (*ratio cognoscendi, la vérité de la science*) and the order of being (*ratio essendi, la vérité de la chose*). The order of knowledge, or the analytic order, follows the order of things as they are known. Consequently, an analytic presentation of Cartesian metaphysics must, according to Gueroult, begin with one's own existence established by means of the *Cogito*, the first thing which is known to us, and proceed from there to the existence of other things, e.g. God and the material world, whose knowledge depends on the knowledge of oneself. The order of being, or the synthetic order, on the other hand, proceeds in quite a different way as Gueroult understands it, presenting things in an order that reflects the *real* dependencies that things have with respect to one another, independent of our knowledge of them. Consequently, on this understanding of the distinction, a synthetic presentation of Cartesian metaphysics must begin not with the self and the *Cogito*, but with God, the real cause on which all else, including one's own existence, depends.

Although Descartes himself never presents an account of the distinction between analysis and synthesis in quite these terms, a plausible case can be made that this is what he had in mind. Descartes distinguishes between the order of knowledge and the order of being in a passage from the *Rules for the Direction of Mind* which Gueroult often cites as support for this position: "Individual things ought to be viewed differently in relation to the order they have with respect to our knowledge, than if we speak of them as they really exist" (AT X, 418). While Descartes does not explicitly use the terms "analysis" and "synthesis" in this connection, it is natural to associate this distinction between the order of knowledge and the order of things with the distinction Descartes draws between the two *rationes demonstrandi* in the *Second Replies*, as Gueroult does. The order of things "with respect to our knowledge" in the *Regulae* seems exactly what Descartes is referring to some years later when he characterizes the analytic *ratio demonstrandi* as showing the "true way by which a thing is discovered." While synthesis is not characterized in terms that directly suggest the order of being, there is nothing in the characterization Descartes gives in the *Second Replies* which prevents identifying synthesis with order of being, thus completing the parallelism between the two passages.[5] Such a conjecture would make reasonable sense of Descartes's remarks as reported by Burman regarding the relative positions of the *a posteriori* and *a priori* arguments for the existence of God in the *Meditations* and the *Principles*. If a synthetic exposition is one that follows the order of being, then one should expect a synthetic treatment of Cartesian metaphysics to put the *a priori* argument, which proceeds from the essence of God to his existence, before the *a posteriori* argument, which proceeds from a particular idea we have to the existence of God as a necessary cause of that idea.

As elegant as Gueroult's interpretation is, it unfortunately will not stand up to the actual texts. Gueroult's thesis offers a plausible and intuitively satisfying account of the different positions of the *a posteriori* and *a priori* arguments for the existence of God in the *Meditations* and the *Principles*. However, his reading runs up against a basic similarity between the two works. Although the two presentations of the metaphysics differ with respect to many important details, the two works seem constructed on largely the same plan. Both works begin with doubt, both proceed from there to the *Cogito*, from the *Cogito* to God, and from God to the external world. Given the similarities between the structures of the two works, it is hard to understand how one could hold that one work follows the order of knowledge and the other work follows the order of being. Something, it seems, must be wrong with

Gueroult's reading; either analysis and synthesis are not connected with the distinction between order of knowledge and order of being, or the *Principles* are not synthetic after all.[6]

However, it may be possible to retain the thesis that the *Meditations* are analytic and the *Principles* synthetic if a different interpretation of these terms can be offered, one that is more consistent with the texts. Edwin Curley presents and argues for such an account in his paper, "Spinoza as an expositor of Descartes."[7] Curley's intuition is simple. We *know* that the *Geometrical Appendix* to the Replies to Objections II is synthetic, and have good reason to believe that the *Principles* are as well. If we are to discover what synthesis is and how it differs from analysis, then the question we must ask is clear: what do the *Principles* and the appendix to the Replies to Objections II have in common that differentiates both of them from the analytic *Meditations*?

Approaching the problem in this way, Curley presents two features which, he claims, differentiate synthetic works from analytic presentations of the same material: the framing of "formal definitions of important concepts," and the "prompt and explicit recognition of eternal truths."[8] In the *Meditations* key concepts, like that of clarity and distinctness, are introduced by examples, rather than by definition, as in the *Principles*. And it is the *Principles*, not the *Meditations*, in which Descartes seems to admit that the *Cogito* depends on the principle that what thinks must exist. Curley's basic strategy might be used to uncover even further differences between the purportedly synthetic *Principles* and *Geometrical Appendix* and the analytic *Meditations*, yielding eventually a rich and interesting account of the distinction between analysis and synthesis, an account that does not suffer from the problem we found in Gueroult. Following Curley's line of thought, one might point out that the *Meditations* is written in the first person, while the *Principles* and the *Geometrical Appendix* are both written impersonally; or, perhaps more substantively, the *Meditations* can be differentiated from the purportedly synthetic works by virtue of the fact that in the *Meditations*, unlike the other two works, we find whole chains of reasoning, including false starts, heuristic arguments meant to motivate particular premises, and strict arguments essential to establish conclusions. The first causal proof for the existence of God as presented in the Third *Meditation* illustrates this well. The argument proper is preceded by an investigation based on the distinction between innate, adventitious, and factitious ideas, an argument that leads, unfortunately, to no certain knowledge (AT VII, 37–40). The causal argument itself, when finally presented, contains a number of lengthy sub-arguments. For example, Descartes gives a long heuristic argument to motivate the premise that there must be at least as much formal reality in the cause as there is objective reality in the effect (AT VII, 40–2). Also, the final conclusion, that God must exist as the cause of our idea of Him, is given only after a lengthy enumeration of our ideas and their possible causes (AT VII, 42–5). This contrasts radically with the presentation of the same argument in the *Principles* and in the *Geometrical Appendix*. In both of these works, there are no false starts or dead ends, and little heuristic argument. The proof and its premises are presented unadorned and bare (see AT VII, 167; AT VIII A, 11–12).

But despite the attractiveness of Curley's account, one large difficulty remains. While Curley's strategy is capable of yielding a plausible account of the distinction that fits the texts, in the end it rests on an unstable foundation. While Curley shows us how the concepts of analysis and synthesis can be made to fit the *Meditations* and the *Principles*, neither he nor Gueroult has shown us why we *ought* to see the texts in that way. Neither has established with sufficient evidence the basic premise in this exercise in interpretation, the claim that Descartes *really saw* the distinction between analysis and synthesis as being relevant to the differences between the *Meditations* and the *Principles*.

No one, of course, can question the claim that Descartes wrote the *Meditations* according to the analytic *ratio demonstrandi*. He explicitly tells us he did this in the Replies to Objections II. But the direct evidence that Descartes wrote the metaphysical part of the *Principles* synthetically is very weak. The *only* textual evidence for this claim comes from the *Conversation with Burman*. But, it must be remembered, these words are not from Descartes' own hand. They are filtered through Burman and almost certainly through Clauberg, and clearly contain a number of mistakes.[9] Thus it is difficult to be sure that the particular wording of any given passage represents Descartes' intentions, particularly when the remarks relate to such an obscure point as the distinction between analysis and synthesis. It is defensible to use that document to support an interpretation drawn from more reliable texts. But it seems questionable to use passages from the *Conversation* as the *basis* of an interpretation, which one must do if one is to maintain that the *Principles* are synthetic.

In addition to the general concerns about the reliability of the *Conversation*, there are some rather more specific reasons for questioning whether Burman's report is trustworthy on this point. Descartes, of course, never directly says that the *Principles* are *not* synthetic, any more than he says that they *are*, outside of the *Conversation*. But it does seem significant that in a number of contexts in which Descartes could quite naturally have connected the *Principles* with the synthetic mode of writing, he does not.

Descartes' correspondence allows us to trace out the history of the *Principles* and the Replies to Objections II with some confidence. Descartes seems to have finished his manuscript of the *Meditations* by April of 1640, for by May 5, 1640 he began to send it out for comment (AT III, 61). During the time he was putting the final touches on the *Meditations*, soliciting objections, and writing the replies that were to be published with them, he began to work on his *Principles*. The earliest reference to the *Principles* is in a letter written to Mersenne on November 11, 1640, where he talks about his intention

> to write a completely ordered course of my philosophy in the form of theses where, without any excess of words, I will present only my conclusions along with the true reasons from which I derive them.
>
> (AT III, 233; cf. AT III, 259–60)

By the end of December, it is clear that Descartes has actually begun to work on the first part, that which contains his metaphysics. He writes Mersenne in a letter of December 31, 1640:

> I have resolved to spend [this year] writing my philosophy in such an order that it can easily be taught. And the first part, that which I am working on now, contains almost the same things as the *Meditations* which you have, except that they are in an entirely different style.
>
> (AT III, 276)

It is only after the *Principles* were in progress that Descartes received the Second Objections, the reply to which contains the discussion of analysis and synthesis. Mersenne promised to send them in December 1640 (AT III, 265), but Descartes does not seem to have received them until January 1641 (AT III, 282). Descartes worked on the response through January and February (AT III, 286, 293), and sent it to Mersenne by early March 1641 (AT III, 328). This raises a serious problem for the thesis that the *Principles* were intended to be synthetic: if Descartes was already well into the metaphysical sections of the *Principles* by the time that he wrote the Replies to Objections II, why does he not mention them? After distinguishing between analysis and synthesis there, Descartes presents "a certain few things [from the *Meditations*] in synthetic style . . . from which, I hope, [my readers] will get some help" (AT VII, 159). If Descartes really thought of his *Principles* as synthetic, it would have been very natural for him to have informed his readers that they could expect the *whole* of his metaphysics in synthetic style in a work then in progress. That he does not mention the *Principles* in this connection is significant.

It could be objected here that Descartes may not have wanted to publicize the *Principles* until they were further along. There is something to this objection, to be sure. When Descartes first tells Mersenne of his new project in November and December of 1640, he does ask him to keep the project secret (AT III, 233, 259). But Descartes seems to have changed his mind fairly soon. In the Replies to Objections IV, in a passage that was written by the end of March 1641, within a month of the completion of the Replies to Objections II, Descartes refers to the work in progress.[10] If he was willing to refer to the *Principles* in answering Arnauld, it seems strange that he would neglect to mention them in the discussion of analysis and synthesis in the Replies to Objections II, if in fact he thought of the new work as being synthetic. Still more difficult to explain is why, if he considered the *Principles* to be synthetic, Descartes would have neglected to refer to them in the French translation of the Replies to Objections II, which appeared in 1647, three years after the *Principles* was published. In the translation there is significant alteration of the sections of the Replies to Objections II dealing with analysis and synthesis, doubtless with Descartes' approval and probably from his own hand. After distinguishing between analysis and synthesis and before giving the example of synthetic argumentation in his *Geometrical Appendix*, Descartes eliminates a large section of the Latin text and replaces it with the following short paragraph:

But, nevertheless, to show how I defer to your advice, I shall try here to imitate the synthesis of the Geometers, and make an abridgement of the principal arguments which I have used to demonstrate the existence of God and the distinction between the human mind and body. This might perhaps serve to lessen the attention required of the reader a bit.

(AT IXA, 123; cf. AT VII, 157–9)

Surely, if Descartes really did think that the metaphysics was presented synthetically in the *Principles*, this would have been a perfect opportunity to tell his readers so, and refer them to that work. That he did not is at least some evidence that the *Principles* were not meant to be synthetic.

It is thus significant, we think, that Descartes does not mention the *Principles* when he talks about analysis and synthesis. But it is perhaps even more significant that he does not talk at all about analysis and synthesis when he discusses the relations between the metaphysics of the *Meditations* and the *Principles*, as he does on a number of occasions outside of the *Conversation*. Sometimes Descartes describes the metaphysics of the *Principles* as an "abrégé" of his philosophy (AT III, 259: AT V, 291; cf. AT IXB, 16). Sometimes Descartes focuses on the fact that the *Principles*, unlike his previous writings, are written in short articles (AT VII, 577), or that the work is a simplified version of his *Meditations*, containing only "my conclusions, with the true arguments from which I derive them" (AT III, 233). Sometimes he informs his correspondents that the principal difference between the two works is that "that which is given at length in the one is considerably shortened in the other, and *vice versa*" (AT III, 276). But *nowhere* in his correspondence or his published writings does Descartes ever mention the distinction between analysis and synthesis in connection with the *Principles*. This would be very strange indeed if Descartes *really* thought that the *Principles* were synthetic.

Thus, it seems reasonable to deny that Descartes intended the *Principles* to be an example of the synthetic *ratio demonstrandi*. But in doing so, we do not want to assert that they are analytic either. The discussion of the *Principles* and their relation to the *Meditations* lacks any reference *at all* to the distinction between analysis and synthesis. This strongly suggests that the distinction between analysis and synthesis may be entirely *irrelevant* to understanding the true relations between the metaphysical arguments of the *Meditations* and the *Principles*.

This position leaves us with a problem: if we cannot appeal to the distinction between analysis and synthesis, how, then, are we to understand the important differences between the two works? It seems to us that there is no clear and simple answer to this question; Descartes' own words and our commonsense are all we have to rely on. The brevity of the metaphysical sections of the *Principles* may be attributed to the fact that Descartes conceived of Part I of the *Principles* as a preface to a scientific treatise, and not as a metaphysical treatise to stand on its own (cf. AT III, 523; AT IXB, 16).[11] Similarly, certain other features of its intended use may explain the use of explicit definitions and quasi-syllogistic argument in the *Principles*. Descartes' hope that his *Principles* might be used as a textbook in the schools might have influenced him to set his arguments out in a more explicit way, more like a typical scholastic textbook, than he did in the *Meditations* (see AT III, 276; AT VII, 577). Also, he seems originally to have conceived of the *Principles* as part of a larger publication, which was to include an annotated scholastic treatise on metaphysics, and an explicit comparison between his philosophy and the philosophy of the schools.[12] This may have induced Descartes to give explicit definitions and careful arguments, so that the similarities and differences between his philosophy and that of the Scholastics would be more apparent to the reader (cf. AT III, 259–60).

These considerations do not explain all of the important differences between the *Meditations* and the *Principles* by any means. For example, they cannot explain why Descartes orders the arguments for the existence of God differently in the two works.[13] Giving up the claim that the *Principles* are synthetic does make the commentator's job somewhat more difficult. But, it seems to us, nothing is gained by trying to explain the differences between the *Meditations* and the *Principles* in terms foreign to Descartes' own conception of their relations.[14]

NOTES

1 References to Descartes' works will generally be given in the text. References are given in standard form to volume and page numbers in *Oeuvres de Descartes*, ed. C. Adam and P. Tannery (Paris: 1897–1913; corrected edition Paris: 1964–75). All translations are our own.

The technical terms "analysis" and "synthesis" come up very infrequently in Descartes's writings. "Analysis" is mentioned in connection with the procedure of the *Meditations* in only one other place, in the Replies to Objections IV (AT VII, 249). All other appearances of the technical terms are in mathematical contexts. See, e.g., AT II, 22, 30, 82, 337, 394, 400, 438, 637; III, 99; VI, 17–18, 20; X, 373. For informal and non-technical uses of the term "analysis," see, e.g., AT I, 236–7; VII, 444, 446. The only place in the corpus where Descartes attempts explicitly to characterize the notions of analysis and synthesis and distinguish between the two is in the passage from the Replies to Objections II that we discuss. In this note, we shall be concerned with the notions of analysis and synthesis only insofar as they have been used by commentators to explain the differences between the *Meditations* and the *Principles*. For more general historical accounts of analysis, synthesis, and the closely related notions of resolution, composition, and method in general, see, e.g., J. Hintikka and U. Remes, *The Method of Analysis* (Dordrecht, 1974); J. Hintikka, "A discourse on Descartes's method," in *Descartes: Critical and Interpretive Essays*, ed. Michael Hooker (Baltimore, Md, 1978), pp. 75–88; and J. H. Randall, *The School of Padua and the Emergence of Modern Science* (Padua, 1961).

2 It is interesting to note that this explanation for the divergence between the *Meditations* and the *Principles* on this point is found in the literature on Descartes even before the first publication of the *Conversation* in 1896. See, e.g., Joseph Millet, *Descartes, sa vie, ses travaux, ses découvertes, avant 1637* (Paris, 1867), pp. 216–17. Millet gives his account as if it were common knowledge, and offers no documentation.

3 For resolutions of this seeming inconsistency, see *Descartes' Conversation with Burman* trans. John Cottingham (Oxford, 1976), pp. 70–1, and Martial Gueroult, *Descartes selon l'ordre des raisons* (Paris, 1953–68), vol. I, pp. 357–8 n. 58.

4 See *Descartes selon l'ordre des raisons* (Paris: 1953 and 1968), vol I, pp. 22–8, 357–60; *Nouvelles réflexions sur la preuve ontologique de Descartes* (Paris, 1955), pp. 17–20; and "La vérité de la science et la vérité de la chose dans les preuves de l'existence de Dieu," in *Descartes* (Cahiers de Royaumont) (Paris, 1957), pp. 108–20, esp. pp. 112–17. This last paper is followed by an interesting discussion (pp. 121–40) to which we shall later refer. The interpretation presented below is taken from the writings here cited. It is fair to say that the distinction between analysis and synthesis as Gueroult draws it plays a central role in his elaborate interpretation of Cartesian metaphysics.

5 Well, *almost* nothing. The somewhat peculiar language of the *Second Replies* does raise something of a problem for relating those two passages and identifying analysis with the order of knowledge and synthesis with the order of being, a problem that Gueroult does not deal with. In the *Second Replies*, analysis is characterized as proceeding *tanquam a priori* and synthesis as proceeding *tanquam a posteriori*. But Descartes, like his contemporaries, identified *a priori* arguments with arguments that proceed from cause to effect, and *a posteriori* arguments with arguments that proceed from effect to cause. See AT I, 250–1, 563; II, 433; IV, 689; XI, 47. And since causes are clearly prior to their effects in the order of things, the Replies to Objections II would thus

seem to identify analysis with the *ratio essendi* and synthesis with the *ratio cognoscendi*, exactly the *opposite* of what Gueroult claims! These passages also raise a more general problem of interpretation. While Gueroult's interpretations of the terms in question are in apparent contradiction with the Replies to Objections II, they are in accord with the traditional understanding of those terms, in accordance with which analysis was almost invariably associated with *a posteriori* arguments from effect to cause, and synthesis with *a priori* arguments from cause to effect. See, e.g., Lisa Jardine's discussion of the Renaissance uses of this terminology in *Francis Bacon: Discovery and the Art of Discourse* (Cambridge, 1974), pp. 249–50, and Louis Couturat's discussion in *La Logique de Leibniz* (Paris: 1901), pp. 176–9. Thus, the obvious reading of the Replies to Objections II makes Descartes' usage of the terms "analysis" and "synthesis" radically at variance with the way in which his contemporaries used them. For different resolutions of these problems, all favourable to the Gueroult thesis, see *Oeuvres philosophiques de Descartes* ed. F. Alquié (Paris, 1963–73), vol. II, p. 582 n. 1; J. Brunschwig, "La preuve ontologique interprétée par M. Gueroult," *Revue Philosophique* 150 (1960): 251–65, esp. pp. 257–9; and J.-M. Beyssade, "L'ordre dans les *Principia*," *Les études philosophiques* (1976): 387–403, esp. pp. 394–5.

6 A similar point is made by J. Brunschwig in "La preuve ontologique interprétée par M. Gueroult," esp. pp. 255–7. Brunschwig's arguments are attacked in B. Rochot, "La preuve ontologique interprétée par M. Gueroult (Response aux 'Objections' de M. Jacques Brunschwig)," and defended in J. Brunchwig, "Reponse aux objections de M. Rochot," *Revue philosophique* 152 (1962): 365–70. The question also arises in the discussion following Gueroult's "La vérité de la science et la vérité de la chose," in remarks made by Hyppolite (pp. 125–6) and Alquié (pp. 134–5). Gueroult's initial response is to say that the *Principles* "*sont quelque chose d'un peu bâtard*" insofar as they are really a mixture of analysis and synthesis (see pp. 126 and 137). This position is also endorsed by Henri Gouhier: see his *La pensée métaphysique de Descartes* (Paris, 1968), p. 109. J.-M. Beyssade works this "L'ordre dans les *Principia* . . ." position out in some detail.

7 In *Speculum Spinozanum*, ed. Siegfried Hessing (London, 1977), pp. 133–42.

8 *ibid.*, pp. 136–7.

9 For recent discussions of the reliability of the *Conversation*, see *Oeuvres philosophiques de Descartes* ed. Alquié, vol. III, pp. 765–7, Roger Ariew's review of *Descartes' Conversation with Burman*, trans. Cottingham, in *Studia Cartesiana* 1 (1979): 183–7, and Cottingham's reply to Ariew, ibid., pp. 187–9. Ariew also shared with us his "Descartes really said that?," given at the Pacific Division Meetings of the APA, March 1980. Curley discusses this question in "Spinoza as an expositor of Descartes," p. 140 n. 9.

10 The reference to the *Principles* is given in AT VII, 254. This reference, which is part of a long discussion of transubstantiation, was not published in the Paris edition of 1641, and first appeared in the Amsterdam edition of 1642. There is strong evidence, though, that it

was written in March 1641. In a letter of March 18, 1641 Descartes refers to the last sheet of his reply to Arnauld, "where I explicate transubstantiation in accordance with my principles," as being in progress (AT III, 340). It seems to have been finished and sent to Mersenne by March 31, 1641 (AT III, 349). Mersenne, though, suggested that he eliminate this passage in order more easily to obtain the approbation of the authorities, a suggestion that Descartes took (AT III, 416). When the Paris edition appeared, the long section on transubstantiation was reduced to a single sentence (given in the textual note to line 21 in AT VII, 252) which *also* contains a reference to his yet to be completed *Principles*. The full discussion was restored for the Amsterdam edition at Descartes' request (AT III, 449).

11 Given this, it might be interesting to compare the metaphysics of the *Principles* with the version of the metaphysics presented in Part IV of the *Discourse*, another work intended as the preface to a scientific work. While the two presentations differ in many important respects, there are some striking similarities between the two. For example, both lack the hypothesis of the Evil Genius, and in both the real distinction between mind and body seems to be proved before Descartes proves that God exists.

12 See AT III, 233, 259–60. The text he mentions in this connection is Eustachius a Sancto Paulo's *Summa philosophica*, published first in Paris in 1609, but reprinted often throughout the seventeenth century. Descartes refers to this as "the best book that has ever been written on this material" (AT III, 232; cf. AT III, 251). Descartes abandoned this project in favor of a straight presentation of his own ideas in part because Eustachius' death on December 26, 1640 prevented Descartes from getting his permission to use his book in that way (AT III, 260, 286), and in part because he came to think that an explicit attack on the Scholastics was not needed (AT III, 470).

13 It should be noted, in this connection, that even if one accepts the claim that the *Principles* are synthetic, this difference between the *Meditations* and the *Principles* is not easily explained. Curley's account of analysis and synthesis, for example, seems to leave this divergence between the two texts unexplained.

14 We would like to thank Roger Ariew, Edwin Curley, Alan Donagan, Harry Frankfurt, and Stephan Voss for helpful discussions and correspondence concerning the matters discussed in this paper.

PROFESSOR COTTINGHAM AND DESCARTES' METHODS OF ANALYSIS AND SYNTHESIS

Stanley Tweyman

In the Replies to Objections II, Descartes draws a contrast between the first principles of geometry and the first principles of metaphysics (the subject-matter of the *Meditations*). In geometry, the primary notions "accord with the use of our senses. Hence there is no difficulty there except in the proper deduction of the consequences" [p. 102]. The method of deduction employed by the geometer Descartes calls synthesis.[1] On the other hand, the first principles of metaphysics

> are by their nature as evident as, or even more evident than, the primary notions which geometricians study; but they conflict with many preconceived opinions derived from the senses which we have got into the habit of holding from our earliest years, and so only those who really concentrate and meditate and withdraw their minds from corporeal things, so far as is possible, will achieve perfect knowledge of them.
>
> (HR II, 111)

To enable the reader to grasp the first principles of metaphysics, Descartes utilizes a method of proof or demonstration which he refers to as analysis:

> Analysis shows the true way by which a thing was methodically discovered and derived . . . so that, if the reader care to follow it and give sufficient attention to everything, he understands the matter no less perfectly and makes it as much his own as if he himself had discovered it . . . I have used in my

Meditations only analysis, which is the best and truest method of teaching.

[pp. 101–2]

Commenting on Descartes' discussion in the Replies to Objections II on the distinction between analysis and synthesis, John Cottingham writes:

> It seems that for any argument one may proceed in two ways: start from basic axioms and work "downwards," unravelling the consequences that follow, or alternatively, start from some complex proposition, and ask how it can be proved, climbing "upwards" until one reaches unassailable axioms. Yet this hardly shows that there are two logically distinct patterns of argument involved . . . [T]he distinction seems to boil down to nothing more than a contrast between moving "downwards" from axioms to a desired result and moving "upwards" from a given proposition until we reach the axioms that generate it.
>
> At this point, one begins to suspect Descartes' triumphant proclamation of his "new method" involves more than a small measure of window dressing, at least as far as his metaphysics is concerned.[2]

In the Preface to the *Principles of Philosophy*, Descartes insists that the *Meditations* (and the other works which he mentions, *Of the Dioptric, Of Meteors*, and *Of Geometry*) should be studied before the *Principles* is read, in order to "sufficiently prepare the mind of readers to accept the *Principles of Philosophy*," or, as he puts it a few lines later, "in order that it [i.e. the *Principles*] may be properly understood" (HR I, 212).[3] We know from the Replies to Objections II that in the *Meditations* Descartes used only the method of analysis. Burman has recorded that, according to Descartes, the method employed in the *Principles of Philosophy* is synthesis: "In the *Principles* [the author's] purpose is exposition, and the procedure is synthetic."[4]

In this paper, I intend to show the nature of Descartes' "analytic" proof of his existence in the Second Meditation, and how this analytic proof of his existence is intended "to prepare the mind of readers" to accept the synthetic proof of his existence in the *Principles of Philosophy*. Once this is done, and the synthetic proof is generated and understood, it will be seen that Cottingham misrepresents the differences between analysis and synthesis.

Descartes begins the Second Meditation with two analytic demonstrations of his existence – the first based on the notion of persuasion, and the second on deception:

> But I was persuaded that there was nothing in the world, that there was no heaven, no earth, that there were no minds, nor any bodies; was I not then likewise persuaded that I did not exist? Not at all: of a surety I myself did exist since I persuaded myself of something [or merely because I thought of something]. But there is some deceiver or other, very powerful and cunning, who employs his ingenuity in deceiving me. Then without doubt I exist also if he deceives me, and let him deceive me as much as he will, he can never cause me to be nothing so long as I think that I am something.
>
> [p. 51]

The "persuasion demonstration" appears to be the following: Descartes affirms something which he cannot doubt – that he was persuaded of something; he then attempts to affirm in thought both that he was persuaded of something and that he does not exist; by finding a repugnancy between these two thoughts (i.e. he cannot affirm in thought both that he was persuaded and that he does not exist), he concludes that his initial thought is necessarily connected with the denial of the second. A similar situation obtains in regard to his second demonstration: he affirms what he cannot doubt – that he has been deceived; he then attempts to affirm in thought both that he was deceived and that he does not exist; by finding a repugnancy between these two thoughts, he concludes that his initial thought is necessarily connected with the denial of the second: if he is deceived, then necessarily he exists.

Once his two analytic demonstrations have been put forth, he asserts: "So that having reflected well and carefully examined all things, we must come to the definite conclusion that this proposition, I am, I exist, is necessarily true each time that I pronounce it, or that I mentally conceive it" [p. 51]. The reference to a conclusion in this passage is not to a conclusion of a syllogistic-type argument. Rather, he means that he is able to hold or assert that he exists in light of his analytic demonstrations which have revealed the necessary connection between being persuaded and existing, and being deceived and existing.

Descartes now goes on to inquire about his nature:

> But I do not yet know clearly enough what I am, I who am

certain that I am; and hence I must be careful to see that I do not imprudently take some other object in place of myself, and thus that I do not go astray in respect of this knowledge that I hold to be the most certain and evident of all that I have formerly learned.

[p. 51]

This passage is not easy to understand. In asking what he is, he warns against imprudently taking some other object in place of himself. However, given that he does not yet know what he is, it is difficult to understand how he can be certain that he has not confused himself with some other object. When we engage in conceptual analysis, we should be able to identify typical instances of the kind of object into whose nature we are inquiring, and then seek to discover its essential features. However, since Descartes denies that he has any knowledge of himself at this stage, he cannot be proposing to analyze the self as he would, for example, analyze the concept of a chair or table. Just how he does gain a knowledge of the self will now be elucidated.

In attempting to determine with certainty what he is, he tells us that he will review his former opinions about himself, "and of my former opinions I shall withdraw all that might even in a small degree be invalidated by the reasons I have just brought forward, in order that there may be nothing left beyond what is absolutely certain and indubitable" [p. 51]. He begins the examination into his previous beliefs about himself by dividing these beliefs into two classes – those beliefs about himself which appear to depend upon the body, and those which appear to depend upon the soul. Those which he formerly held to depend upon the body he rejects at this stage; all functions previously held to belong to the soul are also rejected, except for thought:

But what I am I? . . . Can I affirm that I possess the least of all those things which I have just said pertain to the nature of body? I pause to consider, I revolve all these things in my mind, and I find none of which I can say that it pertains to me . . . Let us pass to the attributes of soul and see if there is any one which is in me . . . What of thinking? I find here that thought is an attribute that belongs to me; it alone cannot be separated from me. I am, I exist, that is certain. But how often? Just when I think; for it might possibly be the case if I ceased entirely to think, that I should likewise cease altogether to exist. I do not now admit anything which is not necessarily true.

[pp. 52–3]

The analytic demonstrations which reveal his nature take the same form as the analytic demonstrations which he employed to prove that he exists. He begins with what he cannot doubt – that he exists. He then attempts to affirm in thought both that he exists and that (a) he is not extended and (b) that he does not think. By finding no repugnancy between the affirmation of his existence and that he is not extended, he rejects the claim that his existence is inseparable from himself as extended; on the other hand, by finding a repugnancy between the affirmation of his existence and that he does not think (i.e. he cannot affirm in thought both that he exists and that he does not think), he concludes that his initial thought is necessarily connected with the denial of the second, namely, if he exists, then he must think.

I realize, of course, that this formulation of the analytic demonstration of the necessary connection between thought and existence runs counter to accepted interpretations of Descartes: it is typically granted that the connection is discovered between thought and existence, and not between existence and thought. Nevertheless, as I have now shown, in the case of the *Meditations*, the certainty of Descartes' existence is discovered *before* he comes to know that thinking is his essential feature. Accordingly, in the *Meditations*, the connection which is initially discovered is between existence and thought.

This reading of the Second Meditation explains how he can be certain that he has not "imprudently take[n] some other object in place of myself." Given the necessary connection between existence and thought, to think of oneself as existing is already to think of oneself as thinking – even if we are not yet aware of this necessary connection. (Similarly, given the necessary connection between figure and extension, and motion and duration, when we think of something moving and of something figured, we are already thinking the passage of time and that the object is extended respectively, even if we are not attending to these features.) Therefore, when Descartes asks what he is, now that he knows that he exists, he is asking for the feature or features which are inseparable from his awareness of his existence – what must also be thought when he thinks of his existence. It is clear that in asking

152

what he is, Descartes is not engaging in what we would refer to as conceptual analysis in the manner outlined earlier.

We are now able to explain why Descartes says: "I am, I exist, that is certain. But how often? Just when I think; for it might possibly be the case if I ceased entirely to think, that I should likewise cease altogether to exist." The formulation *Cogito ergo sum* employed in the *Principles* and elsewhere is useful to show the *sufficiency* of thinking to existence – if I think then I must exist. The *Cogito*, however, cannot be used to show the *necessity* of thinking to existing – which is (at least part of)[5] what the passage under consideration is asserting – for it would involve denying the antecedent. On the other hand, once it is recognized that at this stage in the *Meditations* the connection being affirmed is between existence and thought, we understand that the necessity of thinking to existing is established through *modus tollens*. Now, it is true that Descartes says that "it *might possibly* be the case if I ceased entirely to think, that I should likewise cease altogether to exist." And it is also true that normally where something is claimed to be a necessary condition for the existence of something else, the words "might possibly" (which I have italicized) would not be included: if thinking is a necessary condition of his existence, then if he ceases to think he must cease to exist. However, we must take into account that Descartes has not established that his essence is *only* to think, or that insofar as he thinks he cannot also be corporeal. Descartes urges both in the Second Meditation and in the Replies to Objections III[6] that knowing that he exists as a thinking thing is not a proof that he is not corporeal. His proof for this appears in the Sixth Meditation. If his essence is to some extent also corporeal, then perhaps insofar as he is a body, he can continue to exist, even though all thinking has ceased. This is why at this point he speculates, rather than asserts, that the cessation of thought might bring it about that he will cease "altogether" to exist. If he is more than a thinking thing, then his non-thinking nature may continue, even if he ceases to exist as a thinking thing.

I now turn to the second concern of this paper, namely, how does Descartes' treatment of the self in the Second Meditation help to prepare the mind of readers to accept the *Cogito* in Principle VII? The first six Principles deal with what can be doubted, and, at the beginning of Principle VII, Descartes enumerates the extent of his doubt, while at the same time proving that this doubt cannot extend to the self insofar as it thinks:

> While we thus reject all that of which we can possibly doubt, and feign that it is false, it is easy to suppose that there is no God, nor heaven, nor bodies, and that we possess neither hands, nor feet, nor indeed any body; but we cannot in the same way conceive that we who doubt these things are not; for there is a contradiction in conceiving that what thinks does not at the same time as it thinks, exist. And hence this conclusion *I think, therefore I am,* is the first and most certain of all that occurs to one who philosophizes in an orderly way.
>
> (HR I, 220)

In two different places – Principle X and in the conversation with Burman – Descartes insists that the demonstration of his existence in Principle VII involves the major premise "in order to think we must be" or "whatever thinks is:"

> And when I stated that this proposition *I think, therefore I am* is the first and most certain which presents itself to those who philosophize in orderly fashion, I did not for all that deny that we must first of all know *what is knowledge, what is existence, and what is certainty,* and that *in order to think we must be,* and such like; but because these are notions of the simplest possible kind, which of themselves give us no knowledge of anything that exists, I did not think them worthy of being put on record.
>
> (HR I, 222)

> Before this inference, "I think, therefore I am", the major "whatever thinks is" can be known; for it is in reality prior to my inference, and my inference depends upon it. This is why the author says in the *Principles* that the major premise comes first, namely because implicitly it is always presupposed and prior.
>
> (CB, 4)

Therefore, when he tells us in Principle VII that "there is a contradiction in conceiving that what thinks does not at the same time as it thinks, exist," he must mean the logical contradiction present in the following argument:

Whatever thinks exists
I think
_____

∴ I do not exist

There is a contradiction in concluding from the premises in this argument "I do not exist," because what follows from these premises is "I do exist." What is interesting for our purpose is that there is no concern with a proof for the major premise, whatever thinks exists, and no proof in the first six *Principles* that his essence is to think. In the *Principles*, the discussion pertaining to himself as a thinking thing appears in Principles VIII and IX, i.e. it appears *after* the proof of his existence. In other words, the *Principles* treats "whatever thinks exists" as being already known; similarly, that Descartes' essence is to think is taken for granted in the *Principles*. That both of these matters are countenanced in the *Principles* can be explained by recalling that we were told that the *Meditations* should be read and understood before attempting to read the *Principles*. Now, in light of his analytic proofs in the Second Meditation, we have already seen why he holds that his essence is to think. What must now be addressed is why Descartes believes that the *Meditations* has prepared the reader to accept the major premise "whatever thinks exists" – a premise which nowhere appears in the *Meditations*. In fact, given his assertion that only analysis was used in the *Meditations*, no major premise could have there been employed in establishing his existence.

To understand the role of the Second Meditation in providing the major premise "whatever thinks exists," we must understand the major steps in the Second Meditation. Thus far we have seen that (a) Descartes provides the two analytic demonstrations of his existence – the first based on the fact that he was persuaded of something, and the second based on the fact that he has been deceived; and (b) that Descartes uses analysis to demonstrate that his existence is necessarily connected to thinking. In the third step, the Second Meditation attempts to elucidate what it means to say that he is a thinking thing:

> But what then am I? A thing that thinks. What is a thing which thinks? It is a thing which doubts, understands, [conceives], affirms, denies, wills, refuses, which also imagines feels.
>
> [p. 54]

Descartes' analytic demonstrations of what it is to be a thing which thinks take the same form as his previous demonstrations in the Second Meditation: if he affirms that he is a thing which thinks and denies that he is a being who doubts, or understands, etc., then he

155

can no longer think that he is a thing which thinks. And Descartes states this in the paragraph following the passage quoted above: "Is there likewise any one of these attributes which can be distinguished from my thought, or which might be said to be separated from myself?"

Although Descartes began the Second Meditation by affirming the necessary connection between being persuaded of something and existing, and being deceived and existing, by the third stage of the Second Meditation he realizes that when he offered his two analytic demonstrations in the first stage of the Second Meditation, the first relatum in each demonstration – "being persuaded of something" and "being deceived" – is nothing but a mode of thought. Accordingly, in place of "I was persuaded of something" and "I was deceived," he can now substitute "that I think." We are able to see, therefore, that by the end of the third stage of the Second Meditation, Descartes has come to understand that if he thinks then he exists.

The major premise revealed in Principle X and elsewhere for proving his existence in Principle VII is "whatever thinks exists." In the Replies to Objections II, Descartes explains that "whatever thinks exists" is learned "from the experience of the individual – that unless he exists he cannot think. For our mind is so constituted by nature that general propositions are formed out of the knowledge of particulars" (HR II, 38). In other words, once the inseparability of thought and existence is intuited in the case of an individual, the general proposition can then be inferred. It is in this manner, then, that Descartes is able to approach the *Principles of Philosophy* with a major premise for this syllogism in Principle VII.

In light of our discussion above regarding the Second Meditation and seventh Principle, we are able to see that, at least insofar as Descartes' proofs of his existence are concerned, Cottingham's characterization of the differences between synthesis and analysis – "start from basic axioms and work 'downwards', unravelling the consequences that follow [synthesis], or alternatively, start from some complex proposition, and ask how it can be proved, climbing 'upwards' until one reaches unassailable axioms [analysis]" – misrepresents the nature and function of each type of proof. Analysis involves a search for first principles (this is its nature). However, it does not proceed from the conclusion of an argument and ascend to unassailable axioms.

Analysis is involved exclusively with first principles and with removing the (sensory) prejudice which keeps the mind from attending sufficiently to them and grasping their self-evidence. And, at least in regard to the analytic proof of his existence in the Second Meditation, we have seen that this prejudice is not removed by proceeding "upwards" from some conclusion or other, but rather by getting the reader to grasp certain necessary connections between ideas, e.g. between being persuaded of something and existing, and being deceived and existing. Since no arguments (premises and conclusions) are involved, analysis cannot differ from synthesis simply in terms of the "direction" of the inquiry. Synthesis does involve deductive arguments, and, as we have seen, the premises can be those arrived at by the analytic mode of proof. However, the mind must be properly prepared in order to grasp the self-evidence of these premises. Descartes is adamant that this preparation involves the removal of prejudice. The removal of this prejudice cannot be accomplished simply by following the argument from its conclusion to its premises. By the time the premises are formulated, all prejudice must have been removed. For Descartes, more is involved in accepting a first principle than having it brought forward. On Cottingham's interpretation, this, by itself, would be adequate.

NOTES

1 "Synthesis . . . demonstrates the conclusion clearly and employs a long series of definitions, postulates, axioms, theorems and problems, so that if anyone denies one of the conclusions, it can be shown at once that it is contained in what has gone before, and hence the reader, however argumentative or stubborn he may be, is compelled to give his assent" [p. 102].
2 John Cottingham, *A History of Western Philosophy 4 – The Rationalists* (New York: Oxford University Press, 1988).
3 References to passages not reproduced in the present volume are to the two-volume set, *The Philosophical Works of Descartes*, trans. Elizabeth S. Haldane and G. R. T. Ross (Cambridge: Cambridge University Press, 1911), and are noted in the text as HR followed by the relevant volume and page number.
4 *Descartes' Conversation with Burman*, trans. John Cottingham (Oxford: Clarendon Press, 1976).
5 What more is being considered will be discussed later in this paragraph.
6 In the Second Meditation, he writes: "I am not a collection of members which we call the human body . . . But perhaps it is true that these same things which I supposed were non-existent because they are

unknown to me, are really not different from the self which I know. I am not sure about this, I shall not dispute about it now; I can only give judgment on things that are known to me. I know that I exist, and I inquire what I am, I whom I know to exist. But it is very certain that the knowledge of my existence taken in its precise significance does not depend on things whose existence is not yet known to me; consequently it does not depend on those which I can feign in imagination" [p. 53].

Similarly, in the Replies to Objections III, he writes: "*A thing that thinks*, he says, *may be something corporeal; and the opposite of this has been assumed; not proved.* But really I did not assume the opposite, neither did I use it as a basis for my argument; I left it wholly undetermined until Meditation VI, in which its proof is given" (HR II, 63).

ANALYSIS IN THE *MEDITATIONS*: THE QUEST FOR CLEAR AND DISTINCT IDEAS

E. M. Curley

I begin with a fact about the way Descartes wrote his *Meditations*: that he conceived them as illustrating a very special way of proving things, a way peculiarly appropriate to metaphysics, a way he called the analytic manner of demonstration. This much, I think, would generally be admitted, and admitted to be important.

But what does this fact mean? What do we know about the *Meditations* when we know that they were written in the analytic mode? And why is this manner of demonstration peculiarly appropriate to metaphysics? So far as I can see, there is no general agreement on an answer to these questions.[1] And if we accept the Cartesian proposition that disagreement indicates that no party to the dispute has knowledge (AT X, 363, VI, 8), then we must say that no one knows, at this stage, what that important fact means.

We know well enough, of course, what Descartes *says* it means. Mersenne had suggested in the Replies to Objections II (AT VII, 128) that Descartes should present his reasoning in the *Meditations* *more geometrico*, prefacing it with the necessary definitions, postulates, and axioms, so that all readers might be able to satisfy themselves at a glance that the reasoning was sound. In his Replies to Objections II (AT VII, 155) [p. 102] Descartes counters he has already been writing in the way characteristic of the geometers, that it is necessary to distinguish between the geometric order and the geometric manner of demonstrating. Order requires simply that the things first proposed be known without the aid of anything that follows, and that the rest be demonstrated solely from the things that precede them. Descartes claims that he has tried to follow this order very accurately in his *Meditations*.

But presenting things in the right order – which Descartes implies is the essence of the geometrical method – may be done in either of two ways. One can use analysis, which "shows the true way by which the thing has been discovered, methodically, and as it were, a priori" (AT VII, 155) [p. 101]; or one can use synthesis, which proceeds "as it were a posteriori . . . and, indeed, demonstrates clearly its conclusions using a long series of definitions, postulates, axioms, theorems, and problems". In general, the advantage of analysis is that, for the right reader, it yields a deeper understanding. If readers are willing to follow it and to attend sufficiently to everything, they will understand the matter as perfectly as if they had discovered it themselves. The advantage of synthesis is that it can force the assent even of a hostile or inattentive reader. If s/he denies any of the conclusions, we can show him/her immediately that it is contained in antecedent propositions which s/he has presumably accepted.

Because it can yield a deeper understanding, analysis is the best method for teaching even in mathematics, where everyone readily accepts the first notions, and there is no difficulty in attaining a clear and distinct perception of them. But in metaphysics, where the first notions are more remote from the sense, and may even be in conflict with prejudices encouraged by the senses, a clear and distinct perception of those notions is more difficult, and ready agreement to them cannot be presumed. So in metaphysics analysis is much the more appropriate way of presenting things than in synthesis.

That, more or less,[2] is what Descartes *says*. But what does it mean? The first thing that is apt to strike a modern reader is the claim that the analytic mode proceeds "as it were a priori," while the synthetic mode proceeds "as it were a posteriori." If synthesis is exemplified by the best-known work of ancient mathematics, Euclid's *Elements of Geometry*, or by the exposition *more geometrico* which Descartes appends to the Replies to Objections II, then it is no small surprise to see it characterized as an a posteriori method. The commentators[3] may come to our aid here, pointing out that in medieval and seventeenth-century usage, the terms *a priori* and *a posteriori* had a different sense from the one they have nowadays, that an a priori argument was one proceeding from cause to effect, whereas an a posteriori argument was one proceeding from effect to cause. But though Descartes no doubt understands these terms that way, it is hard to see that the *Meditations* exemplify a procedure that is, in that sense, a priori. The *Meditations* begin, on the face of it, with a proof of the existence of the self, proceed to proofs of the existence of God, and then move on to a proof of the existence of the world, that is, they go from effect to cause and back again to effect. And the proof of God's existence which is given the apparently privileged position, that is, the first proof, is an argument from one of God's effects, my idea of God, to His existence as its cause. So the first thing which is apt to strike us about the characterization of these two modes of proof is likely only to confuse us.[4]

We are left then with the idea that the analytic mode of presentation recapitulates a viable method of discovery,[5] whereas the synthetic mode, insofar as it begins from a series of definitions, postulates, and axioms, does not. That much may be correct, and potentially illuminating. But it is also potentially misleading. In an earlier attack on this problem,[6] I argued that it seriously misled Spinoza.

Spinoza's first venture into print was an exposition *more geometrico* of Descartes' *Principles of Philosophy*. Spinoza was well aware of Descartes' distinction between analysis and synthesis, and he took himself, in his exposition of Descartes, to be putting into the synthetic mode work Descartes had written in the analytic mode, just as Descartes himself had done at the end of the Replies to Objections II. Whereas there Descartes had presented synthetically a fragment of the analytic Meditations, in his own work Spinoza undertook to present synthetically a large portion of the analytic Principles.

But if we may trust the *Conversation with Burman*,[7] the *Principles* are already written in the synthetic mode, so there is no need to recast them to make them a synthetic work. In that earlier article, trusting the *Conversation with Burman*, I inferred that Spinoza had been misled by the apparent absence of formal apparatus in the *Principles* and had not seen its essential similarity to the clearly synthetic Geometric Exposition at the end of the Replies to Objections II.

The *Principles* does not *begin* with a long series of definitions, as the Geometric Exposition does. But it does at least regularly offer explicit formal definitions of central terms,[8] whereas the *Meditations* typically introduces central terms in a more informal way, by providing an instance of the concept being defined.[9] That is why, when we are seeking a formal definition of some concept like clarity and distinctness, or thought, or substance, we tend to go to the *Principles of Philosophy* rather than to the *Meditations*.

Similarly, the *Principles* does not *begin* with a list of axioms, as the Geometric Exposition does. But it does recognize, in a more forthright way than does the *Meditations*, the role of axioms, or common notions, or eternal truths, in the argument from the self to God to the world. That is why Burman finds a tension between the *Meditations* and the *Principles*. Citing the passage from the Second Replies in which Descartes had said that

> when we perceive that we are thinking things, that is a first notion which is not inferred from any syllogism, nor does someone who says "I think, therefore, I am or exist" deduce existence from thought by a syllogism,

(AT VII, 140)

Burman asks whether Descartes had not asserted the opposite in *Principles* 1, 10, when he said that, in claiming "I think, therefore, I exist" to be the first and most certain proposition of all those that might occur to someone philosophizing in the proper order:

> I did not on that account deny that before this one must know what thought is, what existence and certainty are, and also that it is impossible that what thinks should not exist.

(AT VIII–1, 8)

The reason for this tension, I suggested, is that the analytic method requires postponement of the recognition of the role of general principles until after we have found ourselves deploying them in particular cases. For the nature of our mind is to form general propositions from the knowledge of particulars.[10] In the beginning of the *Meditations* Descartes is tracing the course of a man who is beginning to philosophize, and who attends only to what he *knows* that he knows.[11] At first, Descartes' meditator is a sensual man, a man too attached to the senses, as we all are before philosophy, and he is not aware of his innate knowledge of these eternal truths.

So far I have been stating a problem and outlining[12] a solution I had presented earlier. Although that earlier article has been subjected to some criticism,[13] I still believe that its central thesis is correct. In what follows I propose to develop the thesis more fully, to extend it to problems I had ignored before, and to modify it in certain non-essential respects.

The central thesis might be stated as follows: Descartes' argument in the *Meditations* requires him to deploy concepts and principles which are very abstract and removed from anything we might think we had learned directly from the senses, concepts, and principles which we may understand implicitly, but which we will normally not understand explicitly in a way that is clear and distinct; it requires Descartes to use principles which the ordinary person of *bon sens* will know, but will not know that s/he knows. So the essential task of the analytic method is to bring that knowledge to consciousness, to turn the unclear and indistinct ideas of commonsense into the clear and distinct ideas Descartes needs to make his argument demonstrative.

In the earlier article I stressed Descartes' move from the particular to the general, his introduction of concepts by means of examples, and his postponement of the recognition of general principles, or eternal truths, until after we have seen those principles in operation. It now seems to me that, as far as this goes, it is right, and an important theme in Descartes' thought. But it does not go far enough. There is more to the process of acquiring clear and distinct ideas than that.

What I should now stress is Descartes' use of what I have come to call a dialectical method. By a dialectical method I mean the essentially Platonic procedure[14] of beginning with a conjecture, considering what can be said against that conjecture, and then revising the conjecture in whatever ways the objections suggest. The initial conjecture may be (typically, will be) a false start, in the sense that it will ultimately be rejected in the form in which it is first proposed. But typically it will also be a proposition which recommends itself to commonsense.[15] The process of conjecture, refutation, and revision may be repeated indefinitely until the inquirer reaches a result to which s/he can find no further objection. If the initial conjecture was not a totally false start (and normally it will not have been), something of what it asserted will survive in the final result. Descartes explicitly recognizes what I am calling the dialectical character of his method in the Replies to Objections IV, when he writes that

the analytic manner of writing which I followed permits me to sometimes make suppositions which have not yet been sufficiently examined, as was evident in the First Meditation, where I had assumed many things which I subsequently refuted.

(AT VII, 249)

Examples of this sort of procedure are not limited to the First Meditation; they abound throughout the whole work. I begin with two clear cases.

Descartes' argument for the real distinction between mind and body requires him first to have clear and distinct ideas of both the mind and the body (AT VII, 78) [p. 91]. And though the work of acquiring clarity about these ideas really begins in the First Meditation, it will be most convenient for us to start with the Second. No sooner does Descartes recognize *that* he is than he asks himself *what* he is (AT VII, 25) [p. 52]. He begins by asking what he previously thought he was, as a way of eliciting the kind of answer a person would naturally give to this question before he began to philosophize.[16] He thought he was a man, but what is that? To answer as a scholastic philosopher would, that man is a rational animal, is not helpful, since it only raises questions more difficult than the original question: "What is an animal? What is it to be rational?" The Scholastic answer would be a false start which contains no usable truth in it. So Descartes resolves to "attend rather to what occurred to my thought previously, whenever I reflected spontaneously and naturally on what I was" (AT VII, 25–6) [p. 52]. I thought of myself as a composite of body and soul. And this is not an unhelpful answer. For while my pre-philosophic concepts of body and soul may have been confused, they had some truth in them.

Previously I thought of the body as

> whatever is apt to be bounded by some shape, to be circums-
> cribed by a place, to fill space in such a way that every other
> body is excluded from it, to be perceived by touch, sight,
> hearing, taste or smell, and also to move in various ways.

(AT VII, 26) [p. 52]

Now some of what Descartes had previously thought body to be was wrong. For example, one of the many morals Descartes will draw from his analysis of the piece of wax is that the perception of a physical object is not an act of sight or touch, as he had previously thought, but an inspection of the mind alone (AT VII, 31) [p. 57]. But some elements in Descartes' pre-philosophic conception of body are right, and to be retained. Body *is* whatever is apt to be

164

bounded by a shape, to be circumscribed by a place, and to fill space.

The process of rendering our idea of body clear and distinct is a very gradual one, which occupies Descartes throughout the *Meditations*. What it essentially involves is sorting out what is and what is not to be retained in our pre-philosophic conception of body, and exploring the implications of those elements which are to be retained. The reason Descartes' statement about the essential nature of material things in the Fifth Meditation (AT VII, 63) [p. 81] can be so brief is that he has already laid a great deal of the groundwork for it in the preceding Meditations.[17]

Descartes goes through an analogous procedure with his pre-philosophic concept of mind (*mens*) or soul (*anima*). Here the very choice of terminology is significant. Descartes uses both *mens* and *anima* to refer to the same thing, a thinking thing. But though both terms, in that sense, mean the same, Descartes generally prefers the term *mens* because he feels that the term *anima* has unfortunate connotations. It suggests something corporeal.[18] So it is no accident that, in Descartes' first self-conscious discussion of the nature of the mind in the *Meditations*, he should choose to designate it by the term *anima*. In this exceptional context, he wants to suggest those usually unfortunate connotations:

> It occurred to me also that I am nourished, that I walk, sense, and think, all of which actions I referred to the soul (*anima*). But what this soul was, I either did not consider, or else [FV: if I did consider it] I imagined it to be a something-I-know-not-what, something very subtle, like wind, or fire, or air, which was infused throughout the grosser parts of me.
>
> (AT VII, 26) [p. 52]

One of the things Descartes must do, in order to clarify this pre-philosophic concept, is to recognize that not all the activities he had previously ascribed to the soul are necessarily to be ascribed to it. Nutrition and motion clearly presuppose the existence of a body (AT VII, 27) [p. 52]. But Descartes is proceeding, at this point, on the assumption that he has no body. So he cannot ascribe nutrition or motion to the soul. The case of sensation is more difficult. At first the meditator is inclined to say that sensation requires a body, and hence is not to be ascribed to the soul (AT VII, 27) [p. 54]. Later he realizes that it is possible to conceive of sensation as not necessarily involving a body, but only a peculiar kind of thought, the kind of thought in which we perceive corporeal things as if through the senses (AT VII, 29) [pp. 54–5]. And conceived this way, sensation is properly attributed to the soul, as are all thought processes. Thinking is a property he cannot deny to himself, since any hypothesis he might entertain in an attempt to cast doubt on his thinking would imply that he thinks.[19]

So the only thing that is left of his pre-philosophic conception of himself is that he is a soul conceived as a thing that thinks (AT VII, 27, line 13) [p. 53]. And at this point he introduces the term *mens* as a synonym for "thinking thing." Henceforth the term *mens* will displace the term *anima* as the preferred pre-philosophic term for referring to the thinking things.[20] Descartes remarks that the meaning of the term *mens* was previously unknown to him, which must mean that previously he had no clear concept of the mind. He has, after all, frequently used the term before in the *Meditations* in a perfectly natural and correct way which did not seem to carry any particular theoretical load.[21] This substitution of a term without misleading connotations for a term which definitely does have misleading connotations is another part of the process of clarifying our pre-philosophic conception of the mind, or soul.

After having explained once what a thinking thing is by enumerating various synonyms – *mens, animus, intellectus,* and *ratio* – Descartes returns to the topic later when he enumerates the various activities which exemplify thought: doubting, understanding, affirming, denying, willing, not willing, imagining, and sensing (AT VII, 28, line 20) [p. 54]. This list is not arbitrary. There is a rationale for each element in it. But to discuss that rationale would carry us too far afield and involve repetition of things I have already said elsewhere.[22] Suffice it for now to say that this is part of the process of achieving clarity and distinctness in our idea of the mind or soul.

So far our examples of Descartes at work on the clarification of concepts have involved concepts expressed by terms well entrenched in ordinary language: *body, soul, mind,* and *thought*. Descartes takes the meaning each term has in ordinary language, represented by his own pre-philosophic concept, as a starting-point. But of course he is not interested simply in giving an analysis of ordinary language. Ordinary language reflects a metaphysic which may have some truth in it, but which should not be accepted uncritically. While it may be the first word, it is certainly not the last word.

But sometimes it is not even the first word. Some of the concepts

166

Descartes is anxious to develop are not expressed by terms well entrenched in ordinary language. Consider the term *idea*, which is central to Descartes' proofs of the existence of God, but which also figures largely in his developing analysis of the concept of mind, since all thought, according to Descartes, involves ideation. As a Latin term, the word *idea* does not have a home in ordinary language; it is rare in classical Latin, a borrowing from the Greek, which came to be used by medieval philosophers to signify "the forms of the perceptions of the divine mind."[23] Descartes' use of it in connection with human thought was novel and the source of much confusion among his readers.

In the *Meditations* Descartes' official explanation of the meaning of this term occurs rather early in the Third Meditation:

> But now order seems to require[24] that first I distribute all thoughts into certain kinds and inquire in which of these truth or falsity properly consists. Some of my thoughts are, as it were, images of things, and it is to these alone that the term "idea" properly applies, as when I think of a man, or a chimera, or the heavens, or an angel, or God.
>
> (AT VII, 36–7) [p. 60]

Note that what we have here is a combination of definition by example and definition by metaphor. Ideas are like images. In this case, as we shall see, it is the metaphor, not the examples, which carries the weight of the explanation.

Descartes' enumeration of the other kinds of thought explains why I said above that ideation is essential to all thought, and incidentally sheds a bit more light on the concept of ideation:

> Other thoughts have other forms: when I will, when I fear, when I affirm, when I deny, I always, indeed, apprehend some thing as the subject of my thought, but I also include something more than the likeness of that thing.

So ideation involves apprehending something as the subject of my thought, an apprehension which in turn involves a likeness of the thing thought of. And when I will something or judge something, I always have an idea of that thing, to which I then add something else. This theory of the nature of thought will be explored further in the Fourth Meditation, when Descartes analyzes the nature of judgment.[25] What interests me here is the way Descartes has prepared us for it in earlier passages of the *Meditations*.

167

Descartes' official explanation of the term *idea* does not represent his first serious use of it in the *Meditations*. That came even earlier in the Third Meditation, when Descartes asked himself what he had previously perceived clearly concerning the objects of the senses, and replied:

> That the very ideas, or (*sive*) thoughts, of such things appear to my mind. Even now I do not deny that those ideas are in me. But it was something else that I used to affirm, and that I also, because of certain habits of belief I had formed, thought I perceived clearly (though really I didn't perceive it): that there are certain things outside me, from which those ideas proceeded, and to which they were completely similar.
>
> (AT VII, 35) [p. 59]

From the point of view of the passage we looked at first, Descartes' official explanation of *idea*, this informal account of ideas must be regarded as imprecise insofar as it simply equates ideas with thoughts. But it is also imprecise in another way. It incorporates a pre-philosophic theory of the nature of sense perception, according to which objects external to us cause us to have thoughts exactly like the objects which cause them. And, as is generally the case, that pre-philosophic theory is a mixture of truth and falsity.

What is true in it will find expression later in the Third Meditation, in the doctrine that the objective reality of an idea requires a cause containing, formally or eminently, as much reality as the idea contains objectively (AT VII, 41) [p. 63].[26] But the qualifications with which this truth is hedged warn us that our thoughts are not exactly like their objects. Not only may they be inaccurate in their representation of reality, as when they represent a square object as round – they may also be radically misleading, as when they represent what is merely a vibration of the air as a sound, inducing us to imagine that there is something in objects like our sensation of sound.[27] So the pre-philosophic theory of perception contains a good deal of falsity.

Descartes does not spring that theory of perception on us without warning in the Third Meditation. He has already suggested it to us as early as the First Meditation. No sooner has Descartes' meditator found in dreams a ground for doubting what he perceives through the senses than his commonsense reasserts itself (AT VII, 19–20) [p. 47]. Suppose I am dreaming, suppose none of those particular things are true which I thought most evident: my eyes are not open, I am not moving my head, or extending my hand, perhaps I even have no hands, no body, still

> I must confess that the things I see in my sleep are like certain painted images of things, which can only be formed according to the likeness of true things. Therefore, at least these general things are true and not imaginary: eyes, head, hands, and the whole body.
>
> [p. 47]

There are limits on the power of the imagination, as is shown by the attempts of painters to conjure up bizarre new creatures. They never come up with anything completely new, they only mix familiar ingredients in new ways. So even if things as general as eyes, heads, hands, and so on, could be imaginary, nevertheless

> I must confess that at least other things, still more simple and universal, are true, and that all those images of things which are in our thought, whether they are true or false, are formed from these simple and universal things as if from their true colors.
>
> [p. 47]

At this stage of the First Meditation Descartes' meditator is an empiricist, not only in the sense that he thinks that our beliefs derive their justification from the evidence of the senses (AT VII, 18) [p. 46], but also in the sense that he holds the classic empiricist theory of the origin of our concepts: the simple ones must come from experience; complex ones may not answer to anything that exists, so long as they can be compounded from ones that do.

In this form, the pre-philosophic theory will not last long. Before the meditator has left this Adam and Tannery page, s/he will have recognized that the sciences which treat of the simplest and most general things of all, like arithmetic and geometry, "care little" whether their objects exist in nature. This insight will later blossom into the theory of innate ideas touched on in the Third Meditation (AT VII, 38, 39) [pp. 61, 62] and be developed more fully in the Fifth (AT VII, 63–5) [pp. 80–1].[28] But some elements of the theory of perception will be retained. The notion that our thoughts are *like* pictures of things persists throughout the *Meditations*. Here in the First Meditation it is expressed in terms natural to the man who has not yet begun to philosophize, who is inevitably an empiricist. Not only are our thoughts *like* certain painted images of things (AT VII, 19, line 27) [p. 47]; they *are* mental images of things (AT VII, 20, lines 12–14) [p. 48].

By the time the meditator has reached the Third Meditation, he has learned, through the discussion of the wax, to distinguish between the intellect and the imagination. The wax is not perceived by the senses, nor by the faculty of imagination, but by the intellect alone (AT VII, 34) [p. 55]. So when his pre-prephilosophic theory of perception resurfaces at the beginning of the Third Meditation (AT VII, 35) [p. 58], it is expressed, not in terms of images, but in terms of ideas. And this choice of terminology is quite deliberate:

> I used this term because it was already in common use among the philosophers to signify the forms of the perceptions of the divine mind, although we do not recognize any capacity for having images in God. And I had no term more appropriate.
>
> (AT VII, 181)

Since God's thought is free of images, we use a term originally deployed in connection with his thought to express the fact that our thought can be without images. But our theory of the mental activity which this term is now used to designate is developed, by criticism, from a theory to which the person ignorant of philosophy would naturally be drawn.[29]

As with "idea," so with "substance." In classical Latin the technical use of the term *substantia* emerges rather late, as a way of representing the Greek concept of *ousia*. Descartes defines it informally about halfway through the Third Meditation (AT VII, 44) [p. 66] as a thing capable of existing through itself, but he has already been using the term without any kind of definition for several pages, ever since he informed us that ideas of substances contain more objective reality than ideas of modes (AT VII, 40) [p. 63]. How can this use be justified? What has Descartes done to prepare us for it?

If Descartes' usage has any justification at all, it must lie in the analysis of the piece of wax. And, indeed, it seems to me that that passage does prepare us for Descartes' definition of substance. Even though the analysis of the wax does not explicitly use the term *substantia*, it does use the correlative term *modus*, a perfectly ordinary term in Latin, whose most relevant meaning here is "manner" or "way," though it is usually translated "*mode*". By insisting strongly on the distinction between the wax itself and the various ways in which it appears to me – now tasting of honey and smelling of flowers, hard and cold, and so forth, now tasteless, odorless, fluid, hot, and so forth – Descartes prepares us to regard the term *substantia*, when it appears, as simply a very general term for referring to objects conceived as things which may continue to persist in existence in spite of radical changes in the way they exist. Descartes even has another metaphor to help us understand this contrast. The modes of substance are like the hats and coats worn by people I "see" passing in the street; the substance itself is like the people wearing those clothes. Just as I do not, strictly speaking, see the people, but only infer their existence from the clothes which I do see, so I do not, strictly speaking, see the wax, but only infer its existence from the existence of the various modes I perceive through the senses.[30]

This way of introducing the concept of substance, however, is evidently no more than a heuristic device. If we may judge from the *Synopsis of the Meditations* (AT VII, 14) [p. 42] Descartes does not really think the wax is a very satisfactory example of a substance. In outlining there the proof of the immortality of the soul which he confesses that he has not given in the *Meditations*, Descartes observes that the proof depends on an explanation of the whole of physics. This is necessary, first,

> in order to know that, in general, all substances, or things which must be created by God to exist, are incorruptible by their nature, and can never cease to exist unless they are reduced to nothing by the same God's denying them his concurrence . . .

Descartes would infer from this that while body, taken in general, is indeed a substance, and so never ceases to exist (unless destroyed by God), particular bodies, like "the human body, insofar as it differs from other bodies, is only composed of a certain configuration of members, and other accidents of the same kind." The human body is not a substance, since it "becomes different simply because the shape of certain of its parts is changed, from which it follows that the body very easily perishes." I take this to mean, not that the body perishes as soon as *any* of its modes changes – then the body would indeed perish all too easily – but that there are certain parts of the body whose existing configuration is critical to the body's continued functioning as a body. So presumably the human body cannot survive just any change in its modes, and neither, presumably, can the wax.

In the absence of the fuller explanation which Descartes hinted might appear in his physics, we can only speculate about what this means. But one thing seems quite clear: the human body's status as a substance is not thrown into doubt simply by its dependence on God for maintenance in existence. For that dependence is something the body shares with the mind. If it were sufficient to make the body not a substance, then the mind too would not be a substance. But Descartes is quite clear in this passage that he thinks the mind is a substance, capable of surviving *any* change in its modes. It is on this that he proposes to base a proof of its immortality. So any attempt to explain the apparent claim of the *Synopsis*, that there is only one material substance, by appeal to the definition of substance as an independent being (see *Principles* I, 51) seems premature. (Only those who are prepared to discount Descartes' claim to believe in the immortality of the soul are entitled to deploy that line of reasoning. No doubt there are still interpreters of Descartes who would regard that suspicion as reasonable. To such interpreters I have nothing to say.)

So far I have been explaining the way in which the Descartes of the *Meditations* explains the central concepts of his metaphysics without using the kind of formal definition that appears in the Geometric Exposition or the *Principles of Philosophy*. My choice of examples has not been accidental. I have been guided by the list of definitions which forms the first section of the Geometric Exposition (AT VII, 160–2). And I believe that I have shown how most of the concepts there defined, or at least most of the most important ones, are explained in the *Meditations*.

But I have saved for last the most important concept: that of God. If there is any notion not readily grasped by those mired in the senses, any notion whose introduction must be carefully prepared by dialectical argument, it is the notion of God as conceived by Descartes, the concept of a purely spiritual being who is infinite in every respect. And yet we must, according to Descartes, not only conceive of God, but know that He exists, if we are to have any certainty about anything (AT VII, 36) [p. 60].

No one will need to be reminded that the concept of God is introduced in the First Meditation, in the context of a doubt about the simplest propositions of mathematics. What we must attend to now is the way in which the concept is introduced. As our previous discussion might lead us to expect, God is first mentioned as a being in whom Descartes has long believed – which is to say that his belief in God is one he has held from an early age, and hence, uncritically. Later (AT VII, 36) [p. 59] he will refer back to this belief as a preconceived opinion. If what I have been arguing is correct, Descartes' characterization of belief in God as part of his pre-philosophic theory of the world will imply not only that the belief does not rest on any firm foundations,[31] but also that it involves a mixture of truth and falsity. And it is not evident what Descartes might later think was false in this belief, given that initially he had conceived of God simply as a being who can do all things, and who had, in particular, created him.

As soon as Descartes has introduced this conception of God, he begins to raise doubts about what it implies. *If* God can do anything, then presumably He can cause me to be mistaken, even in my beliefs about the things that seem easiest to understand. But *perhaps* He didn't want to deceive me. For He *is said to be (dicitur)* supremely good. But *if* He is supremely good, and *if* He can do anything he wishes, why does He allow me sometimes to be deceived? There can be no doubt that sometimes I am deceived. Except for this last, the reasoning here is extremely tentative, a fact which Descartes emphasizes by suggesting that some might prefer to deny the existence of a God so powerful, rather than believe that all other things are so uncertain. And, indeed, in the final paragraph of the First Meditation Descartes resolves to conduct his subsequent meditations, not on the hypothesis of a supremely good God, who is the source of truth, but on the hypothesis of an Evil Spirit (*malignus genius*), supremely powerful and cunning, who has done everything he could to deceive him.

Note that by the end of the First Meditation, the two characteristics in Descartes' original definition of God have grown to four. God is not merely an omnipotent creator, but a supremely good source of truth. His goodness is not just something others say of Him, but an essential characteristic in Descartes' conception of Him. This is shown by Descartes' decision to withhold the name "God" from the omnipotent deceiver he conceives in the final paragraph.[32] An omnipotent being who is not good would not be God.

But this, of course, does not solve the problem of the possibility of divine deception. Perhaps the term "God" should be reserved for a being who combines all the attributes mentioned so far: omnipotence, supreme goodness, being the creator, and being a source of truth. Perhaps what we mean by the term "God" is just a being who has all those attributes. But our possibly arbitrary definition cannot legislate such a being into existence. We cannot solve the problem of the possibility of divine deception simply by listing the various attributes contained in our concept of God. For those attributes may not all be combined in one being. Perhaps there is no God in the sense in which we understand that notion. Perhaps the closest approximation in reality to God as we conceive Him is a being who has only some, but not all of the attributes contained in our concept of God. Perhaps our creator is a being who is omnipotent, but not supremely good and not a source of truth. In order not to violate the conventions of our language, we shall call him the Evil Spirit, understanding by that term a being who combines the following attributes: omnipotence, being the creator of all things other than himself, and being supremely malicious. How do I know that it is not the Evil Spirit who is my creator?[33]

As I read the *Meditations*, Descartes' answer to this is that, on reflection, we find the concept of the Evil Spirit to be incoherent. The attributes just enumerated as defining the Evil Spirit cannot be combined in one being, for the attributes involved in our concept of God are necessarily connected with one another. But seeing why this is so requires a close examination of the way Descartes develops the concept of God in the remaining Meditations.

Meanwhile, we must also note that even though Descartes' conception of God has grown more complex in the space of a few paragraphs, it is still not easy to see what there is in it that is false. None of the four characteristics that define the conception of God Descartes has reached here will be rejected by the end of the *Meditations*. I suggest that, if his concept of God is confused at this stage, it is primarily because the characteristics he has so far identified, while essential to God, in the sense that God would not be God without them, do not strictly speaking state the essence of God, but only certain necessary consequences of His essence.[34] We might add that Descartes is also uncertain what these characteristics imply and how they are related to each other. More of that later.

The Second Meditation does nothing, so far as I can see, to enrich Descartes' concept of God. God is perhaps referred to once, when Descartes asks: "Is there some God, or whatever I shall call Him, who sends me these very thoughts?" (AT VII, 24) [p. 51]. But the expression "some God," combining as it does the equivalent of an indefinite article (*aliquis*) with a proper name (*Deus* capitalized), and Descartes' uncertainty about what to call this hypothetical deceiver, only indicate the level of his confusion. In subequent references to the deceiver in that Meditation (AT VII, 25, 26) [p. 51] Descartes carefully refrains from calling him God.

At the beginning of the Third Meditation, God reappears (AT VII, 36), conceived vaguely once again (*aliquis Deus*), and conceived as a potential deceiver regarding the truths of mathematics. Because of this possibility, we must consider whether God does really exist, and whether He can be a deceiver, and the examination of these questions requires us to develop more fully our initial concept of God. At first this is done in the manner of the First Meditation, by enumerating the attributes our idea of God represents Him as having. There are two such lists, in fact:

(1) That [sc. idea] by which I understand a supreme God, eternal, infinite, omniscient, omnipotent, and creator of all the things there are, apart from himself.[35]
(2) By the term God I understand a certain infinite substance, independent, supremely intelligent, supremely powerful, and by whom both I myself, and also everything else that exists – if anything else does exist – have been created.[36]

These two lists display some interesting differences from one another,[37] but what interests me most are their differences from what preceded them and what follows them. That Descartes has added a number of attributes not mentioned in the First Meditation is evident, as is the fact that he has omitted the attribute which apparently caused trouble for the deceiving God hypothesis in the First Meditation: goodness.

I suggest that these variations reveal an inherent defect in this way of proceeding. Although Descartes will shortly say that his idea of God is most clear and distinct (*maxime clara & distincta*, AT VII, 46), I take it that he really regards the enumeration of attributes as not ultimately a satisfactory way of clarifying this concept. No sooner has he made the bold claim that he has a most clear and distinct idea of God, than he leaps from the listing of particular attributes to a general formula covering them all. He has included these several perfections in his idea of God because fundamentally this idea is the idea of a supremely perfect and infinite being (AT VII, 46) [p. 68].

This is a decisive moment in the dialectic. It provides a rationale for thinking of all these various attributes as attributes of one being.

Descartes now has a principle which determines what should or should not appear on any list of attributes:

> Whatever I perceive clearly and distinctly that is real and true and that implies some perfection, the whole of it is contained in this [FV: idea]. It does not matter that I do not comprehend the infinite, or that there are innumerable things in God which I cannot comprehend, and perhaps will not even be able to attain any conception of.
>
> (AT VII, 46) [pp. 67–8]

It does not matter that Descartes' analysis of his idea of God cannot be exhaustive, because now, at least, he has a principle for deciding individual cases. Insofar as this principle entails that this or that feature will appear on the list, a list which an infinite intellect could extend to infinity, it explains why precisely those features are involved in our concept of God. And insofar as it entails other previously unsuspected characteristics,[38] it shows itself to define the idea of a true and immutable nature, not an arbitrary fiction.[39]

But its most important consequence is that it explains why these various features cannot be clearly conceived in isolation from each other: "One of the chief perfections I understand to be in God is the unity, simplicity or (sive) inseparability of all those things that are in God" (AT VII, 50) [000]. With this deduction from the concept of God as a supremely perfect being, one of the principal confusions of the earlier Meditations has been removed. If the perfections are inseparable from one another, then the concept of the Evil Spirit as a supremely powerful being is revealed to be a concept involving a contradiction.[40] The perfection of omnipotence cannot exist in isolation from the perfection of goodness. Hence Descartes will conclude, by the end of the Third Meditation, that the God he has an idea of, as a being possessing all perfections, cannot be a deceiver (AT VII, 52) [p. 72]. For it is manifest by the natural light that all fraud and deception depend on some defect.

So far so good. It is easy enough to see that over the course of the first three Meditations Descartes has been gradually clarifying his initial concept of God. But it is also easy to imagine that by the end of the Third Meditation the process is complete. Does Descartes not claim, when he introduces the concept of God as a supremely perfect being (AT VII, 46, line 8) [p. 66] to have an idea of God which is most clear and distinct (maxime clara et distincta)?

We must, of course, answer "yes" to this last question. But doing so does not commit us to regarding the process of clarification as complete. When Descartes or, rather, his meditator, repeats his claim to possess a clear and distinct idea of God at the end of the paragraph just cited (AT VII, 46, line 28) [p. 67] he introduces an interesting qualification: "the idea I have of God is the clearest and most distinct of all [the ideas] that are in me." The meditator's idea of God may well be clearer and more distinct than any other idea he has and still not be as clear and distinct as it needs to be for the subsequent argument.

Having a clear and distinct idea of a thing, or of a kind of thing, I have been assuming, is a matter of seeing what is and what is not involved in being that thing or a thing of that kind. More precisely, it is a matter of recognizing that there are certain properties we cannot but ascribe to a thing of that kind (clarity) and others which we are not at all compelled to ascribe to it (distinctness).

The meditator's idea of God will not be as clear and distinct as Descartes would like it to be until he recognizes that he cannot think of God except as existing (AT VII, 66 and 67) [p. 82] that God is the only being to whose essence existence belongs (AT VII, 68) [p. 84] that there cannot be two or more Gods (ibid.). So the ontological argument of the Fifth Meditation is not, as it might appear, a kind of afterthought in which Descartes returns to a proposition already satisfactorily proven earlier. It is, rather, the culmination of Descartes' search for a clear and distinct idea of God, a culmination to which the clarifications of the preceding Meditations were a necessary preliminary.

To recognize these implications of the idea of God, the meditator must already have attained a certain level of clarity. He must, first of all, have risen from the idea of God as possessing this or that perfection to the idea of God as possessing all the perfections, whatever they may be.[41] That is what the dialectic of the Third Meditation contributes to the quest. But the meditator must also have recognized that his idea of God as a supremely perfect being is free of contradiction. That is why the dialectic of the Fourth Meditation is necessary before the ontological argument can be advanced.

To say this is to claim that Descartes anticipated a criticism of his version of the ontological argument which Leibniz pressed repeatedly: that Descartes had assumed too easily the possibility of a supremely perfect being.[42] To be sure, Descartes does not undertake, in the manner of Leibniz, an a priori proof of the compatibility of all perfections. But he does make it a criterion of a clear and distinct perception that it not involve a contradiction (cf. AT VII, 71) [p. 60]. And he does at least attempt to remove from his idea of God what he perceives as the most dangerous threat of contradiction.

From the beginning he had conceived of God as his creator. But as he comes to see that he conceives of God also as a supremely perfect being, it becomes increasingly urgent to understand how a supremely perfect being could be the creator of a manifestly imperfect being. To achieve this understanding is the project of the Fourth Meditation. Whether or not we think Descartes is successful in that project, we must at least recognize that success there is essential to a proper presentation of the ontological argument. When Descartes is presenting his thoughts in the best of all possible orders, the ontological argument must be postponed until after the arguments of the Third and Fourth Meditations, for the best order does not simply assume that we possess the requisite clear and distinct ideas; it shows a process by which someone with confused ideas can acquire clear and distinct ones. Conversely, when Descartes allows himself to assume possession of a clear and distinct idea of God, he can begin, as he does in his synthetic works, with the ontological argument.[43]

Ultimately, I think, Descartes' project does fail. His attempt to solve one mystery leads only to a deeper mystery. To explain how a perfect being can be the creator of an imperfect being, he ascribes to the imperfect being a freedom which will, in the end, be no easier to reconcile with the perfection of his creator than error was.[44] But that is a story for another day. My project here has simply been to explain what in practice the use of the analytic method in the Meditations comes to. And I think we have seen enough examples now of the kind of thing which I claim is characteristic of this method to have a clearer and more distinct idea of the nature of analysis in the Meditations.[45]

NOTES

1 For a representative selection of previous treatments of this issue, see L. J. Beck, *The Method of Descartes* (Oxford: Clarendon Press, 1952), ch. 18; G. Buchdahl, *Metaphysics and the Philosophy of Science* (Cambridge, Mass.: MIT Press, 1969), pp. 118–47; J. Hintikka, "A discourse

on Descartes' method", in M. Hooker, *Descartes': Critical and Interpretive Essays* (Baltimore, Md: Johns Hopkins Press, 1978), reprinted in this volume; M. Gueroult, *Descartes selon l'ordre des raisons* (Paris: Vrin, 1953) 1:22–8, 357–60; J.-M. Beyssade, "L'ordre dans les *Principia*," *Les études philosophiques* (1976): 387–403.

2 "More" because decisions about what to quote, what to paraphrase, what to omit, how to translate what is quoted, and how to paraphrase what is paraphrased, all involve some element of interpretation; "less" because I have deliberately omitted certain prima facie important claims, some because I think they are apt to be misleading in the end, others because I want to postpone them for later attention.

3 See, for example, Alquié's annotation of the French version of Descartes' reply, in *Descartes, Oeuvres philosophiques*, ed. F. Alquié (Paris: Garnier, 1967), 2: 581–5.

4 A full account of this passage would have to explain what reservations Descartes has in mind when he says that analysis is "as it were" (*tanquam*) an a priori procedure (and similarly, *mutatis mutandis*, for synthesis). Cf. Beyssade, "L'ordre dans les *Principia*." It would also have to explain why Descartes says, in a parenthesis (AT VII, 156), that often, in synthesis, the proof itself is more a priori than in analysis.

5 In fact, Descartes claims more than just that it shows a *viable* method of discovery. He claims that it shows the *true* way the thing was discovered. See the passage cited below in n.7. But I take that claim with a grain of salt.

6 "Spinoza as an expositor of Descartes," in *Speculum Spinozanum*, ed. S. Hessing (London: Routledge & Kegan Paul, 1977), pp. 133–42.

7 See *Descartes' Conversation with Burman*, trans. John Cottingham (Oxford: Clarendon Press, 1976), p. 12. Since this work is at best Burman's record of Descartes' replies to his questions, and since the text may be corrupt for a variety of reasons, it must be treated with some suspicion, particularly where it seems to contradict Descartes' own works. For an interesting discussion of the reliability of the *Conversation*, see an article forthcoming in the *Archiv für Geschichte der Philosophie*, by Roger Ariew, "Infinite and indefinite in Descartes' *Conversation with Burman*."

In this case Burman's report of Descartes' reply contradicts Descartes' claim in the Replies to Objections II that the analytic method is the best one for teaching. In my earlier article I suggested (without argument) that Descartes might have changed his mind about which method was best for teaching. Beyssade, in his excellent edition of the conversation (*Descartes, L'entretien avec Burman* (Paris: PUF, 1981), 42), cites a letter to Mersenne of December 31, 1640 (*Oeuvres philosophiques*, ed. Alquié II, 307) in which Descartes, referring to the *Principles*, says that he is engaged in writing his philosophy in such a way that it can easily be taught. This letter evidently was written before the Replies to Objections II were written (see the article by Garber and Cohen, cited below in n. 13, pp. 143–4), so it does not show a change of mind after the Replies to Objections II. But it does show that, even in writings which are incontestably Cartesian,

Descartes was of two minds about what method was best for teaching.

8 In the article cited above, I mentioned the definitions of thought (*Principles* I, 9) and clarity and distinctness (*Principles* I, 45). I might have added those of substance (I, 51), attribute (I, 56), and the natural light (I, 30).

9 In the article cited above, I mentioned the introduction of the concepts of clarity and distinctness via the example of the wax, and the explanation of thought at AT VII, 28. Analogously, the concept of the natural light is introduced in the *Meditations* by giving examples of things known by it (AT VII, 38–9) [p. 62]. But, clearly, not all of Descartes' central concepts will be open to that mode of explanation. Most importantly, the idea of God will not be.

10 See AT VII, 140, and cf. Descartes' Letter to Clerselier (Alquié II, 841–2). Since the general propositions grasped in these contexts would be eternal truths, this is not any ordinary induction. The move from the particular to the general would be like what is sometimes referred to in discussions of Aristotle as an intuitive induction, i.e. a process not of reasoning but of direct insight into first principles, "mediated psychologically by a review of particular instances" (W. D. Ross, *Aristotle* (New York: Meridian, 1959), p. 44, cf. p. 211). I make no attempt to judge whether this represents a just interpretation of Aristotle. Cf. Jonathan Barnes's notes to *Posterior Analytics* B, 19, in his edition of that work (Oxford: Clarendon Press, 1975), pp. 248–60.

11 Cf. the *Conversation with Burman*, p. 3.

12 But not simply summarizing. The text and the footnotes provide additional evidence in favor of that interpretation, some of which I had not noticed when I wrote the earlier article.

13 By Daniel Garber and Lesley Cohen, in "A point of order: analysis, synthesis, and Descartes' *Principles*," *Archiv für Geschichte der Philosophie* 64 (1982): 136–47 (reprinted in this volume). Garber and Cohen primarily challenge the claim that the *Principles* was written according to the synthetic method, pointing out that our only direct evidence for this comes from the (suspect) *Conversation with Burman* and that, on various occasions when Descartes might have been expected to call attention to this synthetic character, he did not do so. I am inclined to think that the explanation for this silence is that Descartes recognized that the *Principles* did not have the formal features his audience would expect in a synthetic treatise, that he did not have the patience for the kind of labour that would be involved in a full-scale treatment of the whole of philosophy *more geometrico*, and that he did not want to arouse expectations he had no intention of satisfying. For the purposes of this article, whose concern is with the *Meditations*, I have no need to defend the claim that the *Principles* is synthetic. It will be enough to compare the *Meditations* with the Geometic Exposition. But I do, in fact, still think that the *Principles* is fundamentally a synthetic work. For the purposes of my earlier article, it would be sufficient if it were, as Gueroult and Gouhier have suggested (in *Descartes* (Paris: Cahiers de Royaumont,

1957), pp. 108–40, and *La pensée métaphysique de Descartes* (Paris: Vrin, 1968), p. 109), a hybrid work, combining features of both methods.

14 A procedure Plato gives examples of in nearly all the dialogues, but which he theorizes about most helpfully in the *Republic*, 531e–540. I take it that for all their respect for the axiomatic procedures of the mathematicians, neither Plato nor Descartes really finds it satisfactory simply to assume his first principles without argument. The problem is to find a way of arguing for first principles which will not permit the cry of dogmatism to be raised in turn about the principles of the argument.

15 That is, propositions which would be accepted by all or by most people, particularly those uncorrupted by the false philosophy taught in the schools. Unlike Aristotle, who also conceived of dialectic as a path to first principles (*Topics* I, i–ii), Descartes would not give special standing to "the wise."

16 So it is not only in the First Meditation that Descartes makes his meditator begin with confused ideas. The procedure is used repeatedly in the *Meditations*, in the Third (AT VII, 38), in the Fourth (AT VII, 54), in the Fifth (AT VII, 66), and in the Sixth (AT VII, 74ff.). Part of Descartes' justification for this procedure lies in his conviction that old habits of belief are hard to break (cf. AT VII, 22, 29), and that we must, therefore, be weaned from them gradually. But partly it lies in his confidence that the perceptions of a man untutored by philosophy (and therefore uncorrupted by false philosophy) must contain some truth.

17 Beginning in the First Meditation (AT VII, 20) and continuing throughout the early meditations (e.g. in AT VII, 30–1, 43–5). I have discussed this in more detail in ch. 8 of *Descartes against the Skeptics* (Cambridge, Mass.: Harvard University Press, 1978).

18 "In good Latin *anima* signifies *air* or *breath*, from which usage I believe it has been transferred to signify the *mind* [*mens*]; that is why I said it is often taken for something corporeal," Letter to Mersenne, April 21, 1641 (Alquié II, 327); cf. AT VII, 161.

19 Here I assume an interpretation argued for at length in *Descartes against the Skeptics*, ch. 4.

20 The list of synonyms given at AT VII, 27, lines 13–14 does contain the term *animus*, which translators have sometimes rendered *soul*. But while classical usage of *animus* and *anima* certainly overlaps (see the entries in the *Oxford Latin Dictionary*), classical authors do sometimes make a distinction which Descartes surely intends here. Lewis & Short cites the following from Nonius Marcellus: *Animus est quo sapimus, anima, qua vivintus.* It is not easy, however, to find a good term in English with which to make the distinction.

21 Descartes frequently uses the term *mens* or its cognates (e.g. *amens, demens*) in a non-reflective way earlier in the *Meditations* (e.g. at AT VII, 17, 19, 21). Particularly interesting is AT VII, 25, since a doubt about the existence of minds had *not* been suggested in the First Meditation.

22 See *Descartes against the Skeptics*, pp. 187–8. It is interesting to note that when essentially the same list is repeated at the beginning of the

Third Meditation (AT VII, 34), the French version adds two further activities of the mind: loving and hating (AT IX, 27). Beyssade suggests (personal correspondence, April 4, 1984) a reason for the addition: that between 1641 (the date of the Latin text) and 1647 (the date of the French translation) Descartes has developed his theory of intellectual love and hate (see the letter to Chanut of February 1, 1647). Beyssade, however, finds it curious that memory is omitted from the list.

23 On the history of the term *idea*, see H. A. Wolfson, "Extradeical and intradeical interpretations of the Platonic ideas," in his *Religious Philosophy* (Cambridge, Mass.: Harvard University Press, 1961). For Descartes' sensitivity to this history, see his reply to Hobbes (AT VII, 181) cited below. For classical usage, see the *Oxford Latin Dictionary*.

24 Here, as is often the case, the French version differs. And here, as is rarely the case, it seems virtually certain that the variation is one in which we should see Descartes' hand: "And so that I can have the opportunity to examine this without interrupting the order of meditation I have proposed for myself, which is to pass gradually from the notions I first find in my mind to those I can find there subsequently, I must first divide . . ." (AT IX, 29). This whole paper might be regarded as a commentary on that passage.

25 And in the Fifth, when Descartes develops the theory of innate ideas mentioned in the Third Meditation. I return to this below. For now the point is simply that the analysis of the concept of mind is far from complete in the Second Meditation.

26 Cf. the Geometrical Exposition, comments on Axiom V.

27 I take my example from the first chapter of *Le monde*, where this pre-philosophic belief occupies center stage.

28 I take it that a theory of innate ideas is implied in the First Meditation when Descartes suggests (AT VII, 20–1) [p. 48] that the truths of mathematics are not touched by the dream argument, and so require the hypothesis of a deceiving God to render them doubtful. If mathematics cares little whether its objects exist in nature, it cannot be affected by an argument casting doubt on the evidence of the senses, which are preeminently a way of learning what exists in nature. If mathematics is a science indifferent to the exemplification of its objects in physical nature, then even its fundamental concepts are not to be thought of as having been derived from experience.

29 For more on Descartes' concept of ideas, see my article "Descartes, Spinoza, and the ethics of belief," in *Spinoza: Essays in Interpretation*, ed. M. Mandelbaum and E. Freeman (La Salle, Ill.: Open Court, 1975).

30 Cf. *Principles*, I, 52.

31 This does not, however, mean that it cannot serve perfectly well as a ground for doubting the truths of mathematics in the First Meditation. See *Descartes against the Skeptics*, chs 3–5.

32 Some have thought that Evil Spirit is not in fact omnipotent, largely because Descartes never seems to mention doubt about mathematical truths in connection with him. For example, mathematical prop-

ositions are not included in the list of prior beliefs to be rejected in the final paragraph of the First Meditation, or in the second and third paragraphs of the Second Meditation. See R. Kennington, "The finitude of Descartes' Evil Genius," *Journal of the History of Ideas* 32 (1971): 441–6. And it appears that traditionally demons were conceived as limited in power, capable of acting on the mind only by presenting deceptive sense experiences. See Tullio Gregory, "Dio ingannatore e genio maligno," *Giornale critico della filosofia italiana* (1975): 477–516. If the Evil Spirit were finite in power, this might explain why Descartes says in the Third Meditation (AT VII, 36) that the only reason he had doubted the truths of mathematics was because "some God" could have given him such a nature that he could be deceived about the most manifest things.

Nevertheless, when Descartes introduces the demon at AT VII, 22, he calls him *summe potentem*, a phrase repeated with reference to the *deceptor nescio quis* at AT VII, 25. Similarly the *deceptorem aliquem* at AT VII, 26 is *potentis simum*. Although Descartes does hold that supreme power and malignity are incompatible (see AT V, 150), it appears that his meditator does not appreciate that fact at this point of the *Meditations*.

33 Note that, in shifting from God to the deceiver, we shift from a being in whom we have long believed, though no doubt without adequate warrant for our belief, to one whose epistemic status is more dubious. No doubt belief in demons was more common in Descartes' time than in ours, but belief in omnipotent demons must have been rare even then. See Gregory, "Dio ingannatore e genio maligno." This illustrates what I think is an important fact about the *Meditations*: that a ground of doubt need not be probable on the evidence, nor even believed; it is sufficient that it is not known to be false. For more on this, see *Descartes against the Skeptics*.

34 This way of putting things is perhaps not one Descartes himself would choose; my reading here, and throughout this essay, owes much to Spinoza.

35 AT VII, 40. The French version adds: "immutable" (AT IX, 32).

36 AT VII, 45. The French version adds: "eternal and immutable" (AT IX, 35–6).

37 As Professor Rodis-Lewis points out, in the notes to her bilingual edition, *Meditationes de prima philosophia/Méditations métaphysiques* (Paris: Vrin, 1978), p. 45, *independent* replaces *eternal*; but according to the First Replies these two attributes are necessarily connected (AT VII, 119).

38 E.g. that there is nothing potential in his idea of God (AT VII, 47, 51) or that God has the power of existing *per se* (AT VII, 50).

39 This will be essential to the ontological argument. Cf. the Replies to Objections I (AT VII, 117) and *Descartes against the Skeptics*, pp. 148–52.

40 See the *Conversation with Burman*, p. 4.

41 Cf. AT VII, 67: "For although it is not necessary for me ever to have any thought of God, nevertheless, as often as it does please me to

think of the first and supreme being, and to draw, as it were, the idea of Him from the treasury of my mind, it is necessary for me to attribute all perfections to Him, even if I do not then enumerate all of them or attend to them individually."

42 See, for example, Leibniz's Letter to Oldenburg of December 28, 1675, in L. Loemker, *Leibniz: Philosophical Papers and Letters* (Dordrecht: Reidel, 1969), p. 166.

43 In the article cited above in n. 13, Garber and Cohen complained that "even if one accepts the claim that the *Principles* are synthetic, this difference between the *Meditations* and the *Principles* [viz. that the order of the arguments for the existence of God is different in the two works, the order in the *Principles* are synthetic, this difference between the *Meditations* and the *Principles* corresponding to that in the Geometric Exposition] is not easily explained. Curley's account of analysis and synthesis, for example, seems to leave this divergence between the two texts unexplained" (p. 146n). Certainly my earlier article on this topic offered no explanation of that phenomenon. But I would contend that the natural extension of it presented in this article meets the challenge.

44 Cf. *Principles* I, 40–1.

45 I leave for another day the difficult question of whether the analytic method of the *Meditations* is the same as the analytic method of the *Regulae*. But as readers of *Descartes against the Skeptics* might expect, I think we should not be surprised if they are not the same, and should not presume that the *Regulae* can be used to interpret the *Meditations*. Some previous discussions of analysis seem to me to have assumed too easily that the two methods are essentially the same.

THE ONTOLOGICAL PROOF WITHIN THE ORDER OF REASONS

Georges J. D. Moyal

The place the ontological proof occupies in the *Meditations* became the focus of a sustained debate between Professors H. Gouhier and M. Gueroult when the latter's *Descartes selon l'ordre des raisons* first appeared. The debate, in turn, gave rise to *Nouvelles réflexions sur la preuve ontologique*, a monograph in which Professor Gueroult deployed, in minute details, a distinction of decisive importance for understanding the *Meditations*: the distinction between the metaphysical level ("plan métaphysique") and the level of nature ("plan de la nature") in the Cartesian itinerary; without it, indeed, many a passage of the *Meditations* would remain opaque.

It seems to me, however, that another way of envisioning the question of the role of the ontological proof presents itself, and that it is possible to resolve the debate without having recourse to this distinction. Not that it loses thereby any of its usefulness: on the contrary, it remains indispensable for understanding many a Cartesian doctrine, notably, that of free will.[1] Nevertheless, it seems to me that its role in this debate need not be as important as Professor Gueroult makes out in his *Nouvelles réflexions*.

I propose, therefore, to take up again the question of the role of the ontological proof in the *Meditations* without resorting to this distinction, and to examine thereafter how this interpretation may help resolve the debate which pitted him against Professor Gouhier.

I

The *Meditations* must undoubtedly be included amongst those rare works in which each word, each expression is carefully chosen, has its specific significance and plays a very precise role in the whole: it is therefore incumbent upon every commentator to suspect the most ordinary expression in this work to be linked to other passages, however distant in the text they may be, however surprising their juxtaposition may appear at first blush. A brief passage in the First Meditation requires just such a treatment in order to account for the ontological proof.

Immediately after having conjured the possibility of a deceiving deity, Descartes writes: "there may in fact be some people who would prefer to deny [the existence of] so powerful a God rather than believe that everything else is uncertain. Let us not oppose them [for the present] but grant them that everything said [here] about God is a fiction."[2] The question this passage raises is that of knowing where, in the *Meditations*, is to be found the answer to the position adopted here by these "people." Evidently, "Let us not oppose them [for the present]" intimates that they will be answered. However, Descartes does not indicate where this answer is to be found; or, at least, he does not indicate it explicitly.

There are, in fact, three possibilities: either (a) they are answered immediately;[3] or (b) any of the three proofs for the existence of God, wherever it may occur, should suffice to answer them; or, last (c), this answer is to be found at a specific location only, and only one of the three proofs is aimed at them. Of these three possibilities, only the last, to my mind, is the correct one.

Indeed, the first alternative cannot be maintained. For these opponents do not object only to the Cartesian attempt to doubt the truths of mathematics. They are not readers finding themselves suddenly compelled to become atheists by the apparent absurdity involved in doubting the simplest truths of reason. Their atheism is not foisted on them at all: Descartes merely seeks to take up, through their stance, the position of a humanism (or of a rationalism) for which the hypothesis of a God – whether He be a deceiver or not – is superfluous. Theirs is an atheistic humanism which contents itself with a rational science, and finds in it all the satisfactions, actual or anticipated, which reason demands. There is indeed, therefore, an "upset", as Professor F. Alquié notes, immediately after the quoted passage.[4] But this upset does not constitute Descartes' answer: it can only justify the move to doubt the truths of reason. Its force resides only in compelling the admission that, if God did not exist, there would be all the more reason to doubt the certainties to which they cling.

They could nevertheless insist, and maintain that truths of reason are the only ones we can cling to, however false they may be in the eyes of a being endowed with supra-rational faculties, and capable of knowing therefore their falsehood: since we have, and can have, no access to His vantage-point, we must remain content with what appears to us to be certain: the truths of mathematics, for instance.

Descartes, however, has not undertaken to persuade them of the possibility of a deceiving deity merely to shake their confidence in the truths of reason. "Let us not oppose them for the present" shows, on the contrary, that the answer they are to get must also convince them that God exists. Otherwise – and this is important – their humanism would constitute an alternative to the system Descartes proposes quite as viable, on the whole, as its rival, since it would end up being identical with it save for its denial of God.

Yet it is this very possibility which Descartes admits provisionally, by not opposing it "for the present."

But now their position consists of two tenets: atheism, and the reliability of the truths of reason. Moreover, the two are interdependent: God does not exist since reason suffices to account for the universe; the divine hypothesis is therefore superfluous.[5] Descartes must therefore not only attack their atheism but also show that the link they maintain between the two tenets is unsustainable. He must therefore attack this link and not just the two doctrines separately.

If so, we must recognize that neither the proofs in Meditation III nor the analysis of judgment and error in Meditation IV are sufficient to dispose of their doctrine. For nothing in them undermines the link they maintain between the two claims. All the less so, since there is no question of Descartes *demonstrating* to them that mathematical certainties are not reliable; Descartes knows quite well that these truths are reliable and will remain. He seeks to prove to them rather that these certainties depend on God's existence. But since they insist on their reliability independently of God, Descartes must postpone answering them: he must first uncover the foundations of this reliability, since it constitutes the only point on which he and they will agree, the only point from which the debate with them may then begin.

These foundations, however, are not uncovered until after Meditation III: they are obtained, in part, from the analysis contained in Meditation IV. Hence, the proofs in Meditation III could not be intended for them, since the problem of God's existence does not arise, for them, within the context of a hyperbolical doubt such as is attacked in the Third Meditation: they do not share this doubt. The second alternative is therefore eliminated.

This leads us naturally to conclude that it is only in the Fifth Meditation that Descartes undertakes to refute their atheism. And, indeed, a number of indications in this Meditation show that it is precisely then that Descartes takes up the debate that opposes him to these objectors.

For indeed, Meditation V assimilates the ontological proof to mathematical demonstrations: if one is to assent to the latter's conclusions, one must also assent to the conclusion of the a priori proof, since the foundations of their veracity are identical; in both cases, it is only the clarity and distinction with which they present themselves which ensure that these proofs are sound. But now, if the mathematician should take the trouble to find out what justifies the certainty he acknowledges in mathematical proofs, he must recognize, according to Descartes, that it is founded only on the evidence (i.e. the clarity and distinctness) of the ideas contained in them. Since the ontological proof, likewise, only involves clear and distinct ideas, the atheistic mathematician must necessarily admit the error of his atheism, and this on the strength of evidence at least equal to that which he admits in mathematics.

Let us now turn to the text. The Fifth Meditation marks the beginning of the application of the criterion of truth, henceforth guaranteed by God: after Meditation IV, there only remains the task of sifting ideas as they present themselves, retaining those that are evident and rejecting the rest. It so happens that the first perceptions to occur, then, are those of the mathematical determinations of material or extended substance, hence the rehabilitation of the geometrical sciences. But similarly, to the extent that it is conformable to the model of geometrical demonstrations, the ontological proof must compel our assent. Indeed, Descartes, as he reviews it in detail, highlights the resemblances it bears to mathematical demonstrations; and even that which should constitute a difference between them – the existence of its object and the non-existence of theirs – is not sufficient to deny its mathematical character. There are other differences to be noticed: for instance, certain mathematical demonstrations begin with definitions; they thus start from something arbitrary; Descartes argues that the ontological proof does not resemble these.[6] Other proofs, such as *reductiones ad absurdum*, start off from false suppositions;[7] yet

188

others begin with fictitous ideas.[8] The ontological proof resembles none of these. It resembles instead those which begin with evident truths and conclude with other truths. If, lastly, the atheistic geometer is concerned that a certain logical remoteness, and hence, a certain implausibility *ab initio*, separates him from acknowledging the existence of God, Descartes can reassure him:

> Some of the things I clearly and distinctly perceive are obvious to everyone, while others are discovered only by those who look more closely and investigate more carefully; but once they have been discovered, the latter are judged to be just as certain as the former. In the case of a right-angled triangle, for example, the fact that the square on the hypoteneuse is equal to the square on the other two sides is not so readily apparent as the fact that the hypoteneuse subtends the largest angle; but once one has seen it, one believes it just as strongly. But as regards God, if I were not overwhelmed by preconceived opinions, and if the images of things perceived by the senses did not besiege my thought on every side, I would certainly acknowledge him sooner and more easily than anything else.[9]

In short, the analogy is complete: nothing distinguishes this proof from geometrical demonstrations.

However, there is more: even before attempting to highlight its mathematical character, Descartes proclaims clearly that the ontological proof would lose none of its compelling force even if one were to withhold one's assent to what he has put forth in the preceding Meditations: "even if it turned out that not everything on which I have meditated in these past days is true, I ought still to regard the existence of God as having at least the same level of certainty as I have hitherto attributed to the truths of mathematics."[10] It is this text, more particularly, which leads me to think that it is indeed those "who would prefer to deny the existence of such a powerful God rather than to believe that everything else is uncertain" whom he addresses at last. For it indicates that this proof should recommend itself to them by its sole conformity to the standards of mathematical demonstrations, and this even if they have refused to follow the itinerary which involves doubting the reliability of reason in order to ensure its foundations, and which Descartes follows through Meditations II, III and IV. It is this text which constitutes, in short, the second abutment of a bridge spanning these three Meditations, and which enables Cartesian rationalism to come to grips with this atheistic humanism at last.

We must not forget, however, that if Descartes addresses a particular audience here, he also addresses, through its objections, a wider audience: his readers. Hence, when he undertakes to answer the first, he makes it the representative of a philosophical doctrine which exhausts the gamut of possibilities he must review to satisfy this larger audience; the latter, because of its heterogeneity, is neutral and is thus prepared to countenance the complex itinerary Descartes follows. It is therefore by a *detour* that the ontological proof finds its place in the order of reasons. A detour, indeed, for what we have just seen of it suggests that it constitutes an interruption; the very text quoted just now ("even if it turned out that not everything on which I have meditated in these past days is true") shows that this proof would still hold even if it were detached from the preceding Meditations. But it is not detached from them at all: it does fit within a specific order, though not quite that proposed by Professor Gueroult.

Once again, we must go back to the First Meditation in order to identify the particular order Descartes follows. "Let us not oppose them for the present" will help us here also. It introduces, as we have seen, the possibility of a doctrine the possible truth of which Descartes must envision, even though he does not seek to make it his: the doctrine that certain knowledge can be had without God's assistance, and which therefore dispenses with God's existence. It introduces therefore one of the horns of a dilemma which can be formulated thus: either certainty depends on God or it is obtainable independently of His existence. If the first, then God exists and guarantees it: this corresponds to the itinerary followed in Meditations III and IV. If the latter, then analysis shows that the conditions of (mathematical) certainty are such that they enable us to discover the existence of God: this corresponds to the argumentation in Meditation V. Hence, in either case God's existence must be acknowledged.

It appears then that the ontological proof, presented here as the second horn of this dilemma, can be inserted in the order of reasons in that it answers an alternative hitherto held aside by Descartes: that of a rational but atheistic science. Descartes has set for himself the goal not merely of defeating a radical skepticism which, in any case, he alone enunciates, but also of replying to a more prevalent skepticism, one which acknowledges the reliability of mathematics but dispenses with the hypothesis that God exists. Moreover, Descartes does not consider that, on the strength of having answered the former, he has, *a fortiori*, answered the latter. Both positions are distinct and call for distinct answers; for the ordinary skeptic can very well attach no importance to the proofs in *Meditation III*. Indeed they would not recommend themselves to his assent since they do not display a mathematical form. He could content himself with the analysis of error and of the means of avoiding it without feeling compelled to admit the existence of God.

II

So much for the two theses. What now of the *link* uniting them?

The fact is that the ontological proof's insertion in the order of reasons can be seen from a second perspective as well. It makes possible the solution to a problem which both Descartes and the atheistic geometer share: that of the eternal character of eternal truths.[11] For it is not enough for Descartes to have convinced the atheistic geometer of the necessity of acknowledging the existence of God on the basis of the latter's own criteria of evidence; he must also be convinced that God is the necessary condition of knowledge.

But now, although the Fourth Meditation has brought out the role of a God who guarantees the truth of the clear and distinct, it has done nothing with regard to the immutable character of eternal truths. Descartes shows that God guarantees also the immutability of eternal truths by addressing the atheistic geometer. For it is this immutability which accounts for the confidence that led him to dispense with a God who seemed to him foreign to the rule of evidence.[12] Descartes undertakes to shake this confidence by bringing out the necessity for it to be based on God's existence: the atheistic geometer's assurance would be worthless unless it were founded on the immutability of eternal truths, and unless this immutability itself were justified by the only being capable of guaranteeing it – an Eternal Being. All this, in accordance with the very criteria of evidence acknowledged by the atheistic geometer.

Accordingly, the geometer must recognize not only that God exists and guarantees the certainty of his knowledge, but also that the link between these two things holds in the reverse order to that which the ontological proof presents: it is not the nature of the clear and distinct which compels me to accept the existence of God; it is rather that because God exists, I am compelled to accept certain truths as well as their permanence, i.e. their immutability. Descartes thereby completes the reversal: it is through this manoeuver that he proves to the atheistic humanist the primacy of the idea of God over those of mathematics; that not only is it necessary to follow the Cartesian itinerary, but also that it is the only one possible, and that, consequently, the humanist alternative to it cannot be as sound as Descartes', something which he had accepted provisionally by "not opposing it for the present." The atheistic geometer should have followed him right from the First Meditation; in refusing to do so, he merely postponed the condemnation of his error, a condemnation which he now finds himself compelled to utter himself. This is what explains the paragraph – pivotal, if any such there be – in the Fifth Meditation, in which Descartes maintains: "Although it needed close attention for me to perceive this truth [*sc.* that God exists], I am now just as certain of it as I am of everything else which appears most certain; and what is more, I see that the certainty of all other things depends on it, so that without it nothing can be perfectly known."[13] Descartes clearly shows that this perfection in knowledge pertains to the immutability of eternal truths when, dealing with the possibility of inconstant beliefs the atheistic geometer might have, he adds, immediately after:

> Admittedly my nature is such that so long as I perceive something very clearly and distinctly I cannot but believe it to be true. But my nature is also such that I cannot fix my mental vision continually on the same thing, so as to keep perceiving it clearly; and often the memory of a previously made judgment may come back, when I am no longer attending to the arguments which led me to make it. And so other arguments can now occur to me which might easily undermine my opinion, if I did not possess knowledge of God; and so I should thus never have true and certain knowledge about anything, but only shifting and changeable opinions.[14]

If such is the case, we must conclude that this last paragraph, far from dealing with a supposed divine guarantee of memory, as some may have believed, merely establishes instead the basis of a belief in the permanence of eternal truths: it shows that what they are about will remain such, indefinitely, since God has willed it so by creating them eternal.[15]

Thus, the ontological proof does indeed fit in the order of reasons, and meets it at both ends: it is introduced by the necessity not to omit anything, and in particular, not to omit a reply to atheistic rationalism; and it introduces the account of the eternity of eternal truths, hitherto omitted, but necessary for the Sixth Meditation. To be sure, Descartes does not give it the same importance he gives to the other proofs of God's existence. When he writes "I ought still to regard the existence of God as having at least the same level of certainty as I have hitherto attributed to the truths of mathematics,"[16] he implies that if one adopts the mathematical approach, one thereby uses a procedure which lessens its importance by making the truth of God's existence subsidiary to the truths of mathematics. It is, in fact, the reverse which ought to be acknowledged: it is God's existence which guarantees the truth of the clear and distinct. Whether the atheistic geometer agrees to follow him through the Third and Fourth Meditations or not, he will have to admit God's existence. And it will be to his advantage to admit the primacy of this truth if he wishes to be assured, in mathematics, of the constancy of the truth of his beliefs, and of their invulnerability to doubt. This dilemma, with which Descartes confronts the atheistic geometer, originates in the First Meditation, for it is only there that is envisioned the disjunction between the two means of arriving at God's existence.

Unlike the others, the Fifth Meditation does not exhibit any thematic unity at first sight. But if what is argued here is sound, one can find in it a conducting thread: it adds, to the conditions of truth uncovered in the Fourth, the conditions of the eternity of eternal truths – a necessary prerequiste step for the founding of physics in the Sixth. But it also enables Descartes now to tie together threads of argumentation first loosened in the First Meditation: it is this other function which gives it a heterogeneous appearance. It is not unified; it unifies.

III

There only remains now the task of relating this interpretation to the debate between Professors Gouhier and Gueroult.

M. Gouhier finds it quite surprising – and not without cause – that the ontological proof should depend on the proofs in the Third

Meditation. "What we cannot understand well," he writes, "is a rational proof of the existence of God which includes, in the preliminaries on which it is founded, another rational proof of Gods existence. If I undertake to demonstrate rationally God's existence, is it not because, at the outset, I acknowledge the possibility that God might not exist?"[17] This suggests that, according to M. Gouhier, there would be, undoubtedly, nothing to prevent the order of proofs in Meditations III and V from being other than it is. That is in fact what he implies, two pages later:

> Whether there be a Deity deceiving me or not, I perceive necessary existence in the idea of God. Whether the proof be *a priori* or *a posteriori*, what is essential for Descartes is that it should bear on God viewed as a Perfect Being; for a moment's reflexion is enough for us to see that His perfection excludes deception. Whether *a priori* or *a posteriori*, the demonstration leads directly to a God whose veracity is posited at the same time as is His existence.[18]

Even if we agree that M. Gouhier is right on this last point, the fact remains that Descartes would not pass up the least opportunity to order his proofs one way rather than another, for as little as that one of them should happen to be connected to this or that point in the unfolding of the *Meditations*; so that even if the ontological proof's appearance in the Fifth Meditation is "fortuitous,"[19] a mere association of ideas would still suffice to explain its appearance there and not elsewhere.

But there are, in fact, much better reasons to reject M. Gouhier's claim. When he writes, "Whether there be a Deity deceiving me or not, I perceive necessary existence in the idea of God," he also suggests that this perception suffices to establish God's existence. Which is not the case. Or, rather, which would not be the case if the ontological proof followed the Second Meditation immediately. For one would then have to agree that the perception of this relation between the idea of existence and the idea of God overcomes, the way the *Cogito* does, the Evil Genius hypothesis. It would also have to be the case that the divine guarantee is already available at the end of this Meditation. But neither of these conditions is fulfilled. What explains that the proof by effects rightfully belongs in the Third Meditation while the ontological proof does not, is that the former establishes the link between God's existence and my own and that my existence is ascertained in spite of the Evil

Genius's attempts to deceive me. Such is not the case for the a priori proof. In reality, it is because God's existence can be so intimately tied to my own that it can be demonstrated in the Third Meditation. The link between these two existences is immediate; it is quite appropriate to speak of an order of reasons holding between the *Cogito* and God's existence, but this order would be disrupted if Descartes proceeded any differently. For it is as much the innateness of the idea of God in me as the fact that I am created in His image which operate in the Third Meditation to ensure this tight link between God and myself, and to thwart thereby the Evil Genius.[20]

If, consequently, there are reasons to believe that the proofs of God's existence are indeed where the order of reasons requires them to be according to Descartes, does this mean that M. Gouhier's criticism misses its target? No, for the fact remains that a proof must not presuppose its conclusion: God's non-existence must remain a possibility at the outset. The ontological proof, contrary to what M. Gueroult maintained about it at first, far from being aimed at those who are not or who have ceased to be atheists, is aimed rather at those who have not renounced their atheism, and who have not even wanted to rid themselves of their prejudices: they have seen no necessity to do so, contenting themselves with mathematical truths and doubting only the necessity of tying them to God's existence.

Does it then follow that M. Gueroult's thesis is false? Not if we confine ourselves to the necessity of making the a priori proof depend on the order of reasons. This dependence, however, is not what M. Gueroult makes it out to be, not even in his *Nouvelles réflexions*. Yet this latter work expresses the thesis which comes closest to our present interpretation.[21]

M. Gueroult is indeed right to insist that the ontological proof has its place in the order of reasons; he is equally right to admit, following M. Gouhier's criticisms, that it is not necessary for it to be aimed at those who are not or who have ceased to be atheists. The proof is indeed one in the strictest sense of the term; and this implies that it must acknowledge, *ab initio*, the possible non-existence of God; it would otherwise beg the question. But in order to do this, it is not necessary to weaken the main thesis in *Descartes selon l'ordre des raisons*. It is sufficient simply to recognize that the order of reasons follows a different path from the one both Professor Gouhier and he have in mind: this path is not unilinear, but a bifurcation. Descartes sets a dilemma in the First Meditation, a dilemma both branches of which reach the same point: either one admits the possibility of a deceiving deity and one must then call in doubt the certainty of mathematical truths, or one denies the existence of a God however conceived, and one clings (as a foundation to truth) to the reliability of mathematics. In either case, one is compelled to reach the existence of a non-deceiving God who guarantees the certainty of the clear and distinct as well as the constancy of eternal truths. The order of reasons is undisturbed: it undergoes no interruption. But to say that it undergoes no interruption does not entail that it could not so bifurcate, at the outset, that when Descartes ensures that he has omitted nothing, he should not have to deal with both branches of this fork, instead of just one.

That being said, the two branches do not have equal merit in his eyes. It is indeed the first which, in principle, guarantees the second. Metaphysical doubt can and must affect the ontological proof, since it only provides mathematical certainty: the sort of certainty which has been called into doubt in the First Meditation through the hypothesis of a deceiving deity. M. Gueroult is therefore right to insist on the superiority of the proofs by effects relative to the a priori proof.

It is evident that, when M. Gueroult weakens his claims in his *Nouvelles réflexions*, the position he then adopts is an uncomfortable one since it must reconcile (a) a unilinear path for the order of reasons, (b) the ontological proof's dependence on the a posteriori proofs, and (c) the logical independence of the premises of the a priori proof. These three conditions are indeed difficult to satisfy at the same time. But the problem is resolved, it seems to me, the minute one sees that "order" does not necessarily mean linear succession of reasons or discoveries; nothing precludes order from being somewhat more complex (however minute the degree of complexity), or the meditator, concerned to exhaust all conceivable alternatives, from allowing his train of thought to take a sidestep now and then, even if this means coming back to it later, to satisfy the same concern, not to omit anything, and thus ensure against error.

NOTES

1 Cf. note 19 below.
2 *Meditation I*, in *The Philosophical Writings of Descartes*, trans. John Cottingham, Robert Stoothoff and Dugald Murdoch (Cambridge: Cambridge University Press, 1984) (hereafter CSM), vol. II, p. 14. I

shall, when quoting from it, bring the occasional minor modification to this translation. Here, the inserts appearing in square brackets – the first occurring in CSM, the other two not – reflect de Luynes' French translation. The reader may want to refer to the debate that the first two occasioned between M. Vincent Carraud and myself, in issues 19 and 20 of the *Bulletin cartésien* (itself published in *Archives de Philosophie* 54 (1991): 71–2, and 55 (1992): 3–9, respectively).

3 This answer would, then, be the very next sentence in the text ("According to their supposition, then, I have arrived at my present state by fate or chance or a continuous chain of events, or by some other means; yet since deception and error seem to be imperfections, the less powerful they make my original cause, the more likely it is that I am so imperfect as to be deceived all the time.") and would merely address their refusal to doubt the truths of mathematics, not their denial of the existence of God; something which the controverted words, "for the present" seem to rule out.

4 In his edition of *Oeuvres philosophiques de Descartes*, 3 vols (Paris: Garnier, 1963–73), III, 410 n. 1.

5 This does not contradict in any way our earlier denial that their atheism is foisted on them by a dilemma compelling them to choose between the possibility of a deceiving God and the loss of mathematical certainties; for we are not to view them as readers who come by their doctrines as they proceed in their reading of the *Meditations*, but rather as representatives of a position forming a logical, not a chronological, whole.

6 "And it must not be objected at this point that while it is indeed necessary for me to suppose that God exists, once I have made the *supposition* that he has all perfections . . . nevertheless *the original supposition was not necessary*" (CSM II, 46; emphasis mine).

7 "Similarly, the objection would run, it is not necessary for me to think that all quadrilaterals can be inscribed in a circle; but given this supposition, it will be necessary for me to admit that a rhombus can be inscribed in a circle – which is patently false" (ibid.).

8 "I understand that this idea is not something fictitious which is dependent on my thought" (CSM II, 47).

9 CSM II, 47.

10 CSM II, 45.

11 Thus Professor Alquié writes, in his edition of the text: "In this passage, divine veracity is not called upon to guarantee the memory of the evidence, but the continuity, the maintenance of that evidence, in the face of all possible doubt . . . the certainty which accompanies the atheist's clear knowledge can be shaken . . . it is therefore not the certainty of a true science. Contrariwise, the knowledge acquired at the end of the *Meditations* and founded on God can no longer be shaken. It is a true and certain science." (*Oeuvres philosophiques de Descartes'* vol. II, p. 565 n. 2.)

12 It is appropriate to recall here the description to be found in the *First Meditation*: they are geometers "who would rather deny the existence of so powerful a God". But what does this power amount to if not to

ensuring that I err each time I number the sides of a square? And if such is God's power, it includes, as well, the opposite power to make it so that the number of sides a square has should never vary: it is the constancy of the realities enunciated by mathematical truths which must be referred to divine power, and which must be so referred using the very type of evidence which the geometer acknowledges.

13 *CSM* II, 48.

14 ibid.

15 This reading becomes the easier to grant when it is pointed out that the word "memory," as Descartes uses it in this and related passages, belongs to the class which Gilbert Ryle calls "success-words" (cf. *The Concept of Mind* (New York, 1962), pp. 149–53). For just as the analysis of "knowledge" entails the truth of the known proposition (it is impossible to know what is not the case), so too it is impossible to remember what was not the case, what did not take place. It is this sense of "remember" which clarifies Descartes' claim that "Now [that] I have perceived that God exists . . . even if I am no longer attending to the arguments which led me to judge that this [*sc.*, something, other than God's existence, perceived clearly and distinctly in the past] is true, provided I remember that I clearly and distinctly perceived it, there are no counter-arguments which can be adduced to make me doubt it, but on the contrary I have true and certain knowledge of it" (*CSM* II, 48 [000]). For if I remember having clearly and distinctly perceived it, then indeed I did so perceive it. There is no question here of Descartes making the case for a divine guarantee of memory: such a claim would fly in the face of evidence and conflict with his views on the fallibility of memory and on the clear and distinct. Professor Alquié, commenting on this text, has well observed that "in this passage, knowledge of God is not called on to provide a foundation for memory or for the remembrance of the evident, but – what is different – to provide a foundation for what is evident now so that it may subsist, and not be recalled into doubt thereafter" (*Oeuvres philosophiques de Descartes*, vol. II, pp. 477–8 n. 3.

16 CSM II, 45.

17 H. Gouhier, "La preuve ontologique de Descartes: A propos d'un livre récent", *Revue Internationale de Philosophie* 8: 28 (1954): 299.

18 ibid., p. 301. It must be observed here that Professor Gouhier seems briefly to have glimpsed an interpretation such as the one presented here, but did not stop at it. He writes: "Here is another possible reading: forget what has gone on before; the [ontological] proof enjoys, minimally, the certainty that the reasonable man [*l'honnête homme*] allows to mathematical truths, and which represents, in his eyes, the highest certainty; naturally, after what has gone on before, it is the existence of God which in the eyes of the philosopher, represents this highest certainty, since mathematical truths are unable to free themselves of metaphysical doubt." But he diverges from this reading immediately after, when he adds that "to suspend the conclusions of the preceding Meditations would be a way of interrupting the 'order of reasons'." (ibid., p. 302).

19 The word is Professor Gouhier's (ibid., p. 300), and so is the suggestion that the ontological proof may owe its presence in *Meditation V* to a mere association of ideas, rather than to the order of reasons.

20 The tightness of the link between God's existence and my own is nowhere so well expressed as in an article by R. F. McRae entitled "Innate ideas:" "Here we must note that Descartes says that the idea of God 'is innate in me just as the idea of myself is innate in me'. He says moreover that 'it is not essential that the mark [of the workman imprinted on his work] should be something different from the work itself'. Thus, he explains to Gassendi, a picture whose inimitable technique showed that it was painted by Apelles could be said to carry the mark which Apelles imprinted on all his pictures. This makes it clear that it is *on my nature* not *in my mind* – that God has imprinted his mark. That is why reflection on the self of which I am conscious yields not only the idea of what I am, but the idea of God too. The two ideas are innate in the same sense" (in *Cartesian Studies*, ed. R. J. Butler (Oxford: Blackwell, 1972), p. 42).

21 Attention might be drawn here to the fact that the atheistic geometer's certainty is "blind," so to speak: it arises out of an assent *imposed* by the clarity and distinctness of the ideas he contemplates. He is, in this regard, *passive* with respect to them. What Descartes urges him to do is to apply his own methods of analysis to the idea of this certainty, to acquire a critical awareness of it and to gain control of the assent that he gives as much to mathematics as to other truths. The atheistic geometer can thus move from the level of nature to the metaphysical level, and thereby acquire this absolute freedom of assent. It is on this that, in many ways, I share Professor Gueroult's views (cf. *Nouvelles réflexions*, p. 97). (This notion of an absolute freedom of assent is examined by me in detail in another article, "The unity of Descartes's conception of freedom," *International Studies in Philosophy* 19(1) (1987): 33–51.)

SELECTED
BIBLIOGRAPHY

BOOKS

Arnauld, Antoine (trans.). *On True and False Ideas: New Objections to Descartes' Meditations and Descartes' Replies.* Lewiston: Mellon Press, 1990.

Beck, Leslie John. *The Metaphysics of Descartes: A Study of the Meditations.* Oxford: Clarendon Press, 1965.

—— *The Method of Descartes: A Study of the Regulae.* Oxford: Clarendon Press, 1952.

Biffle, Christopher. *A Guided Tour of René Descartes' "Meditations on First Philosophy."* Mountain View: Mayfield, 1989.

Bordo, Susan R. *The Flight to Objectivity: Essays on Cartesianism and Culture.* Albany: Suny Press, 1987.

Broadie, Frederick. *An Approach to Descartes' Meditations.* London: Athlone Press, 1970.

Champigny, Robert. *Sense, Antisense, Nonsense.* Gainesville: University Press of Florida, 1986.

Charpentier, Thomas Victor. *Essai sur la méthode de Descartes.* Delagrave, 1869.

Cottingham, John. *Descartes.* Oxford: Blackwell, 1986.

—— *The Rationalists: A History of Western Philosophy.* Oxford: Oxford University Press, 1988.

Curley, E. M. *Descartes against the Skeptics.* Cambridge: Modern Age, 1978.

Doney, W. (ed.). *Descartes: A Collection of Critical Essays.* Garden City: University of Notre Dame Press, 1968.

—— *Eternal Truths and the Cartesian Circle: A Collection of Studies.* New York & London: Garland, 1987.

Feinberg, Joel (ed.). *Reason and Responsibility.* Belmont: Wadsworth Publishing Co., 1989.

Frankfurt, Harry G. *Demons, Dreamers, and Madmen: The Defense of Reason in Descartes' Meditations.* Indianapolis: Bobbs-Merrill, 1970.

Gouhier, H. *La pensée métaphysique de Descartes.* Paris, 1968.

Gueroult, M. *Descartes selon l'ordre des raisons.* Paris: Aubier-Montaigne,

1953; 2nd edn, 1968.

Gueroult, Martial, and Ariew, Roger (trans.). *The Soul and God: Descartes' Philosophy interpreted according to the Order of Reasons*. Minneapolis: University of Minnesota Press, 1984.

Hintikka, J., and Unto, R. *The Method of Analysis*. Dordrecht: D. Reidel, 1974.

Hooker, Michael (ed.). *Descartes: Critical and Interpretive Essays*. Baltimore: Johns Hopkins University Press, 1978.

Katz, Jerrold J. *Cogitations: A Study of the "Cogito" in Relation to the Philosophy of Logic and Language and a Study of them in Relation to the "Cogito"*. Oxford: Oxford University Press, 1986.

Kenny, A. *Descartes: A Study of his Philosophy*. New York: Random House, 1968.

Lefèvre, R. *La Métaphysique de Descartes*, Paris: Presses universitaires de France, 1959; 2nd edn, 1966; 3rd edn, 1972.

Lennon, T. M., Nicholas, J. M., and Davis, J. W. (eds). *Problems of Cartesianism*. Kingston and Montreal: McGill – Queen's University Press, 1982.

Mackenzie, Patrick T. *The Problems of Philosophers: An Introduction*. Buffalo: Prometheus, 1989.

Malcolm, N. *Dreaming*. London: Routledge & Kegan Paul; New York: Humanities Press, 1959.

Martin, J. (abbé). *Descartes. Première Méditation, avec une notice biographique et une étude sur la philosophie de Descartes*. Paris: Poussielgue, 1882.

Merrylees, W. A. *Descartes: An Examination of some Features of his Metaphysics and Method*. Melbourne: Melbourne University Press, 1943.

Rodis-Lewis, Geneviève (ed.). *Méthode et métaphysique chez Descartes: Etudes en français*. New York and London: Garland, 1987.

Rorty, Amélie Oksenberg (ed.). *Essays on Descartes' Meditations*. Berkeley: University of California Press, 1986.

Schouls, P. A. *The Imposition of Method: A Study of Descartes and Locke*. Oxford: Clarendon Press, 1980.

Serrus, Charles. *La Méthode de Descartes et son application à la métaphysique*. Alcan, 1933.

Sesonske, A., and Fleming, N. (eds). *Meta-Meditations: Studies in Descartes*. Belmont: Wadsworth Publishing Co., 1965.

Smith, Norman Kemp. *Studies in Cartesian Philosophy*. London: Macmillan, 1902; reprinted New York: Russell & Russell, 1962.

Soffer, Walter. *From Science to Subjectivity: An Interpretation of Descartes' "Meditations"*. New York: Greenwood Press, 1987.

Tweyman, Stanley. *Descartes and Hume: Selected Topics*. Delmar: Caravan Press, 1989.

Versfeld, Marthinius. *An Essay on the Metaphysics of Descartes*. London: Methuen, 1940.

Williams, B. *Descartes: The Project of Pure Inquiry*. Atlantic Highlands: Humanities Press, 1978.

ARTICLES

Abhraham, W. E. "Disentangling the 'Cogito'," *Mind* 83 (1974): 75–94.

Aldrich, Virgil C. "Descartes' method of doubt: an interpretation and appreciation," *Philosophy of Science* 4 (1937): 395–411, 521–45. [Commemorative lecture].

Allaire, E. B. "The circle of ideas and the circularity of the *Meditations*," *Dialogue* (Canada) 5 (1966): 131–153.

Alston, W. F. "The ontological argument revisited," *Philosophical Review* 69 (1960): 452–74.

Anderson, D. R. "Three views of the *Cogito*," *Kinesis* 13 (1983–4): 11–20.

Arthur, Richard T. W. "Continuous creation, continuous time: a refutation of the alleged discontinuity of Cartesian time," *Journal of the History of Philosophy* 26 (1988): 349–75.

Ashworth, E. J. "Descartes' theory of objective reality," *The New Scholasticism* 49 (1975): 331–40.

Attig, Thomas. "Descartes and circularity: the precipitous rush to defense," *The Modern Schoolman* 54 (1977): 368–78.

—— "Husserl's interpretation and critique of Descartes in his 'Cartesian Meditations'," *The Modern Schoolman* 55 (1978): 271–81.

Ayer, Alfred Jules. "Cogito ergo sum," *Analysis* (1953): 27–31.

—— "I think, therefore I am," in his *The Problem of Knowledge*. London, Macmillan, 1956, pp. 45–54. Reprinted Harmondsworth: Penguin Books.

Baier, Annette. "The idea of true God in Descartes," in *Essays on Descartes' Meditations*, ed. Amélie Oksenberg Rorty. Berkeley: University of California Press, 1986, pp. 359–87.

Balz, A. G. A. "Concerning the ontological argument," *Review of Metaphysics* 7 (1953): 207–24.

Bannan, John F. "Theories of truth and methodic doubt," *The Modern Schoolman* 58 (1981): 107–13.

Baumer, Michael R. "Sketch for a modal interpretation of Descartes *Cogito*," *Philosophy Research Archives* 11 (1985): 635–55.

Beck, L. J. "Cogitatio in Descartes," *Cartesio nel terzo centenario del discorso del metodo* 35 (1937): 41–52.

—— "Descartes' cogito reexamined," *Philosophy and Phenomenological Research* 14 (1953–4): 212–20.

Beck, R. N. "Some remarks on logic and the *Cogito*," in *Cartesian Essays*, ed. B. Magnus and J. B. Wilbur, The Hague: Martinus Nijhoff, 1969, pp. 57–64.

Bell, P. "Poesy and argument in Descartes' *Meditations*," *Newsletter of the Society for Seventeenth-century French Studies* 3 (1981): 71–8.

Bencivenga, E. "Descartes, dreaming, and Professor Wilson," *Journal of the History of Philosophy* 21 (1983): 75–85.

Beneš, Jaroslav. "L'importance des Méditations métaphysiques du Descartes au point de vue de sa méthode," *Congrès Descartes: Travaux du IXe Congrès International de Philosophie*, Paris, 1937.

—— "Quomodo Cartesius problema criticum posuerit et solverit," *Divus Thomas* (Piacenza) 40 (1937): 472–87.

Bergoffen, Debra B. "Cartesian dialectics and the autonomy of reason," *International Studies in Philosophy* 13 (1981): 1–8.

—— "Cartesian doubt as methodology: reflective imagination and philosophical freedom," *Proceedings of the American Catholic Philosophical Association* 50 (1976): 186–95.

Berleant, A. "On the circularity of the Cogito", *Philosophy and Phenomenological Research* 26 (1965–6): 431–3.

Berthet, J. "La méthode de Descartes avant le Discours," *Revue de métaphysique et de morale* 4 (1896): 399–415.

Bestor, T. W. "There are no certain indications by which we may clearly distinguish wakefulness from sleep," *Journal of Thought* 13 (1978): 216–25.

Beth, E. W. "*Cogito ergo sum*: Raisonnement ou intuition?," *Dialectica* 12 (1959): 223–35.

Beyssade, Jean-Marie. "Descartes on freedom of the will," *Graduate Faculty Philosophy Journal* 13 (1988): 81–96.

—— " 'Mais quoi ce sont des fous': sur un passage controverse de la 'Première Méditation'," *Revue de métaphysique et de morale* (1973): 273–94.

Beyssade, Michelle. "System and training in Descartes' 'Meditations'," *Graduate Faculty Philosophy Journal* 13 (1988): 97–114.

Beyssade, Michelle and Beyssade, Jean-Marie. "Des Méditations métaphysiques aux Méditations de Philosophie Première: pourquoi retraduire Descartes?", *Revue de métaphysique et de morale* 94 (1989): 23–36.

Blackwell, R. J. "Reflections on Descartes' methods of analysis and synthesis," in *History of Philosophy in the Making: A Symposium of Essays to Honor Professor James D. Collins on his 65th Birthday*, ed. by L. J. Thro. Washington, DC, 1982, pp. 119–132.

Blumenfeld, D., and Blumenfeld, J. B. "Can I know that I am not dreaming?," in *Descartes: Critical and Interpretive Essays*, ed. Michael Hooker. Baltimore: Johns Hopkins University Press, 1978, pp. 234–55.

Boardman, W. S. "Dreams, dramas, and scepticism," *Philosophical Quarterly* (Scotland) 29 (1979): 220–8.

Bolton, Martha. "Confused and obscure ideas of sense," in *Essays on Descartes' Meditations*, ed. Amélie Oksenberg Rorty. Berkeley: University of California Press, 1986, pp. 389–403.

Boos, W. "A self-referential *Cogito*," *Philosophical Studies* 44 (1983): 269–90.

Booth, C. S. "Cogito: performance or existential inconsistency?," *Journal of Critical Analysis* 4 (1972–3): 1–8.

Botkin, R. "Descartes' First Meditation: a point of contact for contemporary philosophical methods," *Southern Journal of Philosophy* 10 (1972): 353–8.

—— "What can we do when dreaming: a reply to Professor Davis," *Southern Journal of Philosophy* 10 (1972): 367–72.

Bouwsma O.K. "Descartes' evil genius," *Philosophical Review* 58 (1949): 141–51.

—— "Descartes' scepticism of the senses," *Mind: A Quarterly Review of Psychology and Philosophy* 54 (1945): 312–23.

—— "Failure I: are dreams illusions?" in *Toward a New Sensibility: Essays of O. K. Bouwsma*, ed. by J. L. Craft and R. E. Hustwit. Lincoln, Nebr.: 1982, pp. 61–88.

Boyer, Charles (SJ). "Le cogito dans Saint Augustin," *Cartesio nel terzo centenario del discorso del metodo* 35 (1937): 79–83, and CD 1: 1937, 89–92.

Bracken, Henry. "Descartes–Orwell–Chomsky: three philosophers of the demonic," *The Human Context* 4 (1972): 523–51.

Bréhier, Emile. "The creation of the eternal truths in Descartes's system," in *Descartes: A Collection of Critical Essays*, ed. Willis Doney. London: University of Notre Dame Press, 1968, pp. 192–208.

Brodeur, Jean-Paul. "Thèse et performance dans les 'Méditations' de Descartes," *Dialogue* (Canada) 14 (1975): 51–79.

Broughton, J. "Skepticism and the Cartesian circle," *Canadian Journal of Philosophy* 14 (1984): 593–616.

Buchdahl, Gerd. "Descartes: method and metaphysics" in *Metaphysics and the Philosophy of Science*. Cambridge, Mass.: MIT Press, 1969, pp. 79–180.

Burkey, John. "Descartes, skepticism, and Husserl's hermeneutic practice," *Husserl Studies* 7.1 (1990): 1–27.

Calhoun, David H. "God and self: ontology and intersubjectivity", *The Journal of Value Inquiry* 22 (1988): 23–38.

Carney, J. D. "*Cogito, ergo sum* and *Sum res cogitans*," *Philosophical Review* 71 (1962): 492–96.

Carr, D. "The 'Fifth Meditation' and Husserl's Cartesianism," *Philosophy and Phenomenological Research* 34 (1973–4): 14–35.

Carriero, John. "The First Meditation," *Pacific Philosophical Quarterly* 68: 3–4 (1987): 222–48.

—— "The Second Meditation and the essence of the mind," in *Essays on Descartes' Meditations*, ed. Amélie Oksenberg Rorty. Berkeley: University of California Press, 1986, pp. 199–221.

Caton, H. P. "Analytic history of philosophy: the case of Descartes," *Philosophical Forum* 12 (1981): 273–94.

—— "Descartes' anonymous writings: a recapituation," *The Southern Journal of Philosophy* 20 (1982): 299–311.

—— "Kennington on Descartes' evil genius" *Journal of the History of Ideas* 34 (1973): 639–41.

—— "On the interpretation of the *Meditations*," *Man and World* 3 (1970): 224–45

—— "Rejoinder: the cunning of the evil demon", *Journal of the History of Ideas* 34 (1973): 643–4.

—— "Will and reason in Descartes' theory of error," *The Journal of Philosophy* 72: 27 (1975): 87–104.

Chappell, Vere. "The theory of ideas," in *Essays on Descartes' Meditations*, ed. Amélie Oksenberg Rorty. Berkeley: University of California Press, 1986, pp. 177–98.

Charlton, William. "La certitude cartésienne", *Archives de Philosophie* 38 (1975): 595–601.

Chinn, E. Y. "A journey around the Cartesian circle," *Philosophy Research Archives* 9 (1983): 279–92.

Chopra, Y. N. "The Cogito and the certainty of one's own existence," *Journal of the History of Philosophy* 12: 2 (1974): 171–9.

Clarke, D. M. "Descartes' use of 'demonstration' and 'deduction'," *The Modern Schoolman* 54 (1976–7): 333–44.

Cook, Monte "The alleged ambiguity of 'idea' in Descartes' philosophy," *Southwestern Journal of Philosophy* 6 (1975): 87–94.

—— "Descartes' doubt of minds," *Dialogue* (Canada) 27 (1988): 31–9.

Coolidge, Julian L. "The origin of analytic geometry," *Osiris: Studies in the History and Philosophy of Science* 1 (1936): 231–50.

Costa, M. J. "What Cartesian ideas are not," *Journal of the History of Philosophy* 21 (1983): 537–49.

Cottingham, John. "Descartes' *Sixth Meditation*: The external world, nature and human experience", *Philosophy*, Suppl. 20 (1986): 73–89.

—— "Mathematics in the First Meditation: a reply to Professor O'Briant," *Studia Leibnitiana* 10 (1978): 113–15.

—— "The role of the malignant demon," *Studia Leibnitiana* 8 (1976): 257–64.

Cress, D. "Does Descartes have two 'ontological arguments'?", *International Studies in Philosophy* 7 (1975): 155–66.

Crocker, S. F. "Descartes' ontological argument and the existing thinker," 53 *The Modern Schoolman* (1975–6): 347–77.

Cummins, R. "Epistemology and the Cartesian circle", *Theoria* 41 (1975): 112–24.

Curley, E. M. "Analysis in the *Meditations*: the quest for clear and distinct ideas," in *Essays on Descartes' Meditations*, ed. Amélie Oksenberg Rorty. Berkeley: University of California Press, 1986, pp. 153–76.

—— "Descartes on the creation of the eternal truths," *Philosophical Review* 93 (1984): 569–97.

—— "Dreaming and conceptual revision," *Australasian Journal of Philosophy* 53 (1975): 119–41.

Daniel, S. H. "Doubts and doubting in Descartes," *The Modern Schoolman* 56 (1978–9): 57–65.

Danto, A. "The representational character of ideas and the problem of the external world," in *Descartes: Critical and Interpretive Essays*, ed. Michael Hooker. Baltimore: The Johns Hopkins University Press, 1978, pp. 287–98.

Dascal, Marcelo. "On the role of metaphysics in Descartes' thought," *Man and World* 4 (1971): 460–70.

Davies, K. "The impersonal formulation of the Cogito," *Analysis* 41 (1980–1), 134–7.

Davis, R. "Dreams and dreaming: a reply to Professor Botkin," *Southern Journal of Philosophy* 10 (1972): 373–8.

—— "I have on rare occasions while half asleep been deceived," *Southern Journal of Philosophy* 10 (1972): 373–8.

Delahunty, R. "Descartes' cosmological argument," *Philosophical Quarterly* (Scotland) 30 (1980): 34–46.

Deutscher, Max. "Stories, pictures, arguments," *Philosophy* 62 (1987): 159–70.

Diaz, J. A. "Cartesian analyticity", *Southern Journal of Philosophy* 26: 1 (1988): 47–55.

Dietl, P. J. "The feasibility of hyperbolical doubt," *Philosophical Studies* 20 (1969): 70–3.

Dilley, F. B. "Descartes' cosmological argument," *Monist* 54 (1970): 427–40.

Dixit, Shriniwas. "Descartes' dogmatism," *Philosophical Quarterly* (India) 22 (1949–50): 175–8.

Donagan, A. "Descartes's 'synthetic' treatment of the real distinction between mind and body," in *Descartes: Critical and Interpretive Essays*, ed. Michael Hooker. Baltimore: The Johns Hopkins University Press, 1978, pp. 186–196.

Doney, Willis. "The Cartesian circle," *Journal of the History of Ideas* 16 (1955): 324–38.

—— "Curley and Wilson on Descartes," *Philosophy Research Archives* 6 (1980): 1376.

—— "Descartes' conception of perfect knowledge", *Journal of the History of Philosophy*, 8: 4 (1970): 387–403.

—— "The geometrical presentation of Descartes's a priori proof," in *Descartes: Critical and Interpretive Essays*, ed. Michael Hooker. Baltimore: The Johns Hopkins University Press, 1978, pp. 1–25.

Dore, C. "Descartes's Meditation V: proof of God's existence," in *The Existence and Nature of God*, ed. A. J. Freddoso. Notre Dame, Ind.: University of Notre Dame Press 1983, pp. 143–60.

Dorter, K. "First Philosophy: metaphysics or epistemology?," *Dialogue* (Canada) 11 (1972): 1–22.

—— "Science and religion in Descartes' 'Meditations'," *Thomist* 37 (1973): 313–40.

Dräseke, Johannes. "Zu René Descartes' cogito ergo sum," *Archiv für Geschichte der Philosophie* 32 (1919–20): 45–55.

Dreisbach, D. F. "Circularity and consistency in Descartes," *Canadian Journal of Philosophy* 8 (1978): 59–78.

Dreyfus, Ginette. "Discussion sur le 'cogito' et l'axiome 'pour penser il faut être'," *Revue internationale de philosophie* 6 (1952): 117–25.

Drury, S. "The relationship of substance and simple natures in the philosophy of Descartes," *Canadian Journal of Philosophy*, Suppl. 4 (1978): 37–58.

Dupré, L. "Alternatives to the Cogito," *The Review of Metaphysics* 160 (1987): 687–716.

Dyksterhuis, E. J. "La méthode et les essais de Descartes," in *Descartes et les cartésianisme hollandais*. Paris: Presses Universitaires de France, 1950, pp. 21–44.

Elliot, Robert, and Smith, Michael. "Descartes, God and the evil spirit," *Sophia* 17 (1978): 33–6.

Erde, E. L. "Analyticity, the Cogito, and self-knowledge in Descartes' *Meditations*," *Southwestern Journal of Philosophy* 6: 1 (1975): 79–85.

Evans, J. L. "Error and the will," *Philosophy* 38 (1963): 136–48.

Fafara, Richard J. "An Eighth Set of Objections to Descartes's 'Meditations'?," *The Modern Schoolman* 57 (1979): 25–44.

Farkas, Viorica. "Dreaming in Descartes à la Wilson," *Philosophy Research*

Archives 11 (1985): 111–25.

—— "Epistemic appraisal and the Cartesian circle," *Philosophical Studies* 27: 1 (1975): 37–55.

Feldman, F. "On the performatory interpretation of the *Cogito*," *Philosophical Review* 82 (1973): 345–63.

Field, R. W. "Descartes' proof of the existence of matter," *Mind* 94:374 (1985): 244–9.

Flage, Daniel E. "Descartes's Cogito," *Historical Philosophical Quarterly* 2 (1985): 163–78.

Flew, A. "Philosophical doubt and Cartesian certainty," in *An Introduction to Western Philosophy*. Indianapolis: 1971, pp. 302–30.

Forguson, Lynd. "Multi-media 'Meditations'," *Teaching Philosophy* 5 (1982): 301–9.

Foti, Veronique. "The functions and ordering of the theistic arguments in Descartes' 'Meditations'," *Auslegung* 4 (1976): 7–20.

Frankfurt, H. G. "Descartes' discussion of his existence in the Second Meditation," *Philosophical Review* 3: 75 (1966): 329–56.

—— "Descartes on the consistency of reason," in *Descartes: Critical and Interpretive Essays*, ed. Michael Hooker. Battimore: The Johns Hopkins University Press, 1978, pp. 26–39.

—— "Descartes on the creation of the eternal truths," *Philosophical Review* 86 (1977): 36–57.

—— "Descartes' validation of reason", *American Philosophical Quarterly* 2 (1965): 149–56.

—— "Memory and the Cartesian circle," *Philosophical Review* 71 (1962): 504–11.

Funkenstein, A. "Descartes, eternal truths, and the divine omnipotence," *Studies in the History and Philosophy of Science* 6 (1975): 185–99.

Garber, Daniel. "Science and certainty in Descartes," in *Descartes: Critical and Interpretive Essays*, ed. Michael Hooker. Baltimore: The Johns Hopkins University Press, 1978, pp. 114–51.

—— "The scientific background to Descartes' *Meditations*," in *Essays on Descartes' Meditations*, ed. Amélie Oksenberg Rorty. Berkeley: University of California Press, 1986, pp. 81–116.

Garber, Daniel, and Cohen, Lesley. "A point of order: analysis, synthesis, and Descartes's *Principles*," *Archiv für Geschichte der Philosophie* 64 (1982): 134–47.

Garns, Rudy L. "Descartes and indubitability," *Southern Journal of Philosophy* 26: 1 (1988): 83–100.

Gavin, William J. "The meaning of a person," *Existential Psychiatry* 7 (1969): 33–5.

Gewirth, Alan. "The Cartesian circle," *The Philosophical Review* 50 (1941): 368–95.

—— "The Cartesian circle reconsidered," *The Journal of Philosophy* 67 (1970): 668–85.

—— "Clearness and distinctness in Descartes," *Philosophy* 18 (1943): 17–36.

—— "Experience and the non-mathematical in the Cartesian method," *Journal of the History of Ideas* 2 (1941): 183–210.

Glouberman, M. "God incorporated," *Sophia* (Australia) 26: 3 (1987):

13–21.

—— "Mind and body: two real distinctions," *Southern Journal of Philosophy* 22 (1984): 347–60.

—— "The structure of Cartesian scepticism," *Southern Journal of Philosophy* 21 (1983): 343–57.

Gombay, A. " '*Cogito ergo sum*': inference or argument?", in *Cartesian Studies*, ed. R. J. Butler. Oxford: Clarendon Press, 1972, pp. 71–88.

—— "Descartes and madness," in *Early Modern Philosophy*, ed. Georges J., D. Moyal and Stanley Tweyman. Delmar: Caravan Press, 1986, pp. 21–33.

Gonda, J. "Kennington's Descartes and Eddington's two tables," *Graduate Faculty Philosophy Journal* 11: 2, (1986) (*Essays in Honor of Richard Kennington*, ed. M. Davis), pp. 111–21.

Götterbarn, D. "An equivocation in Descartes' proof for knowledge of the eternal world," *Idealistic Studies* 1 (1971): 142–8.

Gouhier, H. "L'ordre des raisons selon Descartes," in *Cahiers de Royaumont, Philosophie no. II*. Paris: Editions de Minuit, 1957.

—— "La preuve ontologique de Descartes," *Revue international de philosophie* 7: 28 (1954): 299.

—— "La veracité divine dans la Méditation VI," *Les études philosophiques* (1956): 296–310.

Goyard-Fabre, S. "Descartes et la méthode," *Ecole des lettres* 63 (1972): 37–41.

Grene, M. "Idea and judgement in Descartes' *Third Meditation*: an object lesson in philosophical historiography," *The Independent Journal of Philosophy* (*Unabhängige Zeitschrift für Philosophie*) 5–6 (Modernity), (1988): 113–20.

Grimaldi, Nicholas. "Sur la volonté de l'homme chez Descartes et notre ressemblance avec Dieu," *Archives de Philosophie* 50 (1987): 95–107.

Grimm, R. "Cogito, ergo sum," *Theoria* 31 (1965): 159–73.

Groarke, L. "Descartes' First Meditation: something old, something new, something borrowed," *Journal of the History of Philosophy* 22 (1984): 281–301.

Guérin, M. "Le malin génie et l'instauration de la pensée comme philosophie," *Revue de métaphysique et de morale* 79 (1974): 145–76.

Gueroult, M. "Le *cogito* et l'ordre des axiomes métaphysiques dans les *Principia philosophiae Cartesianae* de Spinoza," *Archives de Philosophie* 23 (1960): 171–85.

—— "De la méthode prescrite par Descartes pour comprendre sa philosophie," *Archiv für Geschichte der Philosophie* 44 (1962): 172–84.

Hanfling, Oswald. "Can there be a method of Doubt?," *Philosophy* 59 (1984): 505–11.

Harries, K. "Irrationalism and Cartesian method," *Journal of Existentialism* 6 (1965–6): 295–304.

Harrison, J. "The incorrigibility of the Cogito," *Mind* 93 (1984): 321–35.

Hartnack, J. "A note on the logic of one of Descartes' arguments," *International Philosophical Quarterly* 15 (1975): 181–4.

Hatfield, Gary. "Descartes's *Meditations* as cognitive exercises," *Philosophy and Literature* (1985): 41–58.

—— "The senses and the fleshless eye: the Mediations as cognitive exercises", in *Essays on Descartes' Meditations*, ed. Amélie Oksenberg Rorty. Berkeley: University of California Press, 1986, pp. 45–79.

Hauptli, B. W. "Doubting 'Descartes's self-doubt'," *Philosophy Research Archives* 6 (1980): 1399.

—— "Frankfurt on Descartes: consistency or validation of reason," *International Studies in Philosophy* 15 (1983): 59–70.

Heckmann, H.-D. "What a res cogitans is – and why I am one," *Ratio* 25 (1983): 121–36.

Heimsoeth, Heinz. "Sur quelques rapports des Règles de Descartes avec les Méditations," *Revue de métaphysique et de morale* 21 (1913): 526–36.

Henry, M. "Sur *l'égo du cogito*," in *La passion de la raison*, ed. J. -L. Marion and J. Deprun. Paris: 1983, pp. 97–112.

Hinman, Lawrence M. "Descartes' children: the skeptical legacy of Cartesianism," *The New Scholasticism* 56 (1982): 355–70.

Hintikka, J. "*Cogito, ergo sum* as an inference and a performance," *Philosophical Review* 72 (1963): 487–96.

—— "*Cogito, ergo sum*: inference or performance?," *Philosophical Review* 71 (1962): 3–32.

—— "A discourse on Descartes's method," in *Descartes: Critical and Interpretive Essays*, ed. Michael Hooker. Baltimore: The Johns Hopkins University Press, 1978, pp. 74–88.

Hoenen, S. J. "Descartes's mechanicism," in *Descartes: A Collection of Critical Essays*, ed. Willis Doney. London: University of Notre Dame Press, 1968, pp. 353–68.

Holland, A. J. "Scepticism and causal theories of knowledge," *Mind* 86 (1977): 555–73.

Hooker, M. "Descartes' argument for the claim that his essence is to think," *Grazer Philosophische Studien* 1 (1975): 143–63.

Hughes, Robert D. "Descartes' ontological argument as not identical to the causal arguments," *The New Scholasticism* 49 (1975): 473–85.

—— "Liminaire: le 'cercle' des Méditations: un état des recherches récentes", *Bulletin cartésien* 7 (1978): 1–12.

Humber, J. M. "Clarity, distinctness, the *Cogito* and 'I'," *Idealistic Studies*, 17: 1 (1987): 15–37.

—— "Descartes' ontological argument as non-causal," *The New Scholasticism* 44 (1970): 449–59.

—— "Doubts about Descartes's 'Self-Doubt'," *Philosophical Review* 87 (1978): 253–8.

—— "Recognizing clear and distinct perceptions", *Philosophy and Phenomenological Research* 41 (1980–1): 487–507.

Hunter, J. F. M. "The difference between dreaming and being awake," *Mind* 92 (1983): 80–93.

Idoniboye, D. E. "Descartes and his clear and distinct ideas," *Cahiers philosophiques africains*, (1974): 25–35.

Imlay, R. A. "Descartes' a priori proof for God and the Second Set of Objections to the *Meditations*," *The Modern Schoolman* 63 (1985–6): 111–18.

—— "Descartes' ontological argument," *The New Scholasticism* 43 (1969):

SELECTED BIBLIOGRAPHY

440–8.

—— "Descartes' ontological argument: a causal argument," *The New Scholasticism* 45 (1971): 348–51.

—— "Descartes' two hypotheses of the evil genius," *Studia Leibnitiana* (1980): 205–14.

—— "Dieu, solipsisme et probabilité dans les *Méditations* de Descartes," *Studia Leibnitiana* 20: 1 (1988): 80–6.

—— "Intuition and the Cartesian circle," *Journal of the History of Philosophy* 11: 1 (1973): 19–27.

Immerwahr, J. "Descartes' two cosmological proofs," *The New Scholasticism* 56 (1982): 346–54.

Ishiguro, Hide. "The status of necessity and impossibility in Descartes," in *Essays on Descartes' Meditations*, ed. Amélie Oksenberg Rorty. Berkeley: University of California Press, 1986, pp. 459–71.

Jardine, David W. "Piaget's clay and Descartes' wax," *Educational Theory* 38 (1988): 287–98.

Jennings, Jerry L. "The fallacious origin of the mind-body problem: a reconsideration of Descartes' method and results," *The Journal of Mind and Behavior* (1985): 357–72.

Johnston, J. M. "Cartesian lucidity," *Filosofia* 19 (1968): 663–70.

Katsoff, Louis O. "Cogito ergo sum," *Revue de métaphysique et de morale* 63 (1958): 251–62.

Katz, Jerrold J. "Descartes' *Cogito*," *Pacific Philosophical Quarterly* 68: 3–4 (1987): 175–96.

Keaton, A. E. "Descartes' method," *The Southwestern Journal of Philosophy* 5: 1 (1974): 89–95.

Kelly, Matthew J. "The Cartesian circle: Descartes' response to scepticism," *Journal of Thought* 5: 2 (1970): 64–71.

Kennington, R. "The finitude of Descartes' evil genius," *Journal of the History of Ideas* (1971): 441–6.

Kenny, A. "The Cartesian circle and the eternal truths," *The Journal of Philosophy* 67: 19 (1970): 685–700.

—— "The Cartesian spiral," *Revue internationale de philosophie* 37 (1983): 247–56.

—— "Descartes on ideas," in *Descartes: A Collection of Critical Essays*, ed. Willis Doney. London: University of Notre Dame Press, 1968, pp. 227–49.

—— "Descartes' ontological argument," in *Fact and Existence*, ed. J. Margolis. Oxford: Clarendon Press, 1969, pp. 18–36.

Kinghan, Michael. "The external world sceptic escapes again," *Philosophia* (Israel) 16 (1986): 161–6.

Kosman, L. Aryeh. "The naive narrator: meditation in Descartes' *Meditations*," in *Essays on Descartes' Meditations*, ed. Amélie Oksenberg Rorty. Berkeley: University of California Press, 1986, pp. 21–43.

Kraus, Pamela A. " 'Mens humana: res cogitans' and the doctrine of faculties in Descartes' *Meditationes*," *International Studies in Philosophy* 18: 1 (1986): 1–18.

Kubitz, O. A. "Scepticism and intuition in the philosophy of Descartes," *Philosophical Review* 48 (1939): 472–91.

Kumar, D. "Doubt and Descartes' method," *Visva-Bharati Journal of Philosophy* 3 (1966–7): 101–11.

Kunkel, J. "Dreams, metaphors and scepticism," *Philosophy Today* 25 (1981): 307–16.

La Croix, R. R. "Descartes on God's ability to do the logically impossible," *Canadian Journal of Philosophy* 14 (1984): 455–75.

Lachterman, David R. "*Objectum purae Matheseos*: mathematical construction and the passage from essence to existence," in *Essays on Descartes' Meditations*, ed. Amélie Oksenberg Rorty. Berkeley: University of California Press, 1986, pp. 435–58.

Lang, Berel. "Plotting philosophy: between the acts of philosophical genre," *Philosophy and Literature* 12 (1988): 190–210.

Lascola, R. A. "Descartes' unsound argument," *The New Scholasticism* 52 (1978): 41–53.

LeBlond, Jean. "Cartesian method and classical logic," *The Modern Schoolman* 1: 15 (1937): 4–6.

Levett, M. J. "Note on the alleged Cartesian circle," *Mind: A Quarterly Review of Psychology and Philosophy* 46 (1937): 206–13.

Levin, M. E. "Descartes' proof that he is not his body," *Australasian Journal of Philosophy* 51 (1973): 115–23.

Leyden, W. von. "*Cogito, ergo sum*," *Proceedings of the Aristotelian Society* 63 (1962–3): 67–82.

Lipson, Morris. "Psychological doubt and the Cartesian circle," *Canadian Journal of Philosophy* 19 (1989): 225–46.

Locke, Don. "Mind, matter, and the *Meditations*," *Mind* 90 (1981): 343–66.

Loeb, L. E. "Is there radical dissimulation in Descartes' *Meditations*?," in *Essays on Descartes' Meditations*, ed. Amélie Oksenberg Rorty. Berkeley: University of California Press, 1986, pp. 243–70.

—— "Was Descartes sincere in his appeal to the natural light?," *Journal of the History of Philosophy* 26: 3 (1988): 377–406.

Lott, T. L. "Descartes on phantom limbs," *Mind and Language* 1: 3 (1986): 243–71.

Lucas, Peter G. "Descartes and the wax: rejoinder [to J. J. C. Smart, *q.v.*]," *Philosophical Quarterly* (India) 1 (1951): 348–52.

Luft, Eric V. D. "The Cartesian circle: Hegelian logic to the rescue," *Heythrop Journal* 30 (1989): 403–18.

Macdonald, Margaret. "Sleeping and waking," *Mind: A Quarterly Review of Psychology and Philosophy* 62 (1953): 202–15.

McHugh, Joseph. "Enemy of doubt," *Blackfriars* 10 (1929): 1369–74.

MacIver, A. M. "A note on the ontological proof," *Analysis* 8: 3 (1948): 48.

MacKenzie, Ann Wilbur. "Descartes on life and sense," *Canadian Journal of Philosophy* 19: 2 (1989): 163–92.

—— "Descartes on sensory representation: a study of the *Dioptrics*," *Canadian Journal of Philosophy*, Suppl. 16 (1990): 109–47.

McKinnon, Alastair. "Some conceptual ties in Descartes' 'Meditations'," *Dialogue* (Canada) 18 (1979): 166–174.

MacMurray, John. "The rejection of dualism," in his *The Self as Agent*, The Gifford lectures 1953. London: Faber & Faber, 1957, pp. 62–83.

McRae, R. "Innate ideas," in *Cartesian Studies*, ed. R. J. Butler. Oxford:

Clarendon Press, 1972, 32–54.

Magnus, B. "The modalities of Descartes' proofs for the existence of God," in *Cartesian Essays*, ed. B. Magnus and J. B. Wilbur. The Hague: Mouton, 1969, pp. 77–87.

Malcolm, N. "Descartes' ontological proof," in *Fact and Existence*, ed. J. Margolis. Oxford: Clarendon Press, 1969, pp. 36–43.

—— "Descartes' proof that he is essentially a non-material thing," in *Thought and Knowledge*, ed. N. Malcolm. Ithaca: 1977, pp. 58–84.

—— "Descartes's proof that his essence is thinking," *Philosophical Review* (1965): 315–38.

—— "Dreaming and scepticism," *Philosophical Review* 65 (1956): 14–37.

Manteau-Bonamy, H.-M. "Réflexions critiques sur les Méditations de Descartes," *Revue Thomiste* 63 (1963): 37–72.

Marc-Wogau, K. "Der Zweifel Descartes' und das cogito ergo sum", *Theoria* 20 (1954): 128–52.

—— "The Cartesian doubt and the *Cogito ergo sum*," in his *Philosophical Essays*. Lund: Gleerup, 1967, pp. 41–60.

Margolis, J. " 'I exist'," *Mind* 73 (1964): 571–4.

Margot, J -P. "L'analyse et la synthèse chez Descartes', *De Philosophia* 3 (1982): 33–44.

Marion, Jean-Luc. "The essential incoherence of Descartes' definition of divinity," in *Essays on Descartes' Meditations*, ed. Amélie Oksenberg Rorty. Berkeley: University of California Press, 1986, pp. 297–338.

Marion, M. "Logique et cogito cartésien," *Phi Zéro* 10 (1982): 3–17.

Mark, T. C. "Descartes' proof in Meditation III," *International Studies in Philosophy* 7 (1975): 69–88.

Markie, P. J. "Clear and distinct perception and metaphysical certainty," *Mind* 88 (1979): 97–104.

—— "Dreams and deceivers in Meditation One," *Philosophical Review* 90 (1981): 185–209.

Marlies, Mike. "Doubt, reason, and Cartesian therapy," in *Descartes: Critical and Interpretive Essays*, ed. Michael Hooker. Baltimore: The Johns Hopkins University Press, 1978, pp. 89–113.

Martin, Bradley D. "Descartes' use of 'nature' in the 'Meditations'," *Dialogue* 23 (1981): 37–42.

Martin, Glen T. "A critique of Nietzsche's metaphysical scepticism," *International Studies in Philosophy* 19 (1987): 51–9.

Mathrani, G. N. "A positivist analysis of Descartes' ontological arguments for God," *Philosophical Quarterly* (India) 30 (1957): 183–7.

—— "Descartes' idea of God as the cause of his God-idea: a critical analysis," *Philosophical Quarterly* (India) 33 (1960–1): 249–54.

Mattern, Ruth. "Descartes: 'All things which I conceive clearly and distinctly in corporeal objects are in them'," in *Essays on Descartes' Meditations*, ed. Amélie Oksenberg Rorty. Berkeley: University of California Press, 1986, pp. 473–89.

—— "Descartes's correspondence with Elizabeth: conceiving both the union and distinction of mind and body," in *Descartes: Critical and Interpretive Essays*, ed. Michael Hooker. Baltimore: The Johns Hopkins University Press, 1978, pp. 212–22.

Matthews, Gareth B. "Descartes and the problem of other minds," in *Essays on Descartes' Meditations*, ed. Amélie Oksenberg Rorty. Berkeley: University of California Press, 1986, pp. 141–51.

Merleau-Ponty, Maurice. "Le cogito," in his *Phénoménologie de la perception*. Paris: Gallimard, 1945, pp. 423–68.

Merrill, K. R. "Did Descartes misunderstand the 'Cogito'?," *Studia Cartesiana* 1 (1979): 111–20.

Merrylees, W. A. "Descartes' theory of knowledge," *Australasian Journal of Psychology and Philosophy* 5 (1927): 202–15.

Mesnard, Pierre. "Méditations sur Descartes en la compagnie de Péguy," *Etudes* (Paris) 230 (1937): 450–68.

—— "Les preuves cartésiennes de l'existence de Dieu dans les Méditations métaphysiques," *Cartesio nel terzo centenario del discorso del metodo* 35 (1937): 599–614.

Miles, Murray. "The idea of extension: innate or adventitious? On R. F. McRae's interpretation of Descartes," *Dialogue* (Canada) 27: 1 (1988): 15–30. Réponse de McRae, 24–9; commentaire de M. Miles, ibid., pp. 29–30.

Miller, Dickinson S. "Descartes' myth and Professor Ryle's fallacy," *The Journal of Philosophy* 48 (1951): 270–80.

Miller, Leonard G. "Descartes, mathematics, and God," *Philosophical Review* 66 (1957): 451–65.

Miller, Robert G. "The ontological argument in St Anselm and Descartes," *The Modern Schoolman* 32 (1955): 341–9; 33 (1955–6): 31–8.

Moore, G. E. "Certainty," in *Descartes: A Collection of Critical Essays*, ed. Willis Doney. London: University of Notre Dame Press, 1968, pp. 27–53.

Moreau, Joseph. "Le cercle cartésien," *Revue générale du Centre-Ouest de la France* 44 (1937): 651–61.

Morris, J. M. "Cartesian certainty," *Australasian Journal of Philosophy* 47 (1969): 161–8.

—— "Descartes' natural light," *Journal of the History of Philosophy* 11 (1973): 169–87.

—— "The essential incoherence of Descartes," *Australasian Journal of Philosophy* 50 (1972): 20–9.

—— "What the skeptic cannot doubt," *Philosophical Forum* 11 (1980): 363–88.

Moyal, Georges J. D. "La preuve ontologique dans l'ordre des raisons," *Revue de métaphysique et de morale* 93 (1988): 246–58.

—— " '. . . Quod circulum non commiserim . . .' Quartae responsiones," *Dialogue* (Canada) 28: 4 (1989): 569–88.

—— "Les structures de la vérité chez Descartes," *Dialogue* (Canada) 26: 3 (1987): 465–90.

—— "Veritas aeterna, Deo volente," *Les etudes philosophiques* 4 (1987): 463–87.

Nadler, S. M. "Scientific certainty and the creation of the eternal truths: a problem in Descartes," *Southern Journal of Philosophy* 25: 2 (1987): 175–92.

Nakhnikian, G. "The Cartesian circle revisited," *American Philosophical*

Quarterly 4 (1967): 251–5.

—— "Descartes's dream argument," in *Descartes: Critical and Interpretive Essays*, ed. Michael Hooker. Baltimore: The Johns Hopkins University Press, 1978, pp. 256–86.

—— "Incorrigibility," *Philosophical Quarterly* (Scotland) 18 (1968): 207–15.

—— "On the logic of Cogito *Propositions*," *Nous* 3: 2 (1969): 197–209.

Nason, John W. "Leibniz's attack on the Cartesian doctrine of extension," *Journal for the History of Ideas* 7 (1946): 447–83.

Navarro Cordon, J. M. "Método y filosofia en Descartes," *Anales del seminario de metafisica* 7 (1972): 39–63.

Nelson, J. O. "In defence of Descartes: squaring a reputed circle," *Dialogue* (Canada) 3 (1964–5): 262–72.

Norburn, R. G. "The Cartesian faux-pas and the malignant demon," *Church Quarterly Review* 272 (1946): 127–54.

Normore, Calvin. "Is Descartes' evil spirit finite or infinite?," *Sophia* (Australia) 18: 2 (1979): 28–32.

—— "Meaning and objective being: Descartes and his sources," in *Essays on Descartes' Meditations*, ed. Amélie Oksenberg Rorty. Berkeley: University of California Press, 1986, pp. 223–41.

O'Briant, W. H. "Doubting the truths of mathematics in Descartes' *Meditations*," *Southern Journal of Philosophy* 15 (1977): 527–35.

O'Neil, B. E. "Cartesian simple natures", *Journal of the History of Philosophy* 10: 2 (1972): 161–79.

—— "Epistemological direct realism in Descartes' philosophy," in *Nature Mathematized*, ed. W. R. Shea, Albuquerque, 1974.

Oakes, R. "Material things: a Cartesian conundrum," *Pacific Philosophical Quarterly* 64 (1983): 144–50.

Odegard, D. "Escaping the Cartesian circle," *American Philosophical Quarterly* 21 (1984): 167–73.

Olgiati, Francesco. "Le phènomènisme de Descartes," *Congrès Descartes: Travaux du IXe Congrès International de Philosophie* 1: 36 (1937): 105–10.

Olson, M. A. "Descartes' First *Meditation*: mathematics and the laws of logic," *Journal of the History of Philosophy* 26: 3 (1988): 407–38.

Orenduff, J. M. "The Cartesian circle," *Philosophical Topics* Suppl. (1982): 109–13.

Orenstein, A. "I think, therefore I am not," *International Logic Review* 6 (1975): 166.

Owen, Roberts B. "Truth and error in Descartes," in *Studies in the History of Ideas*, vol. 1. New York: Columbia University Press, 1918, pp. 149–71.

Palmer, H. "The *Cogito* is semi-circular," *International Logic Review* 12 (1981): 5–15.

—— "Must clocks be material?," *Ratio* 14 (1972): 36–44.

Pastore, Annibale. "Approfondimento del pensiero di Descartes," *Filosofia* (Turin) 1 (1950): 229–37.

—— "Novità sulla logica di Descartes," *Archivio di filosofia* (Rome) 4 (1934): 337–49.

Peltz, R. W. "The logic of the Cogito," *Philosophy and Phenomenological Research* 23 (1962–3): 256–62.

Penelhum, T. "Descartes' ontological argument," in *Fact and Existence*, ed. J. Margolis. Oxford: Clarendon Press, 1969, pp. 43–55.

Peukert, K. W. "Der Wille und die Selbstbewegung des Geistes in Descartes *Meditationen*," *Zeitschrift für Philosophische Forschung* 19 (1965): 87–109, 224–47.

Perkinson, H. J. "Descartes's method," in *Since Socrates: Studies in the History of Western Educational Thought*, ed. H. J. Perkinson. New York: 1980, pp. 74–88.

Pintard, René. "Descartes et Gassendi," *Congrès Descartes. Travaux du IXe Congrès International de Philosophie* 2: 36 (1937): 115–22.

Plantinga, Alvin. "Alston on the ontological argument," in *Descartes: A Collection of Critical Essays*, ed. Willis Doney. London: University of Notre Dame Press, 1968, pp. 303–11.

Pompa, L. "The incoherence of the Cartesian *Cogito*," *Inquiry* 27 (1984): 3–21.

Popkin, Richard H. "Charron and Descartes: the fruits of systematic doubt," *The Journal of Philosophy* 51 (1954): 831–7.

—— "Descartes: sceptique malgré lui," in *The History of Scepticism from Erasmus to Descartes*, Assen: 1960, pp. 197–217.

Prichard, H. A. "Descartes's *Meditations*," in *Descartes: A Collection of Critical Essays*, ed. Willis Doney. London: University of Notre Dame Press, 1968, pp. 140–68.

Prior, A. N. "The *Cogito* of Descartes and the concept of self-confirmation," in *The Foundation of Statements and Decisions*, ed. K. Ajdukiewicz. Berlin: 1965, pp. 47–53.

Putnam, Daniel A. "Doubting, thinking, and possible worlds", *Philosophy Research Archives* 9 (1983): 337–46.

Radner, D. "Descartes' notion of the union of mind and body," *Journal of the History of Philosophy* 9 (1971): 159–70.

—— "Thought and consciousness in Descartes," *Journal of the History of Philosophy* 26: 3 (1988): 439–52.

Rahim, S. A. "The Cartesian doubt," *Proceedings of the Pakistan Philosophical Congress* 10 (1963): 250–8.

Rahman, M. Lutfur. "Are clear and distinct ideas true?," *Proceedings of the Pakistan Philosophical Congress* 16 (1970): 150–61.

Rapaport, W. J. "On *Cogito* propositions," *Philosophical Studies* 29 (1976): 63–8.

Rescher, Nicholas. "The legitimacy of doubt," *Review of Metaphysics* 13 (1959–60): 226–34.

Rodis-Lewis, Geneviève. "Création des vérités éternelles, doute suprême et limites de l'impossible chez Descartes," *Papers on French Seventeenth-Century Literature* Suppl. 5, Paris: J. Vrin (1982): 277–318.

—— "Hypothèses sur l'elaboration progressive des Méditations de Descartes," *Archives de Philosophie* 50 (1987): 109–23.

—— "Limitations of the mechanical model in the Cartesian conception of the organism," in *Descartes: Critical and Interpretive Essays*, ed. Michael Hooker. Baltimore: The Johns Hopkins University Press, 1978, pp. 152–70.

—— "On the complementarity of the Méditations III and V: from the 'general rule of evidence' to 'certain science', in *Essays on Descartes' Meditations*, ed. Amélie Oksenberg Rorty. Berkeley: University of California Press, 1986, pp. 271–95.

—— "Quelques compléments sur la création des vérités éternelles," in *Etienne Gilson et nous: La philosophie et son histoire*, ed. M. Couratier. Paris: 1980, pp. 73–7.

Rome, Beatrice K. "Created truth and 'causa sui' in Descartes," *Philosophy and Phenomenological Research* 17 (1956): 66–78.

Rorty, Amélie Oksenberg. "Cartesian passions and the union of mind and body," in *Essays on Descartes' Meditations*, ed. Amélie Oksenberg Rorty. Berkeley: University of California Press, 1986, pp. 513–34.

—— "The structure of Descartes' *Meditations*," in *Essays on Descartes' Meditations*, ed. Amélie Oksenberg Rorty. Berkeley: University of California Press, 1986, pp. 1–20.

Rose, L. E. "The Cartesian circle," *Philosophy and Phenomenological Research* 26 (1965–6): 80–9.

Rose, M. C. "Descartes' malevolent demon," *Proceedings of the American Catholic Philosophical Association* 46 (1972): 157–66.

Rosenthal, David M. "Will and the theory of judgement," in *Essays on Descartes' Meditations*, ed. Amélie Oksenberg Rorty. Berkeley: University of California Press, 1986, pp. 405–34.

Rubidge, Bradley. "Descartes's Meditations and Devotional Meditations," *Journal of the History of Ideas* 51: 1 (1990): 27–49.

Rubin, R. "Descartes' validation of clear and distinct apprehension," *Philosophical Review* 86 (1977): 197–208.

Ryle, Gilbert. "Descartes' myth," in *Descartes: A Collection of Critical Essays*, ed. Willis Doney. London: University of Notre Dame Press, 1968, pp. 338–52.

Saint-Jacques, A. "Le Cogito est-il un premier principe?," *Laval théologique et philosophique* 2 (1955): 100–25.

Salmon, Elizabeth G. "The Cartesian circle," *The New Scholasticism* 12 (1938): 378–91.

Scarrow, D. S. "Descartes on his substance and his essence," *American Philosophical Quarterly* 9 (1972): 18–28.

Scharfstein, B.-A. "Descartes' dreams," *Philosophical Forum* 1 (1968–9): 293–317.

Schiffer, S. "Descartes on his essence," *Philosophical Review* 85 (1976): 21–43.

Schmitt, Frederick F. "Why was Descartes a foundationalist?," in *Essays on Descartes' Meditations*, ed. Amélie Oksenberg Rorty. Berkeley: University of California Press, 1986, pp. 491–512.

Schneier, C. K. "Descartes' proofs for the existence of God: comparison and contrast," *Dialogue* (USA) 23 (1980): 22–6.

Scholz, Heinrich. "Über das Cogito, ergo sum," *Kantstudien* 36 (1931): 126–47.

Schouls, P. A. "Cartesian certainty and the 'natural light'," *Australasian Journal of Philosophy* 48 (1970): 116–19.

—— "The extent of doubt in Descartes' 'Meditations'," *Canadian Journal of Philosophy* 3 (1973): 51–8.

Schrader, David E. "Frankfurt and Descartes: God and logical truth," *Sophia* (Australia) 25: 1 (1986): 4–18.

Schrecker, Paul. "La méthode cartésienne et la logique," *Revue philosophique de la France et de l'étranger* 123 (1937): 336–7.

Sepper, Dennis L. "Imagination, phantasms, and the making of Hobbesian and Cartesian science," *Monist* 71 (1988): 526–42.

Serres, M. "L'évidence, la vision et le tact," *Etudes philosophiques* 23 (1968): 191–5.

—— "Un modèle mathématique du Cogito," *Revue philosophique* 90 (1965): 197–205.

—— "Sur le cercle cartésien," *Revue philosophique* 97 (1972): 311–14.

Sibajiban. "Descartes' doubt," *Philosophy and Phemenological Research* 24 (1963): 106–16.

Sidgwick, H. "On the fundamental doctrines of Descartes," *Mind: A Quarterly Review of Psychology and Philosophy* 7 (1882): 435–40.

Siegler, F. A. "Descartes' doubt," *Mind* 72 (1963): 245–53.

Sievert, D. "Descartes' criteria of truth: conception and perception," *The Modern Schoolman* 56 (1979): 151–60.

—— "Descartes's self-doubt," *Philosophical Review* 84 (1975): 51–69.

—— "Does Descartes doubt everything?," *The New Scholasticism* 53 (1979): 107–17.

—— "Essential truth and the ontological argument," *Southwest Philosophy Review* 1 6:1 (1990): 59–64.

—— "The importance of Descartes's wax example," *Ratio* 21 (1979): 73–84.

Simpson, P. "The dream argument and Descartes' First Meditation," *Auslegung* 9 (1982): 300–10.

Smart, H. J. C. "Descartes and the wax," *Philosophical Quarterly* (India) 1 (1950): 50–7.

Smyth, R. "A metaphysical reading of the First Meditation," *The Philosophical Quarterly* 36 (1986): 483–503.

Snow, A. J. "Descartes' method and the revival of interest in mathematics," *Monist* 33 (1923): 611–17.

Soffer, W. "Descartes, rationality and God," *Thomist* 42 (1978): 666–91.

—— "Dreaming, hyperbole and dogmatism," *Idealistic Studies* 18: 1 (1988): 55–71.

—— "The methodological achievement of Cartesian doubt," *Southern Journal of Philosophy* 16 (1978): 661–74.

Sommers, Fred. "Dualism in Descartes: the logical ground," in *Descartes: Critical and Interpretive Essays*, ed. Michael Hooker. Baltimore: The Johns Hopkins University Press, 1978, pp. 223–33.

Sorensen, Roy A. "Was Descartes' *cogito* a diagonal deduction?," *British Journal for the Philosophy of Science* 37 (1986): 346–51.

Stainsby, H. V. "Descartes' argument for God," *Sophia* (Australia) 6: 3 (1967): 11–16.

Stallknecht, N. P. "The Cogito and its world," *The Personalist* 46 (1965): 52–64.

Steiner, M. "Cartesian scepticism and epistemic logic," *Analysis* 39 (1978–9): 38–41.

Stern, K. "A defense of Cartesian doubt," *Dialogue* (Canada) 17 (1978):

480–9.

Stevens, J. C. "Unknown faculties and Descartes's first proof of the existence of God," *Journal of the History of Philosophy* 16 (1978): 334–8.

—— "Why Descartes' belief that he is not perfect can't be wrong," *The Personalist* 58 (1977): 134.

Stone, J. "Dreaming and certainty," *Philosophical Studies* 45 (1984): 353–68.

Stout, A. K. "The alleged 'petitio principii' in Descartes' appeal to the veracity of God," *Congrès Descartes* 1 (1937): 125–31.

—— "The basis of knowledge in Descartes," *Mind: A Quarterly Review of Psychology and Philosophy* 38 (1929): 330–42, 458–72.

—— "Descartes' proof of the existence of matter," *Mind: A Quarterly Review of Psychology and Philosophy* 41 (1932): 191–207.

Streenivasa Iyengar, K. R. "The nature of Descartes' method", *Congrès Descartes. Travaux du IXe Congrès International de Philosophie* 20: 36 (1937).

Stuart, James D. "Descartes' proof of the external world," *Historical Philosophical Quarterly* 3 (1986): 19–28.

—— "The role of dreaming in Descartes' 'Meditations'," *Southern Journal of Philosophy* 21 (1983): 97–108.

Stubbs, A. C. "Bernard Williams and the Cartesian circle," *Analysis* 40 (1980): 103–8.

Suter, Ronald. "The dream argument," *American Philosophical Quarterly* 13 (1976): 185–94.

—— "*Sum* is a logical consequence of *Cogito*," *Philosophy and Phemenological Research* 32: 2 (1971): 235–40.

Thomas, L. E. "Waking and dreaming," *Analysis* 13 (1953): 121–37.

Thomas, J. "Descartes' trust of clear and distinct perception," *Ratio* 24 (1982): 83–6.

Thornton, Mark T. "Cartesian pains," in *Early Modern Philosophy*, ed. Georges J. D. Moyal and Stanley Tweyman. Delmar: Caravan Press, 1986, pp. 35–64.

Tichỳ, P. "Existence and God," *Journal of Philosophy* 76 (1979): 403–20.

Timoner, K. I. "Descartes' use of some historical elements of the demonstrations in the *Meditations*," *Dialogue* (USA) 23 (1980–1): 14–21.

Tlumak, J. "Certainty and Cartesian method," in *Descartes: Critical and Interpretive Essays*, ed. Michael Hooker. Baltimore: The Johns Hopkins University Press, 1978, pp. 40–73.

—— "Squaring the Cartesian circle," *Southern Journal of Philosophy* 16 (1978): 247–57.

Turbayne, C. M. "Analysis and synthesis," in *The Myth of Metaphor*. New Haven: Yale University Press 1962; rev. edn Columbia: 1970, pp. 228–53.

Tweyman, Stanley. "Descartes' 'demonstrations' of his existence," *Southern Journal of Philosophy* 23: 1 (1985): 101–10.

—— "Descartes' knowledge of God in the Fifth Meditation," *Southern Journal of Philosophy* 26: 2 (1988): 263–75.

—— "Descartes' Second Meditation and Seventh Principle," in *Descartes and Hume: Selected Topics*. Delmar: Caravan Press, 1989.

♦ —— "Deus ex Cartesio," *Studia and Collectanea Cartesiana* I (1979): 167–82.

218

—— "The reliability of reason," in *Cartesian Studies*, ed. R. J. Butler. Oxford: Basil Blackwell, 1972, pp. 122–36.

—— "Truth, no doubt: Descartes' proof that the clear and distinct must be true," *Southern Journal of Philosophy* 19 (1981): 237–58.

Unger, P. "Our knowledge of the external world," *American Philosophical Quarterly* Mon. Oxford, 1970, pp. 40–61.

Van Cleve, J. "Conceivability and the Cartesian argument for dualism," *Pacific Philosophical Quarterly* 64 (1983): 35–45.

Van de Pitte, Frederick P. "Descartes on analogy and other minds," *International Studies in Philosophy* 7 (1975): 89–110.

—— "Intuition and judgment in Descartes' theory of truth," *Journal of the History of Philosophy* 26: 3 (1988): 453–70.

Vendler, Z. "Descartes' res cogitans," in *Res Cogitans: An Essay in Rational Psychology*. Ithaca, 1972, pp. 144–205.

Vernon, T. S. "Descartes' three substances," *Southern Journal of Philosophy* 3 (1965): 122–6.

Vial Larrain, J. de D. "Cogito, ergo sum," *Cuadernos de filosofía* 16 (1976): 17–34.

Vignoles, P -H. "À propos de la première *Méditation* de Descartes," *Cahiers philosophiques* 8 (1981): 87–108.

Vision, G. "*Cogito per cogitationem, ergo sum,*" *Philosophical Forum* 11 (1979–80): 340–62.

Wachbrit, R. "Dreams and representations: a new perspective on dreaming and Cartesian skepticism," *American Philosophical Quarterly* 24: 2 (1987): 171–80.

Wagner, S. I. "Descartes's arguments for mind-body distinctness," *Philosophy and Phenomenological Research* 43 (1982–3): 499–517.

—— "Descartes' Cogito: a generative view," *History of Philosophy Quarterly* 1 (1984): 167–80.

Walsh, W. H. "The limits of reason: Descartes and *Cogito ergo sum,*" in *Metaphysics*. London: 1963, pp. 84–97.

Walton, D. "Performative and existential self-verifyingness," *Dialogue* (Canada) 16 (1977): 128–38.

Watling, J. "Doubt, knowledge and the *Cogito* in Descartes' *Meditations,*" *Philosophy* Suppl. 20 (1986): 57–71.

Watson, John. "The Cartesian Cogito ergo sum and Kant's criticism of rational psychology," *Kantstudien* 2 (1898): 22–49.

Watson, R. A. "The breakdown of Cartesian metaphysics," *Journal of the History of Philosophy* 1 (1963–4): 177–97.

—— "Descartes knows nothing," *History of Philosophy Quarterly* 1 (1984): 399–411.

Weinberg, J. R. "Descartes and the distinction of mind and body," in *Ockham, Descartes, and Hume: Self-Knowledge, Substance, and Causality*. Madison: 1977, pp. 71–82.

—— "The sources and nature of Descartes' *Cogito,*" in *Ockham, Descartes, and Hume: Self-Knowledge, Substance, and Causality*. Madison: 1977, pp. 83–91.

Welbourne, M. "Cartesian madness," *Analysis* 40 (1979–80): 48–50.

Wells, N. J. "Descartes' uncreated eternal truths," *The New Scholasticism* 56

(1982): 185–99.

Wilbur, J. B. "The *Cogito*, an ambiguous performance," in *Cartesian Essays*, ed. B. Magnus and J. B. Wilbur. The Hague: Mouton, 1969, pp. 65–76.

Williams, B. "The certainty of the *Cogito*," *Cahiers de Royaumont* 4 (1962): 40–57.

Williams, Michael. "Descartes and the metaphysics of doubt," in *Essays on Descartes' Meditations*, ed. Amélie Oksenberg Rorty. Berkeley: University of California Press, 1986, pp. 117–39.

Wilson, M. D. "Can I be the cause of my idea of the world? (Descartes on the infinite and indefinite)," in *Essays on Descartes' Meditations*, ed. Amélie Oksenberg Rorty. Berkeley: University of California Press, 1986, pp. 339–58.

—— "Cartesian dualism," in *Descartes: Critical and Interpretive Essays*, ed. Michael Hooker. Baltimore: The Johns Hopkins University Press, 1978, pp. 197–211.

—— "Confused ideas," *Rice University Studies* 63 (1977): 123–37.

—— "Descartes: the epistemological argument for mind-body distinctness," *Nous* 10 (1976): 3–15.

—— "Skepticism without indubitability," *The Journal of Philosophy* 81 (1984): 537–44.

Witcraft, Kelly A. "Cartesian *Meditations* on the human self, God and indubitable knowledge of the external world," *Indian Philosophical Quarterly* Suppl. 15 (1988): 1–19.

Wolz, Henry G. "The double guarantee of Descartes' ideas," *Review of Metaphysics* 3 (1950): 471–89.

—— "The function of the will in Descartes' proofs for the existence of God," *The New Scholasticism* 20 (1946): 295–322.

Wong, D. B. "Cartesian deduction," *Philosophy Research Archives* 8 (1982): 1–19.

Wright, J. N. "Descartes and the wax: rejoinder" (to J. J. C. Smart, *q.v.*) *Philosophical Quarterly* (India) 1 (1951): 348–55.

—— "The method of Descartes," *Philosophical Quarterly* 18: 5 (1955): 78–82.

Yost, R. M. Jr. "Miss Macdonald on sleeping and waking," *Philosophical Quarterly* (India) 5 (1955): 109–24.

SELECTED INDEX TO DESCARTES' *MEDITATIONS ON FIRST PHILOSOPHY*

of 43, 60, 66, 68–70, 73, 83;
infinitude of 74, 79; knowledge
of 35, 44, 72, 73, 85; as a non-
deceiver 85, 92, 93, 100; as not
existing 83–4 perfection of 69,
73

ideas 43, 60, 61, 63, 65, 87;
adventitious 61; of bodies 89;
fictitious 61, 83; innate 61, 71;
produced by objects 92; similar
to objects 89
illusions 50
imagination 44, 47, 53, 55, 56, 57,
58, 76, 86, 87
immortality of soul 41
imperfection 73, 78
indifference 76, 77
infinite 66, 68, 70
inseparability 83
intuition 56

judgement 40, 56, 57, 73, 75, 78,
85

knowledge 49, 57, 58, 59, 75, 80;
as limited 96, 100
knowledge, certain and
evident 40, 85

madness 46
magnitude 80
material/corporeal things/
bodies 88, 92; attributes of 41;
essence of/nature 42, 43, 81, 95;
existence of 44, 77, 86, 92, 93;
ideas of 65, 66, 81; knowledge
of 72, 73, 86
memory 58, 76, 79, 87, 100
metaphysics 37, 60, 102
method 36, 101–3
mind 45, 50, 56, 58, 60, 71, 87,
89, 94, 95; knowability of 58;
nature of 35, 41; as united with
body 83, 94, 95, 97

natural light/light of nature 43,
61, 62, 64, 72, 78, 94
nature 61, 64, 66, 72, 90–1, 93–7
necessity 83
negation 74, 76, 78
non-being 74
nourishment 52

objective reality 64, 67, 92
obscure and confused 65
opinions, false 39, 46

pain 88, 89, 93, 94, 98–9
Pappus 36
passions 89
perception, faculty of 58, 90, 92,
100
perfection 72, 74, 75, 83
persuasion 40, 51, 84
philosophy 35, 37
Physics 48
piece of wax 55–7, 65
pilot in vessel 93
prejudice 36, 40, 41, 84
privation 78
proof 102

quantity 80

reason 61, 62, 75, 76; distinction
of 70; natural 34, 46

science(s) 73
senses 36, 40, 41, 44, 50, 51, 54,
55, 58, 62, 71, 72, 81, 84, 88–90,
92, 94, 95, 100, 102
simple natures 47, 102
soul 34, 35, 37, 41, 43
substance 42, 69, 91, 92
sun, idea of 62, 93
synthesis 102

thinking thing 53, 54, 72, 77, 91,
97
thirst 93, 96, 99, 97
thought 49, 52, 60
time 48
triangle 81, 82, 83, 84, 87
truth 36, 37, 46, 48, 49, 76, 77–81,
84, 93, 95

understanding, faculty of 39, 44,
75–8, 87, 97, 100

waking 86, 90, 100
will 76, 77, 78; as indivisible 78
wisdom 39
workman 34; mark of 71, 74